The fallacies of hope

For Dennis Austin with affection and gratitude

The fallacies of hope

The post-colonial record of the Commonwealth Third World

edited by James Mayall *and* Anthony Payne

Manchester University Press
Manchester and New York
Distributed exclusively in the USA and Canada by St. Martin's Press

Published by Manchester University Press
Oxford Road, Manchester M13 9PL, UK
and Room 400, 175 Fifth Avenue,
New York, NY 10010, USA

Distributed exclusively in the USA and Canada
by St Martin's Press, Inc.,
175 Fifth Avenue, New York, NY 10010, USA

British Library cataloguing in publication data
The Fallacies of hope: the post-colonial record of the Commonwealth Third World.
1. Commonwealth countries. Politics, history
I. Mayall, James II. Payne, Anthony
320.9171241

Library of Congress cataloging in publication data
The Fallacies of hope : the post-colonial record of the Commonwealth Third World/edited by James Mayall and Anthony Payne.
p. cm.
Includes index.
ISBN 0-7190-1760-2
1. Commonwealth of Nations–History. 2. Developing countries–History. 3. Decolonization–History. I. Mayall, James. II. Payne, Anthony, 1952– .
DA16.F35 1890
909'.0971241–dc20 90–40820

ISBN 0 7190 1760 2 *hardback*

Typeset in 10/12 pt Baskerville
by Graphicraft Typesetters Ltd., Hong Kong

Printed in Great Britain
by Billings Limited of Worcester

Contents

Notes on contributors

James Mayall is Reader in International Relations at the London School of Economics.

Anthony Payne is Senior Lecturer in Politics at the University of Sheffield.

Peter Lyon is Reader in International Relations and Academic Secretary of the Institute of Commonwealth Studies at the University of London.

Anirudha Gupta is Professor of International Studies at the Jawaharlal Nehru University in Delhi.

Richard Rathbone is Senior Lecturer in Politics at the School of Oriental and African Studies at the University of London.

Sam Nolutshungu is Lecturer in Government at the University of Manchester.

Paul Sutton is Senior Lecturer in Politics at the University of Hull.

James Craig was a Lecturer in Politics and Administration at the University of Manchester at the time of his death.

Jack Spence is Professor of Politics at the University of Leicester.

1 *James Mayall and Anthony Payne*

Introduction: the hopes and the fallacies

The rise and fall of the British Empire has often been chronicled: its aftermath less so. Perhaps the main reason for this relative neglect lies in an almost natural aversion to anticlimax. The rise of a great power, the rivalries, conquests, even the confusions, through which it establishes and expands its ascendance, have a natural dramatic appeal. So too do the political struggles, social upheavals and military rebellions through which empires are challenged and finally subdued. This is true even where, as in the British case, the battles were largely a ritual affair, staged for effect, between protagonists who were fundamentally intent on collaboration. But when the play is over, what more is there to be said?

I

A story of sorts can be constructed from the determination of human beings to resist change. The commercial and cultural patterns of the Empire, those consumer preferences like the drinking of tea or the playing of cricket which it helped to establish, the rituals of parliamentary procedure and the court room, the habits of thought and discourse, may linger on for a season, so that even now most visitors to Lutyen's secretariat in New Delhi are struck by the way Indian administrative practice echoes the British, and by the continuities between the Queen Emperor's Raj and that of the Nehru dynasty. But such continuities are in reality pale and feeble imitations of the real thing and in time will surely fade from views. As with Roman Britain, their reconstruction will then be the task of archaeologists and philologists, rather than political scientists or contemporary historians.

Nevertheless, from the latter perspective the analogy with Rome is still instructive. The Roman imperial system survived its takeover by the barbarians, but crumbled eventually before the combined onslaught of Muslim and nomadic invasions. Europe turned in on itself; yet, cut off from its Mediterranean trade routes, a new social order, based on the ideal of self-sufficiency, gradually evolved. By the beginning of the eighth century, Hugh Trevor-Roper informs us, European civilisation had shrunk to its lowest point: 'the monastic cell, with its self-contained economy, capable of survival in the oddest places and in the worst times, like a seed in the winter detritus of Nature.'[1] Why should we expect more – or indeed as much – from the aftermath of the British Empire? This question is implicit in much of the work of Dennis Austin to whom the essays in this volume are dedicated. 'The slackening of many of the former bonds of advantage', he writes, 'contrast very sharply with nineteenth century confidence: the present Commonwealth lacks the cohesive force that gave the Victorian Empire its immense attraction.'[2] After the Roman Empire, the European dark ages; after the British Empire, the Commonwealth. The danger of such slick comparisons is obvious but it is worth reflecting on this one a moment longer.

The dark ages can be shown to have nurtured a development of immense historical significance. The imperial state collapsed and its social order disintegrated, but the monks, their eyes steadfastly fixed on another world, conserved the intellectual patrimony of western civilisation for its rediscovery during the Renaissance and propagation following the eighteenth-century Enlightenment. When the British began to dismantle their overseas Empire in 1947, the decision to quit India was greeted with optimism not merely by those to whom power was transferred but by liberal opinion throughout the western world. The bloody accompaniment of partition, and Gandhi's murder by a Hindu fanatic, provided an early foretaste of things to come. But by the early 1950s Nehru's capacity to ignore the contradictory mess of day-to-day political life in favour of the broad sweep of historical progress had restored the optimistic mood. It persisted for another decade, by which time many other African and Caribbean states were also independent. In sum, decolonisation was viewed not as a threat to civilisation, but as proof that civilised (and progressive) values had become embedded not only in western society but veritably across the globe.

II

This extraordinary contrast prompts two questions. Why the optimism? And, does the record of achievement in the forty years since the process began suggest that the hopes that accompanied the transfer of power were misconceived or, at least, greatly exaggerated?

The answer to the first can be aptly provided by paraphrasing Dennis Austin. In Britain, he suggested, as in the rest of imperial Europe, the optimism was partly explained by the fact that the withdrawal of European power from Asia, Africa, the Caribbean and the Pacific did not pose a threat to the existence of the European powers themselves. 'Britain, France, Holland and Belgium still stand in the sense that Rome did not – or Byzantium, or the Pharaohs, or the Han dynasty did not.'[3] Within the successor states to the British Empire the optimism was no doubt partly because the élites which moved into positions of power (as the British moved out) savoured the sweet smell of success. But it was also because they inherited the ideology of British imperial rule, which incorporated two of the most powerful (and optimistic) ideas of our time – liberalism and nationalism. 'Liberalism, born of the Enlightenment, proclaimed the rights of individuals, for which the political shorthand became "adult suffrage". Nationalism, displacing the sovereignty of princes and queens, proclaimed the rights of people, for which the shorthand became "independence".'[4]

A third intellectual legacy should perhaps be added, albeit one that came later and was more muted in its impact – Fabianism or social democracy. With the passage of the Colonial Development and Welfare Act in 1940, notice was served that British rule recognised a commitment to the social and economic well-being of the colonial peoples, thereby bringing to bear on the Empire, during its closing years, some of the dominant values of the emerging social democratic consensus in Britain, and providing a bridge to the post-independence drive to development. The optimism inherent in both liberal and nationalist views of the world sprang originally from a belief that these doctrines were natural – and that what was natural was good. However, the experience of the Great Depression and the Second World War, the one feeding a general and self-defeating retreat behind national defences, the other caused by the need to confront an arrogant and pathological form of nationalism, undermined the credibility of any appeal to a beneficent nature, and it required the post-war modification of both doctrines to accommodate a belief in social and economic engineering, to give them a new lease of life. In the process the successor governments of the Empire were equipped with a programme full of promises, just what they needed to buy the support of their newly 'liberated' constituents.

Were the hopes and expectations generated by this widespread belief in democracy, nation and welfare exaggerated or misconceived? It is this second question to which the authors of this book have addressed themselves. When Dennis Austin surveyed 'the different ways in which the newly independent African governments have tried to acquire authority, use structures of power, and adapt to their purposes the practices of the former colonial state',[5] he borrowed the title of his first chapter – 'The Fallacies of Hope' – from Turner's picture of the West African slave-ship, which hangs in the Boston Museum of Fine Arts. The title certainly captured his own tentative conclusion about the first decade and a half of African independence. In this book we have not only borrowed his title, but attempted to address the same theme in relation to the post-independence record of Commonwealth Third World countries in Asia, the Caribbean and (if the category can be stretched that far) the Mediterranean, as well as Africa. We have also endeavoured to summarise this record in terms of two broader considerations which span the different legacies of Empire – the pursuit of economic development and the protection of human rights.

Nationalism and liberalism (suitably adjusted to accommodate the ideals of social democracy) were, as we have argued, the major intellectual influences shaping the politics of the new Commonwealth Third World. For all that, the record cannot be assessed solely in terms of these doctrines. For much of its later history the British Empire was a major actor in international politics, but the rest of the world never had much influence over the political, or even the economic, behaviour of the colonies. Transition from Empire into Commonwealth was also a transition to a world in which external powers often had a decisive influence on the political and economic development of newly independent countries and where external ties and allegiances were often actively cultivated as a way of maximising the benefits to be derived from independence or raising a regime's international profile. The post-colonial record of the Commonwealth Third World cannot be judged, therefore, merely in terms of the standards set by the departing colonial power and endorsed by the first generation of nationalist leaders. At least, it cannot be judged by these standards as though the rest of the world did not exist.

The truth is that British imperial ideology only developed its national and democratic aspirations fairly late in the day. Indeed, one author has recently argued that the expansion of British imperial power after the loss of the American colonies, and in response to the Jacobin threat of the 1790s, was positively antidemocratic and antiliberal. It was, C. A. Bayly maintains, 'the ferocious reaction of the state and its apparatus to external challenge and internal revolt' that took the British into the Mediterranean, to Malta, Sicily and the Ionian Island, and which compelled them to dismantle the Dutch empire, acquiring the Cape and Ceylon in the process.[6] One might thus argue that it was these military and statist characteristics which created the real legacy of British imperial rule rather than the constitutionalism and free trade of the liberal empire. Be that as it may, it is certainly the case that the wider strategic environment has both imposed constraints and created opportunities for the new states of the Commonwealth of a kind which cannot be properly appreciated if they are studied in isolation from the international system of which they are now a part.

III

That, then, is our agenda. When we turn to examine the actual post-colonial record of Commonwealth Third World countries, it is apparent that many have found the world of statehood gruelling. Most of the states whose political fortunes are discussed – India, Sri Lanka, Ghana, Nigeria – embarked on independence with high hopes and a relatively healthy bank balance. Not many of these hopes have survived. The commitment of many of these countries to democracy is precarious and nearly all are heavily in debt. What went wrong? It is tempting to conclude that their governments, freed from any compelling external discipline, frequently mistook rhetoric for reality. The most squalid power struggles among individuals, ethnic and linguistic groups have been dignified in these countries by the language of nation-building, squandering in the process much of the best of the colonial inheritance. On this first view, poverty and geographical proximity to a major centre of power, rather than relative affluence and strategic remoteness, appear to be a better recipe for political stability and the preservation of democratic values. Not only has Malta avoided the worst excesses of post-colonial corruption and decay, as witnessed the more widely in Asia and Africa, but so too have most of the Commonwealth Caribbean islands – with the two notable exceptions of Guyana and Grenada.

There are nevertheless limits to how much such generalisation (even if true) can teach us about the ways in which the imperial inheritance has been absorbed, accommodated or rejected in different parts of the Commonwealth Third World. Despite the near-universal abuse of power both during and between elections, the tinkering with the independence of the judiciary and the farming of offices in the civil service, it is surprising how resilient the democratic system, and the ideal of universal suffrage on which it is allegedly based, has proved to be. In the Commonwealth Caribbean, elections are regularly held and governments change in a relatively peaceful manner. In India, despite a long history of concessions by the central government to regional and linguistic interests, and some fairly blatant manipulation of the electorate, the habit of state-wide elections is firmly entrenched – as demonstrated most recently in November 1989 – and is not generally thought to be at risk. Even in Sri Lanka, the conduct of elections, albeit effectively ignoring the Tamil minority, has survived, despite what is almost a permanent state of civil war.

Of the Commonwealth countries surveyed here, only in West Africa have the mechanisms of parliamentary government largely failed to take root. In Nigeria, Sam Nolutshungu identifies a vicious circle of post-colonial politics: 'Workers, artisans, small traders and small farmers are not politically organised because there is no democracy, but there can be no democracy because the people are not organised.' Yet, he concludes, in nearly three decades of independence, most of it spent under military rule, 'there has not been a decisive repudiation of the democratic ideal, and those thirty years could conceivably have been much worse from the point of view of all classes of Nigerians'. Could they have been worse for the long-suffering population of Ghana where democratic hopes ran highest, if only because, as the first independent country in sub-Saharan Africa, it acquired a brief if spurious international importance? Dennis Austin recorded the early demise of these hopes in one of the most influential books on post-colonial politics, reviewed here in the light of Ghana's subsequent turbulent history by Richard Rathbone. In his reprise of this work, which 'never ceases to read well', he notes that 'it took some courage implicitly to insist on multi-party democracy as a safeguard of civil and political rights in Africa' at the time Austin was writing. The argument in favour of single-party democracies in the Third World was then being made most forcefully, which makes it worth observing from a contemporary vantage-point that the claim has now long been in disrepute.

In terms of the Commonwealth record on democracy, Ghana in fact presents a final irony. Its present military government has not been noticeably respectful of democratic values; yet under the radical regime of Flight Lieutenant Rawlings it has become the 'flagship' country in the International Monetary Fund and World Bank campaign for African recovery. Western motives are, of course, mixed: behind the sponsorship of Ghanaian recovery is the desire to find a formula under which Africa's debts can be repaid (or at least written off in the decent hope that they will not be repeated). Even so, few would question the existence of an ideological sub-text – the belief that only within a freely operating market economy can the institutions of liberty flourish.

It is not, then, the formal order of democracy which has been the major casualty of the transfer of power from Britain to the successor states of the Empire. Modern civilisation is inherently materialistic, not merely in its underlying structure, but in its aspirations. Democratic pluralism is too closely associated with the conspicuous economic success of the industrial west to be easily displaced as the Commonwealth ideal. It is the content, not the form, of Commonwealth post-colonial democracies that gives rise to the despondency of much of the contemporary writing on these countries.

IV

If there is a general diagnosis of the malaise to put alongside the detailed account of symptoms in different cases, it should most probably be located in the unnatural marriage between nationalism and liberalism in the ideology of the nineteenth-century Empire. When John Stuart Mill followed Coleridge in embracing the seductive ideal of national self-determination, it was because he believed that 'free institutions are next to impossible in a country made up of different nationalities'.[7] In the context of his time there is little doubt that he had the better of the argument with Lord Acton, who maintained, on the contrary, that nationalism was a fatal enemy of the concept of democratic citizenship. Mill agreed that it would have been better if different ethnic identities had been assimilated, or at least educated into political coexistence, within a single civil society before the concept of popular sovereignty had evolved. But he addressed himself to a world where this option was no longer available. From the perspective of the post-colonial Commonwealth, however, it is difficult to avoid the conclusion that it was Acton who was the more percipient.

Anticolonialism borrowed the idiom of national (i.e. cultural) self-determination. But it was very seldom nationalism in the nineteenth-century European sense – that is, a demand that the political map should be redrawn to coincide with a pre-existing cultural or linguistic identity. In most cases, as Nolutshungu points out, the state was not viewed, as in liberal Europe, as the absolutist enemy, to be transformed to a point where it could protect the liberties of civil society:

> The state was dominated by a 'class' that . . . sought to inherit the state, not to subdue it. Having fought the colonial 'ruling class' to a democratic outcome – at least in so far as represented by the granting of a democratic independence constitution – the political class thereafter fought, most of the time, against itself.

Anticolonial nationalist movements derived their solidarity from the solidarity of the colonial 'ruling class'. Having inherited the state, competition for the spoils of office was generally sufficient to undermine the claims of the movement to represent a nascent political nation. In Sri Lanka, Anirudha Gupta concludes, ethnic rivalry was 'the unintended fall-out of the *Swabhasa* movement.' He quotes Bandaranaike: 'Our minds were really fixed at that time on the question of English vs *Swabhasa*. We did not bring our minds to bear . . . on the question of Sinhala vs Tamil.'

Admittedly, ethnic rivalry was not everywhere a necessary or sufficient explanation of the disorder that followed independence. Rathbone notes, for example, that in Ghana while 'some politicians had undoubtedly played regional and ethnic cards in seeking support and in shaping alliances . . . the notion of a unitary Ghana has never been seriously challenged since 1957'. Yet whatever other ingredients are added to the witch's brew – the weakness or non-existence of a national bourgeoisie, the peripheral status and external dependence of the economy, the merciless exploitation of the peasantry by the élite, or even the totalitarian temptations inherent in the colonial state – it is difficult to discount the subversive role of ethnicity over much of the Commonwealth Third World. The two areas where ethnic rivalry has been contained most successfully – the Caribbean and India – are also the parts of the new Commonwealth whose political institutions have the deepest roots and where nationalism, consequently, has been defined in terms of an existing constitutional order rather than against it. In the West Indian islands in particular a distinctive and conservative political culture has developed, helped no doubt by the distance, both in time and mentality, between the population and its African past. As Paul Sutton writes, 'the creole élite at independence wanted no other form of government than the Westminster model, regarding it not as "foreign derived" but as "autochthonous".'

India is of course no stranger to ethnic politics which have often threatened to engulf the state. But the conservatism of Indian society, the deep resistance of the mass of the population to fundamental change, the notorious fragmentation of Hindu society, all impose a tenacious and also torpid stability on Indian political life. As Peter Lyon shows, politics in India have frequently been analysed in terms of the decay of the country's political institutions, and the rise of separatist sentiment at state and regional level. Yet India is a going concern: the freedoms and privileges guaranteed by its constitution (for example, for such groups as the Harijans) may have been abused and manipulated for narrow political ends, but no-one – not even, one suspects, the Sikhs – appears to believe that India will either undergo a revolution or disintegrate! As for the armed forces, Lyon's judgement is that 'the chances of a successful coup . . . have, perhaps, increased in recent years, but not by much'. The functional difficulties of effecting a coup across such a vast and complex country combine with the ingrained professionalism of the Indian army to outweigh still the politicisation engendered by increased involvement in internal law-and-order operations.

In other respects too, scale places India in a category of its own. Not only has the government inherited something of the arrogance of the British in India – Delhi often seems to deal with its smaller neighbours, including Sri Lanka, as geopolitical irritants rather than as genuinely independent countries with which it must do business – but the polity combines a large industrial economy with rural poverty on a massive scale. Village India, with its endlessly complex stratifications, does not fit easily into the modernising nationalist mould. But it does not have to. The Indian middle class, with its distinct but unquestionably modern tastes and attitudes, is large by any standards, certainly large enough to appropriate the institutions and symbols of Indian nationalism for its own ends.

These ends are often unashamedly imperial. (Nostalgia for the Raj is almost as much a growth industry in India as in Britain.) Indeed, it is perhaps not surprising that, in the face of the latent xenophobia and expansionism of this largely North Indian ruling class, many of the heirs of the older Congress tradition are nervous of the concept of Indian nationalism. Pre-colonial India, so the new radicalism has it, was a civilisation rather than a nation-state, and its traditional political rulers, unlike their modern counterparts, did not try to impose a uniform and alien cultural pattern on society. The assertion of a nostalgic cultural authenticity against the predations of an imperial capital – as, for example, in the notorious revival of Sati in Rajasthan – is an odd twist in the story of Indian nationalism. The challenge seems no more likely to succeed there than in other parts of the world where nationalist governments have provoked a kind of cultural Luddism. In India its significance, however, is the evidence it provides of how successful the centre has been in monopolising the language and symbols of the nation for essentially imperial ends. Except on the frontiers of the state, the appeal is for cultural autonomy, not withdrawal from the Indian union. As in many empires, internal rebellion can be dealt with savagely, but so long as the imperial system is not challenged directly, life can go on relatively undisturbed for a very long time.

V

In one respect the Indian experience is not atypical of the Commonwealth Third World, but exemplary. To the extent that the problems of national integration were foreseen at all, excessive reliance was placed on externally assisted programmes of economic and social development as a means of resolving them. The first generation of leaders accepted enthusiastically and largely unquestioningly the optimistic assumptions of post-war development theory. Britain certainly played a part in promoting the belief in the possibilities of macro-economic management and the benign impact of income redistribution within a mixed economy. It was also prominent in championing the return to self-help and neoclassical orthodoxy in the 1980s. But in neither case can the failures of economic policy and performance in the Third World be laid solely at Britain's door. As James Mayall argues, the dream of a 'quick fix' to Third World economic problems is not primarily a legacy of colonial rule. To a much greater extent it is a consequence of competition between the two superpowers for influence in the post-colonial world, and in particular of a United States-led effort to incorporate Third World states in the liberal world economy. Some particular Commonwealth problems arose along the way, mostly as a result of US opposition to trade preferences and the consequences of Britain's final entry into the European Economic Community. For the most part, however, Commonwealth Third World countries were caught up in a wider diplomatic movement which probably created more problems than it solved.

How have they fared economically in this embrace? Mayall emphasises that it is far from easy to establish the answer to that question. The evidence can be looked at in different time-frames and via varying angles of vision. Against the grim human realities of urban poverty, famine and disease, rightly associated in the popular mind with the Third World, there is the hard-headed fact that 'the growth rates of most Third World countries between 1950 and 1975 were high, not only in comparison with their own past experience, but with the rates of the now industrialised countries during the nineteenth century'. The prospect of Third World economic take-off had even reached the point by the mid-1970s that the post-OPEC demand for a 'New International Economic Order' was, for a while at least, taken seriously by western governments precisely because it was thought a shift in the global balance of economic power had indeed taken place. In retrospect, this was no more than an unkind chimera, comprehensively cast aside, outside of East Asia, by the 'new realism' of debt and depression in the 1980s. The structural adjustment programmes imposed on several African and Caribbean Commonwealth countries by the joint agency of the IMF and the World Bank have in fact worsened the social resources of these countries even as their policies are deemed by some to reflect the triumphalist progress of western liberalism (political as well as economic) through the Third World as a whole.

In the end, the welfare record of the Commonwealth Third World has to be judged not in terms of the success or failure of economic policy, let alone by simple reference to growth-rates or balance-of-payments figures, but in terms of the ability of people to enjoy the most basic of political goods – the protection of human rights. Here too the criteria cannot be derived from the history of either British imperialism or decolonisation without reference to the wider international setting, although Britain (together with the United States and France) was certainly prominent in the campaign to put the question of human rights on the international agenda. As Anthony Payne puts it:

> These new states thus took up their place in international society as victors in a struggle but also as graduates of the school of liberal human rights – sometimes, it should be said, disgruntled and dismissive of the colonial legacy, but in the vast majority of cases committed to the fuller implementation of the very social, economic and political values by which imperial rule was first legitimised and ultimately destroyed.

Western powers have nevertheless consistently worked during the post-war period to confine the notion of human rights to a narrow political definition, thereby resisting the wider Third World demand that social and economic considerations be incorporated. In human terms, the two dimensions – 'full bellies in Freedom House'– are clearly complementary and the record of states and societies needs to be judged thus.

A careful review of Commonwealth Third World performance measured in terms of the way in which governments have lived up to human rights commitments does much to puncture the view of Commonwealth exceptionalism. Some Commonwealth countries have done better, but some worse, than countries elsewhere in the Third World. It also calls into question the progressive myth that the post-colonial order is self-evidently morally superior to its predecessor. To the extent that freedom, including the right to go to hell in one's own way, is considered the supreme value, no doubt it is. But in terms of the protection of the fundamental decencies of public life (the chief of which is perhaps the right to a private life free from arbitrary interference by the government) the record is more mixed. On the other hand it does not provide grounds for despair: the Commonwealth is not presiding over the onset of a new dark age. No doubt we should not expect too much; there is certainly much to be gloomy about in the post-colonial world, but there are also islands of enlightenment. The monks in eighth-century Europe knew what to preserve for posterity. 'The peoples of the Commonwealth Third World', Payne concludes, 'know what are the rights they want to be protected, even if they do not currently enjoy them'.

VI

Finally, what of the external environment, and the impact which it has had on the post-colonial record of the Commonwealth Third World? One of the strongest conclusions to emerge from the analyses gathered in this volume is that, in different ways, geopolitical and strategic considerations have frequently had a more determinate influence than have the legacies of British rule. Hopes frequently proved fallacious because they were unrealistic in their own terms, but they were also often undermined by powerful external factors, the force of which had simply not been foreseen by any of the players of the optimistic mood music of the independence moment.

Examples abound. In discussing the Commonwealth Caribbean, Sutton notes that much of the fate of the region has been tied up with a United States strategic preoccupation which only recognises the islands as part of the wider Caribbean Basin. In this geopolitical space global interests are deemed to be at stake – an East-West politics – for which the ultimate price paid by tiny Commonwealth

Grenada was invasion by 'friendly' US marines. Sri Lanka has similarly found its immediate geopolitical environment oppressive, the would-be protector of its interests in this case being the army of another Commonwealth state. Malta's post-colonial history is, in fact, one of the few which illustrates the way in which the wider international system can be used to further national ends. Great powers can afford to be wasteful, indeed conspicuous waste often seems almost as symptomatic of greatness as conspicuous consumption. Small powers must learn to husband their resources if they are to prosper, or even to survive. This is the central theme of the late James Craig's chapter on Malta, an island country whose Mediterranean location between Europe and North Africa represented virtually its only asset at independence. An economy built around a naval base is a fragile inheritance, particularly at a time of British naval contraction. Yet the Maltese government made a virtue out of necessity. By adopting a posture of positive neutrality, and engaging in a measure of diversification, it was able to combine independence with a reasonable level of political stability and modest prosperity. As Craig observes, Malta demonstrates that 'power in international politics is not just about economic strength or military might ... Political leadership is very much a part of the equation'. In particular, strategic competition between the great powers was viewed pragmatically as an asset by successive Maltese leaders, rather than, as in many other parts of the Third World, a constraint on development.

Whether that trick can be pulled off in South Africa is another question. To state the obvious, South Africa is neither a member of the Commonwealth, nor is it a Third World state; yet its problems have dogged the early post-independence history of the Commonwealth Third World like an unwanted ghost, and it has been included in our study for this reason. After all, critics of the Commonwealth case for sanctions against the white South African regime claim that the likely result of such a policy will be to turn a free South Africa into the newest member of the Commonwealth Third World!

Yet if one foreign policy objective has united the disparate new member states of the Commonwealth, it has been opposition to South Africa. Their solidarity in opposing apartheid was largely responsible for South Africa's withdrawal from the Commonwealth. The African states in particular have often seemed to value the organisation primarily as a means of pressuring Britain into applying economic sanctions against the Republic, and as an indirect way of persuading the United States to do the same. Their own independence would not be secure – so the argument ran – until South Africa was also free. The fact that the country has been independent since 1910 and was a founding member of both the League of Nations and the United Nations matters less, in their view, than that its obnoxious social order is indirectly supported by western (above all, British) investment and trade. It would be wrong, though, to conclude that the Commonwealth and Afro-Asian campaign against South Africa has had no influence; at the very least, it has embarrassed the western powers and kept the question of South Africa alive, if only sporadically near the top of the international agenda. Yet Commonwealth and Third World agitation has not seriously shifted the British and American perception that not only is there little that can be done about apartheid from outside the country, but that (in terms of their own strategic and economic interests) there is no pressing need to do very much either.[8]

In this respect western attitudes towards South Africa contrast sharply with their attitudes towards Zimbabwe, where Britain was directly involved and the Commonwealth had an important supporting role to play. Even there, however, it was the perceived shift in the geopolitical and East-West balance that was decisive in galvanising the western powers into action, rather than concern for the abuse of human rights or the erosion of constitutionalism in Rhodesia. The Americans and then the British became concerned that important western interests were at stake only after the conclusion of friendship treaties between the Soviet Union and Angola and Mozambique in the mid-1970s. Similarly, when the Angola–Namibia Accord was finally signed in December 1988, the Commonwealth had virtually nothing to do with it. As Jack Spence rightly argues, 'what made the agreement possible was the combination of superpower midwifery . . . and the discovery of new and unexpected incentives by the local protagonists: Angola, Cuba and South Africa'. The political development of Namibia, as of Zimbabwe before it, will be crucially influenced by the external circumstances which, against the odds, enabled the transfer of power to be negotiated.

And here, no doubt, is the lesson, not only for South Africa but for the Commonwealth Third World too. The situation in South Africa can certainly be debated in terms of the prospects for democracy, with the emergence of the new Mass Democratic Movement a significant indicator of the pre-eminence of the democratic goal in anti-regime politics. It can also be discussed, obviously, in terms of competing nationalisms or the impact of sanctions on the existing level of economic development in the Republic. The breakthrough to political change in South Africa, which may even now be in the process of occurring following the release of Nelson Mandela, will no doubt derive its essence from these internal factors – the interplay of notions of democracy, nation and welfare – but who can doubt that the particular shape, and certainly the character, of any new order as and when it comes, will not be heavily 'brokered' by external forces? The still unfree peoples of South Africa will, in short, have to learn the lesson which the post-colonial period has already taught to so much of the rest of what was the British Empire, namely that their hopes can best be realised (and can perhaps *only* be realised) by working with, rather than against, the grain of the most powerful international economic and political trends of the day.

Notes

1 Hugh Trevor-Roper, *The Rise of Christian Europe*, Thames and Hudson, London, 1965, p. 88.
2 Dennis Austin, 'The British point of no return' in Prosser Gifford and William Roger Louis (eds.), *The Transfer of Power in Africa: Decolonisation 1940–1960*, Yale University Press, New Haven, CT and London, 1982, p. 247.
3 Ibid., p. 225.
4 Dennis Austin, 'Britain, the Commonwealth and South Africa', paper presented to the Commonwealth Relations Seminar of the Institute of Commonwealth Studies, University of London, 25 November 1986, p. 1.
5 Dennis Austin, *Politics in Africa*, University Press of New England, Hanover, NH and London, 1984, p. 1.
6 C. A. Bayly, *Imperial Meridian: The British Empire and the World, 1780–1830*, Longman, London, 1989, p. 102.
7 J. S. Mill, *Representative Government*, ch. 16 (numerous editions).
8 Dennis Austin, *South Africa 1984*, Routledge and Kegan Paul, London, 1985, pp. 62–72.

2 *Peter Lyon*

The first great post-colonial state: India's tryst with destiny

Among the several fashionable frameworks used to analyse India since 1947, that of the 'post-colonial state'[1] is by no means universally acceptable or convincing, even though a plausible case can be made that the various experiences of being colonised by others – whether Persians, Afghans, Portuguese, French or British – have each left some durable legacies. At the very least, however, the term post-colonial, when applied to India, and when intended to signify something more than merely post-independence, implies something of importance about British legacies to India since 1947.[2] Above all else, present-day India is a palimpsest of its rich and varied past, its many colonial subjugations and the eclectic capacity of its indigenous religions and cultures to adapt and survive. These many colonial subjugations include the Mughals certainly no less than the British. Present-day India features too as an ostensible, complex and controversial nation–state in the post-colonial international system or order,[3] of which it is a not insignificant member.

It is tempting, even if over-simple, to depict the main ebbs and flows of India's Union since 1947 in terms of the ups and downs of the Nehru family's activities in national politics – of the Nehru 'dynasty', as Tariq Ali[4] and some others have sardonically characterised it. It is the case so far that the few short times when a member of that family has not been Prime Minister of India seem, in retrospect, to have been mere intervals, episodic arrests in the otherwise long period of political dominance of pan-Indian affairs by this one family – though it should be noted here that the November 1989 general election results may have finally ended this dominance. The drama of governmental changes mirrored by the ups and downs of the Nehru family do, however, provide a convenient framework for this chapter, whose main aims are basically twofold. The first is to trace the course of the play itself by noting briefly the principal characterisations of India since 1947 as advanced by scholarly analysts and commentators. The second is to explore the underlying plot by drawing attention to some of the most important continuing problems faced by India as the first great post-colonial state.

The play

The Nehru era, 1946–64

There was not much euphoria about the last rites of India's passage to independence. Nehru's famous and eloquent 'tryst with destiny' speech on the eve of independence, 15 August 1947,[5] spoke of freedom having come not completely (because of Pakistan, Kashmir, much unfinished business, and the bitterness and traumas of communalism, partition, and the mass killings and displacements of peoples), but 'very substantially'. The murder of Mahatma Gandhi, in January 1948, by a Hindu fanatic who loathed his victim's tolerance towards Muslims and minorities generally, not only gave independent India its first and greatest national martyr,[6] but served also to provide a grim reminder of the continuing plagues of communalism and sectarian violence.

Nehru's conception of what India's government and society should be like was not notably different from that of Attlee (Britain's Prime Minister between 1945 and 1951), though it was expressed much more mellifluously. Fabianesque, mildly optimistic but temperamentally cautious and sceptical, and yet believing firmly in improving people's welfare by means of state enterprise and national planning, Nehru – like Attlee – was also an advocate of a world order without colonialism, though both men were rather vague about what actual steps could, and should, be taken to realise this millennium. If pressed, either of them might have commended the Commonwealth as exemplary in this regard.[7]

Like Ireland in 1921, the price of independence for India in 1947 was partition. What Mahatma Gandhi expressively called the 'vivisection of the subcontinent' was the partition of two great provinces, the Punjab and Bengal, involving immense bloodshed and the displacement of about 20 million people from their homes –

Hindus, Muslims and Sikhs. And soon Kashmir[8] was also partitioned as a result of Indo-Pakistan armed clashes which immediately confirmed and envenomed the relationship of these two neighbours, severed Siamese twins.

It was politically and psychologically important for Nehru, the arch anti-communalist, that the country whose Prime Minister he had become was named not Hindustan but India, and was thus to be regarded as the prime successor of the British Raj. Pakistan was in this sense a secessionist state (and in effect two states, east and west Pakistan, geographically separate but loosely tethered together politically and dominated by west Pakistan's Punjabi majority). The integration of the 550 or more Princely States (more numerous and more complex in character even than the erstwhile Holy Roman Empire in its dying decades) was another massive task assumed from the start and, with the significant exception of Kashmir, resolved rather swiftly, one way or another, mostly in India's favour.[9]

Genuine independence in deed as well as word was to be India's lodestar, Nehru stressed, and on a number of occasions in the early post-independence years, playing one of his familiar roles as schoolmaster–instructor to the nation, he maintained that independence in foreign policy was the clearest and most convincing demonstration of this intent.[10] Yet in the early years after 1947 Stalin's spokesmen were frequently able to castigate Nehru and his lieutenants as 'neo-colonial stooges' and running-dogs or jackals of the imperialists – charges which were given a superficial plausibility, to those who wished to believe them, by India's large sterling balances (accumulated as credit because of Britain's purchases from India during the Second World War), cordial politico-diplomatic ties with Britain, membership of the Commonwealth, and reliance on Britain as its principal supplier of armaments. It was not until the middle 1950s (and notably from the time of Bulganin and Khrushchev's much publicised visit to India in late 1955) that India's independent foreign policy and non-alignment became openly praised in its own right by Soviet leaders, who also endorsed India's claim to Kashmir (a considerable test of friendship, in Indian eyes). Dr S. Gopal, Nehru's official biographer, regards the years 1953–5 as marking the heyday of Nehru and of India's world influence.[11]

The Nehru era faded away rather rapidly in the first four years of the 1960s, undermined dramatically by the shock of military defeat at the hands of China[12] and more insidiously by the waning of the Prime Minister's powers. China's hostility conjured up the spectre of a joint Pakistan–China attack on India, led to agonising reappraisals of the efficacy of non-alignment, and prompted a massive and rapid overhaul of India's whole military capability. Morris-Jones's study of the Indian Parliament,[13] published in 1957, with its epigraph that 'just as Athens was the school for Hellas, so New Delhi has become the school of Asia', conveyed something of the commendations which westerners had generally heaped on India in the 1950s. So, in 1960, a sharp American journalist–author, Selig Harrison, in his book *India: The Most Dangerous Decades*,[14] reshaped the debate by analysing India's condition pessimistically and prophesying that, with the death of her tall leaders and the passing away of the founding fathers, India was likely to have to face increasing fissiparous pressures. Like the Habsburg monarchy in the late-nineteenth and early twentieth centuries, India henceforth would have to combat incipient 'Balkanisation'. Harrison maintained that the three major divisive influences at work were language, caste (and colour) and political parties. With a population expected to reach 500 million by 1971, with regional, economic and political self-interest acutely at work, and more than a dozen major regional languages, with individual states controlled by farmers, wholesalers or money-lenders, India faced a series of authoritarian, political transformations. Harrison was one of the first, perhaps the first, to provide a fully argued exposition for India of the otherwise familiar thesis that, when expectations of progress affect the masses before progress actually comes rapidly enough to satisfy rising expectations, then tensions and 'the most dangerous decades' have dawned. This was one thoughtfully sombre, premature epilogue on the Nehru era.

The Shastri interlude, 1964–6

Lal Bahadur Shastri became Prime Minister of a nation demoralised by defeat at the hands of China, worried by the new bonds Pakistan seemed to be forging with China, and distressed by the death of Nehru, his reputation only somewhat lessened by his last, sad years. The diminutive Shastri (he was only just about five feet tall), lacking much formal education and with no great fluency in English, stood in marked contrast to his Brahminical, patrician, cosmopolitan predecessor. Shastri was perhaps India's most authentically indigenous Prime Minister in the years 1947–89. He had to arrest endemic factionalism within the Congress party, stamp his authority on the upper echelons of national politics and administration, and direct efforts to recover and rebuild India's somewhat tarnished international standing now that the days of relatively easy acceptance of stature and reputation were over. (With pardonable oversimplification *The Economist* had said that India's foreign policy during the late 1940s and 1950s essentially reduced itself to two elements: a frequent international commentary on world events, and the containment of Pakistan.) Now, however, China's test explosion in October 1964 persuaded Shastri to speed up India's own nuclear research.

Shastri seemed to personify the notion that India had an indigenously educated and locally experienced Hindu political leader, that the Nehruvian style of government was over, but that the pursuit of Indian interests was paramount. Personally modest and frugal but determined and surprisingly decisive and courageous, it fell to Shastri in the last six months of his short premiership to have to contend with Pakistan as an adversary. Not one, but two Indo-Pakistan wars were fought in 1965. The first was in the Rann of Kutch, marshy ground where India's western boundary touches what was then west Pakistan's south-western corner. It proved to be only a curtain-raiser for a wider war fought about a month later but along almost the whole of the two countries' respective common boundaries, from Kashmir in the north, through the Punjab, the Rajasthan-Sindh desert, to the Rann of Kutch again. This second Indo-Pakistan war to 1965 was fought to a stalemate (and only later, and retrospectively, was it clearly apparent that its prosecution had done much more to damage Pakistan's than India's political system and economy).[15] It took three months' explicitly Soviet (and implicitly American) diplomatic intervention before a formal peace treaty could be patched up. This was finally achieved and signed, not within the subcontinent, but on Soviet soil in Tashkent in early January 1966, only for Shastri to die of a massive heart attack within hours of the ceremony's conclusion.[16]

Indira Gandhi as Prime Minister, 1966–77

Indira Gandhi, who had been Minister of Information in Shastri's cabinet, was elected to the presidency of the Congress and to be

Prime Minister. Living in the shadow of her famous father, whose political hostess she had been for most of his premiership, she had shown her self-will as early as 1942 by marrying Feroze Gandhi, a Parsi (and no relative of the Mahatma), thus breaking both caste and family tradition since the Nehrus – formerly Kauls – were Kashmiri Brahmins who had set up home in Allahabad. (Feroze died in 1960, leaving behind two sons, Sanjay and Rajiv, whom she successively advanced as her political heirs – first the younger, Sanjay, because of his ambition, until his death in an air crash in June 1980.) When she was elected party leader and Prime Minister, the old-guard syndicate of top politicians who helped to put her there apparently calculated that she would be weak, malleable, and do their bidding. In this assumption they were soon proved wrong. In 1969 she overturned the Congress machine by an incumbency coup which won the Presidency of India for her candidate against that of the party's High Command. This was followed by a snap general election in which her wing, Congress (I) – for Indira – turned Congress (O) – for Organisation – into an impotent rump and gave her a two-thirds majority in the Lok Sabha, the lower house of parliament. Thereafter, she became the dominant political figure in India, her popularity being further increased by victory in the war against Pakistan in 1971. India also tested its own first nuclear implosion in the Rajasthan desert in June 1974. It was termed a peaceful nuclear explosion and served, albeit ambiguously, to announce that India had joined the small world club of nuclear powers.

From 1972 onwards, Mrs Gandhi's autocratic style and the increasingly imperious and capricious behaviour of Sanjay Gandhi combined with mounting factionalism and communalism at the centre and in the regions to generate growing unrest and opposition to 'Indira's Raj'.[17] In June 1975, she proclaimed an Emergency[18] under which civil liberties were restricted, strikes forbidden, the press controlled and much of the democratic system suspended. These clamps stopped, or drove underground, political and industrial unrest and gave a breathing space for some economic recovery and revival. However, other aspects of the Emergency, not least the sterilisation campaign spearheaded by Sanjay, were intensely unpopular, especially amongst Muslims who, rightly or wrongly, believed that it was especially targeted on them.[19]

When a general election was called in March 1977 (a testimony to Mrs Gandhi's determination to restore parliamentary democracy), Congress (I) was heavily defeated. Mrs Gandhi herself lost her seat until re-elected in a by-election in 1978. A judicial commission subsequently convicted her of misuse of power, and the Lok Sabha found her guilty of contempt, for which she was expelled from parliament and sent to gaol for the remaining week of the session. For the first time since 1947 a non-Congress government took office.

The Janata interlude, 1977–9

The Janata coalition government, headed by Morarji Desai, was remarkable for being the only period, until November 1989, when Congress has not been the governing party of India, with commanding majorities in the all-India parliament. The only thread that seemed to unite this otherwise heterogeneous mixture of different factions and interests (each main group headed by an ambitious and usually very aged leader) was suspicion, fear and opposition to Indira Gandhi and her supporters. The professed purpose of the Janata government was, of course, to be different from and better than the previous governments headed by Mrs Gandhi. In foreign policy terms this led to claims that Janata would pursue a 'genuine' non-alignment, not one tilted towards the Soviet Union,[20] of which Mrs Gandhi had been accused. This implied too the need for improvements in Indo-American relations. Two other areas where Janata claimed that it would be an improvement on Mrs Gandhi's practices were within the Commonwealth, where it proposed to be more positive and constructive, and in relations with those regional neighbouring countries which Mrs Gandhi, it was alleged, had alternately ignored or bullied. Initially it did seem as if improvements in India's relations with neighbouring countries, within the Commonwealth, and even with China, were tentatively but constructively under way. But the Vietnamese invasion of Cambodia quickly destroyed early moves towards a Sino/Indian *détente*, and the Soviet invasion of Afghanistan in December 1979, in what turned out to be the dying days of the Janata government, stymied any chance that India might be the constructive leader of South Asian regionalism at this time. Ironically enough, despite pronounced and professed ideological antipathies towards the Soviet Union, the Janata government actually increased Indian dependence on Soviet supplies in certain critical respects (nuclear fuels, oil, and sophisticated weaponry) and relations with the United States did not notably improve.[21]

Mounting factionalism, at first gradually and then more rapidly, sapped and undermined the authority of the Janata government and brought about its eventual collapse in July 1979. It was then succeeded by a very short-lived government which was headed by Charan Singh, leader of the Lok Dal (the party of rich peasant-farmers of north-west India) but which owed its existence to the support of Mrs Gandhi's group of Congress (I) MPs. This situation aptly underlined the heavily personalised quality of political competition and practices at the apex of Indian political life. When that support was soon withdrawn, the precarious and narrow foundation of Charan Singh's political base was laid bare, and for the rest of 1979, from late August onwards, he merely headed a caretaker administration in an ever-denser atmosphere of electioneering.

The long and rather tedious election campaign which occupied the months up to January 1980 was characterised by much personal opportunism, complicated manoeuvrings, behind-the-scenes bargaining and rumours of such bargaining, and took place against a background of continuing and increasing inflation, sporadic outbursts of violence, and unmistakable, if patchy, evidence of deteriorating law and order in some parts of the country. Nor, despite their apparently promising start, were the Janata years in government any better in substance for India's foreign relationships. A combination of rather maladroit moves, ill luck and the persistent lack of real authority at the centre, especially in the last few months, meant that India's behaviour in the world also lacked authority.[22] Janata's eventual electoral defeat at the hands of Congress (I), with Mrs Gandhi still leader, was thus no surprise.

Indira's last four years, 1980–4

Mrs Gandhi's last period of government was characterised by much assurance in her conduct of foreign policy but by continuing and indeed mounting ethnic and religious conflict at home. The latter exploded into violence, especially around the time of elections, whether at state or other levels, and most notably in Kashmir, Assam, Tamil Nadu and the Punjab. There were repeated denials that India was allied with the Soviet Union: the Indo-Soviet treaty of August 1971 was proclaimed as a friendship pact entirely compatible with India's continuing non-alignment and Mrs Gandhi refused Soviet invitations to go to Moscow to celebrate the tenth anniversary of its signing. In practice, there were many demonstrations, from both Moscow and New Delhi, of the continuing cordialities of relations between these two countries.[23] India, alone amongst South Asian governments and one of a very small company in the Third World at large, held back from forthright condemnation of the Soviet invasion of Afghanistan, or the Vietnamese invasion of Cambodia, concentrating instead, according to official spokesmen, on quiet, constructive diplomacy behind the scenes. It is appropriate too to talk of Mrs Gandhi's foreign policy in these years because she took the major roles and decisions, notably when the Non-Aligned Movement's summit was held in New Delhi in March 1983, followed by the Commonwealth Heads of Government meeting in October of the same year. Furthermore, she switched the political and official personnel in the top echelons of the Ministry of External Affairs quite frequently, in terms that left no room for doubt as to who was generally in overall charge.

In this sphere US arms supplies to Pakistan (which had come to be dubbed a front-line state in view of the Soviet invasion and occupation of Afghanistan) continued to be a considerable irritant in New Delhi's dealings with Washington. India and Pakistan nonetheless concluded an agreement in November 1982, and the following March set up a joint commission to promote their bilateral co-operation, tentatively but constructively. Despite China's unequivocal condemnation of both Soviet and Vietnamese policies in these years, India began, and to a limited degree succeeded in bringing about, a process of *détente* with Beijing, slowly and circumspectly amongst officials but more meaningfully at the unofficial level. Annual inter-governmental talks, held in alternate years in Beijing and New Delhi, focused mostly on the border dispute but did not result in agreement.[24] In addition, India continued to have prickly relationships with Bangladesh, Nepal and Sri Lanka, arising from the apprehension these neighbours felt about their region's giant. Even so, the Foreign Ministers of India, Pakistan, Bangladesh, Sri Lanka, Nepal, Bhutan and the Maldives met in New Delhi in early May 1983 and agreed to set up a South Asian regional co-operation forum.[25]

Throughout these four years, as in her earlier terms of office,

Mrs Gandhi continued to affirm faith in the basic policies espoused by her father: socialism, industrialisation, secularism and non-alignment, to which were added the maintenance of the nuclear option and the build-up and modernisation of India's armed forces.[26] She dealt high-handedly with the fissiparous tendencies and regional dissidence which, although afflicting India since independence, had become more pronounced in the 1980s. Her martial reaction to the Sikh demands and campaign for an autonomous – even a secessionist – state in the Punjab led to a murderous revenge when she was assassinated by Sikh members of her own personal bodyguard on 31 October 1984.[27] Some commentators read this as the nemesis of Mrs Gandhi's authoritarian style of democracy, others thought that it would be a prelude to much more communal bloodshed and perhaps the strengthening of Sikh secessionism and the ultimate 'Balkanisation' of India (as both Harrison and Maxwell had earlier warned might happen).

Rajiv's Raj, 1984–9

Soon after succeeding his mother as Prime Minister following her assassination, Rajiv Gandhi successfully consolidated his position with a massive electoral victory, backed by what some observers called a sympathy vote but which is better regarded as a vote for stability and continuity. Rajiv Gandhi's electoral slogans in 1984 were for 'clean' and 'efficient' government. He repeatedly warned of the dangers of a Congress Party dominated by 'power brokers' and rebuked his party in no uncertain terms at its centenary Congress in Bombay in January 1986: 'We [Congress] obey no discipline, no rule, follow no principle of public morality, display no sense of social awareness, show no concern for the public. Corruption is not only tolerated but even regarded as the hallmark of leadership.' These words now seem heavily ironic in the light of what happened to Congress in the November 1989 elections. Rajiv Gandhi's cousin, Arun Nehru, a senior minister at the time (but by 1989 a leader within the ranks of the opposition), said that 'the hunter became the hunted' and that 'the system got the better' of Rajiv. Following the cumulative impact of defeats in state elections and emerging scandals, Mr Gandhi shunted aside those he felt might challenge him and, just like his mother, made loyalty and subservience the test of office.

Rajiv Gandhi's premiership between late 1984 and November

1989 was characterised and trumpeted by many Indian commentators as the start of a new era of economic 'liberalisation' designed to sweep away most of the so-called Permit Raj – that *dirigiste* regime of industrial licensing, extensive control of external trade and domestic investment, which was part and parcel of British imperial rule and was then extended and elevated into claims of comprehensive national economic planning during Jawaharlal Nehru's premiership. However, the shift to more market-orientated policies – carried through in Rajiv Gandhi's early measures of liberalisation – also contributed to the mounting sense of disorientation and fragmentation among India's masses. The economy grew faster in the second half of the 1980s than at any other period since independence. Yet more rapid industrialisation and urbanisation also brought more pollution, turning once rather quiet and clean cities such as Pune (formerly Poona) or Jaipur into industrial nightmares beset with exhaust fumes and debilitating noise.

The benefits of higher growth were largely concentrated on the Indian middle classes – numbering between 100 and 200 million – and have been reflected in rising sales in recent years of passenger cars, TV sets, refrigerators, and other 'luxury' consumer goods. Yet, contrasting with the sharp improvements in living standards for the urban well-to-do, many of the rural poor saw their real earnings diminished by inflation, which began to rise faster than India's historic, so-called Hindu rate of growth. At the same time regional differences of wealth were accentuated, with eastern and central regions of the country generally slipping further into poverty.

Whereas Mrs Gandhi had mostly kept 'business' under a tight leash, her son was markedly disposed to let business have its head. Thus business received much of the blame for the recurrent troubles that beset his administration. The election campaign of 1989 both directly and indirectly took up many of these issues. The one undeniable cause that brought the opposition together was its determination to get Rajiv Gandhi out of office. He was accused of being the personification of all that the nation should feel uncomfortable with – the flashy affluence of the new rich, corruption in public life, the authoritarian and dynastic rule of the Nehru family, the disappearance of 'value-based' politics, the erosion of institutions,[28] and the widening gaps in living standards.[29]

In the late 1980s the name of Bofors, the Swedish group which paid illicit commissions to win a huge arms contract, entered Hindi vocabulary as a current colloquial metaphor, meaning 'dubious broker' or just 'dirty' or 'rotten'. The Bofors affair, and its accompanying disclosures, gave some credence to the charge that Indians at the highest level of government had taken bribes, or had at least received favours, and that elements in the senior ranks of the civil service, the army and the police, the judiciary and Parliament, had been sucked into the subsequent attempts to cover up. Mud from Bofors scattered wide.

The Bofors affair thus added its own morsels of scandal to the tarnishing tales of disrepute by which most of India's central institutions (on which the country's democracy had been founded and still rests) have steadily been discredited and diminished in effectiveness. The apparent success of the beneficiaries of the Bofors transactions in getting away with their gains is widely seen as making a mockery of any official – whether senior civil servant or village functionary – who tries to combat corruption and as encouraging those many without scruples to seek and take ever larger bribes.

Many Indians are reluctant to recognise, however, that some of the changes currently sweeping across their country are also the signs of a more dynamic society which is emerging as a consequence of the discarding of some of the constraints of social immobility and government regulation that have impeded growth in the past. It is an unpalatable fact that in many societies – for example, in the United States of the late nineteenth century or the Italian city-states of the fifteenth century – rapid rates of growth have been accompanied by violence and the rise to power of 'robber barons'. India appears to be no exception.

The plot

So much, then, for the play. What light can an examination of the underlying themes in the plot throw on India's post-colonial history?

Religion, Hinduism and communalism

India is officially a secular state, as defined in its Constitution. Religion and communalism are, however, integral to India's complex and volatile politics, not mere factors standing outside (as the violence of the November 1989 general elections served again to remind us). There are many ways of understanding religion other than that recognised in India's Constitution, where the only institutional space allowed or acknowledged is the plain statement that the Constitution recognises and respects the individual's personal faith. Yet about 85 per cent of India's peoples are Hindu, and Hindu revivalism and assertiveness are playing an increasingly active part in the late 1980s in the politics of India[30] (especially of north-central India, the Indo-Gangetic plains, which is sometimes called the Hindi-speaking heartland or the sacred-cow belt). Jawaharlal Nehru himself was a sincere, even a passionate, secularist and was unrelentingly opposed to communalism. But his daughter and grandson, as Prime Ministers, were on several occasions much more equivocal about communalism and were not entirely unwilling to try to play a communal card for practical electoral purposes. By the time of the communal clashes of the 1989 election campaign some commentators were saying that the epitaph of secularism was being written for India. Hindu revivalism is now clearly viewed with concern by India's many minorities, Muslims and Sikhs not least.

Overall, the Muslims of India are a minority of about 12 per cent, but for a country of about 800 million people that adds up to roughly 100 million. India in fact has the world's largest Muslim population after Indonesia. India's Muslims can recall with pride that their ancestral co-religionists ruled most of northern India as part of the Mogul Empire. Increasingly nowadays they refuse to be treated as second-class citizens and are acutely sensitive to any slight, sometimes imagined rather than intended. The Muslims have generally voted as a block. In 1989 they comprised more than 20 per cent of the electorate in about 98 crucial constituencies in seven states. The lively fortnightly magazine *India Today* calculated, in late October 1989, that the Muslim vote could tip the scales in another 100 constituencies under India's first-past-the-post electoral system. Until 1977 Muslims tended to support Congress, but their defections, mainly in protest at Sanjay Gandhi's mass sterilisation drive, played a key part in the electoral toppling of Indira Gandhi in 1977, and in her election-based return to power in early 1980. As a result of these events, they know their electoral importance and can no longer be taken for granted, especially when communal violence erupts during an election campaign. Indeed, they seem mostly to have voted against Congress in November 1989.

Unrest and violence in the Punjab provoked by militant, and some would-be secessionist, Sikhs, and Mrs Gandhi's heavy-handed attempts to deal with this (especially 'Operation Bluestar', the storming and temporary occupation of the Golden Temple in Amritsar by the army in early June 1984), have also led to heightened communal tension involving bloodshed and ultimately the assassination of Mrs Gandhi. Thereafter, Rajiv Gandhi's inability to produce a successful solution in the Punjab was a considerable contributory factor to the decline in his political reputation and his electoral defeat in 1989. Although Sikhs presently number only about 13 million and therefore comprise just under 2 per cent of India's total population, the Punjab has been an agriculturally rich, highly productive State, the prize exhibit in India's claims to have induced a 'green revolution' of agribusiness on some of the nation's farmlands. Sikhs have hitherto also been of importance, far in excess of their numbers, within India's armed forces. Reconciling the Sikhs and the Punjab State to constructive co-operation within the Indian Union is thus a major and inescapable task for any Indian government in the 1990s.

The national bureaucracy[31]

The top echelon of the Indian Administrative Service (the IAS) served, and still serves, as an all-India mandarinate. These top IAS cadres pride themselves on being at least as good as their predecessors in the Indian Civil Service (the ICS) and, like these forerunners, also regard their service as constituting the 'steel-frame' of the state. Jawaharlal Nehru, after a career before 1947 which caused him to criticise the ICS ethos sharply and repeatedly, came after independence to appreciate and nourish the IAS much more than either his daughter or, still more, his grandson did as Prime Minister. This can be illustrated by reference to their varying treatment of the Planning Commission.

For Nehru, the Planning Commissioners were the principal architects of all-India state building, whereas for Mrs Gandhi, and more markedly for Rajiv Gandhi, this was much less so. Indeed, Rajiv Gandhi on one occasion characterised those on the Planning Commission with the contemptuously dismissive phrase that they were just a 'bunch of jokers' – a sentiment which cannot entirely be attributed to the unfashionability of comprehensive state-directed economic planning in the late 1980s, or as indirect applause for market forces and private entrepreneurship.

A national economy?[32]

Nehru's secularism had a powerful economic dimension – he was determined to improve the material conditions of life for the majority of India's vast population, who at independence still lived, as they always had, in conditions of abject poverty. It was an ambition which he believed required government intervention to forge a truly national and modern economy, although, more problematically, these priorities justified in his mind the relative neglect of the armed services and India's security – at least until the last few years of his life.

Despite some impressive achievements India's economic problems are formidable. Between 1965 and 1980 agricultural production grew at an average rate of 2·8 per cent per year, the so-called Hindu rate of growth. This was not very encouraging, given population growth at about 2 per cent per year, but at least in the 1970s the 'green revolution' enabled the government to achieve the elusive goal of agricultural self-sufficiency. The growth of agricultural production slumped in the 1980s to a mere 0·8 per cent a year, and in 1987 the spectacular failure of the monsoon produced severe drought which adversely affected both agriculture, which had come to account for about 35 per cent of GDP, and hydro-electric power generation.

For the first time for several years the drought dramatised the potential conflict over resource allocations between security and development. Some 5 billion rupees were transferred from the 125 billion rupees defence budget for the financial year 1987/8 to provide drought relief, but the modernisation of India's weaponry and defence equipment continued. Neither re-equipment nor the heavy costs of peace-keeping operations in Sri Lanka appeared to be reflected in defence budget allocations, which at 130 billion rupees for the financial year 1988/9 did not adequately compensate for inflation and was unlikely to meet costs. Unless therefore there are some concealed defence expenditure items, acquisitions orders may have to be cancelled or delayed and training levels reduced.

In other respects, however, the Indian economy performed much better in the second half of the 1980s than most popular impressions of India convey – and the figures show that results were markedly better than in the 1960s and 1970s. The annual increase in real gross domestic product was more than 4½ per cent – giving India the fourth fastest growth rate of the world's twenty-five largest economies. According to World Bank estimates, over the three years from 1985 to 1988, manufacturing output rose by an annual rate of 8–9 per cent at constant prices. Exports in volume terms grew by an average of 10 per cent, which suggests that India has at last begun to improve its share in world markets after slipping back generally during the previous forty years of independence, when exports grew at a meagre trend rate of 2–3 per cent.

Unsurprisingly, however, the distribution of this economic growth has been uneven. In much of rural India living standards have been severely squeezed by rising inflation, and unemployment has grown. (As in China, more emphasis on market forces has helped to widen disparities.) Real growth has been concentrated in certain areas – Bombay and the west coast, the Delhi region and eastern Andhra Pradesh – and has most benefited urban areas and the middle class. The explosive expansion of the consumer market is both providing industry with larger demand and forcing it to be more competitive on quality and cost.

The ambiguous way in which India's economic record is read by many informed commentators was clearly illustrated in a recent assessment by the economics editor of *The Economist*, Clive Crook, in the following terms:

> Between 1950 and 1980 India's income per head grew from $150 to $230, a rise of 1·4 per cent a year. Over the previous 80 years it had grown at less than 0·5 per cent a year. Life expectancy has increased to more than 55 years, and the share of employment in farming has fallen to 67 per cent. India is regarded as a disappointing case. It has every reason to be, for the economic policies of its governments might have been to stifle growth altogether. But over the past few decades even India has achieved faster progress than today's rich countries did during similar stages in their development.[33]

A distinctive foreign policy

Apart from the 1960s (when China deeply discomfited India and when the prospect of a joint Sino-Pakistani assault seemed a real threat to many Indians – until dissipated by India's conclusive victory over Pakistan in 1971), India's foreign policy has generally been regarded as successful, a source of pride to most Indians and thus perhaps as a factor positively aiding state and nation building. India undoubtedly is a distinctive and usually quite explicit presence in almost all important contemporary general international fora – in the UN, UNCTAD, GATT, the Commonwealth, the G77, and the NAM, for example – and quite commonly is accorded or assumes a leading or influential role. This does not mean that India customarily plays the role of the conformist. Indeed, in its opposition to the Nuclear Non-Proliferation Treaty regime and the inclusion of services in the current 'Uruguay Round' of the GATT, many countries would characterise India's persistent advocacy of its own policy preferences as awkward and unrelenting.

Within South Asia, India's occasional willingness to intervene actively in the affairs of its neighbours (in Nepal in the early 1950s and again in 1988–9, in Bangladesh in 1970–1, in the Maldives in 1988, and in Sri Lanka in 1988–9, for example) have earned it the sobriquet, unwelcome to most Indians, of the would-be hegemonical power or bully of South Asia. Suspicion of India's intention is liable to be recurrent in her relations with her neighbours. Such suspicion is structured and situational, given her great size and strength *vis à vis* each and all of these neighbours. Undoubtedly there has been an intensification of regional relations in South Asia in the 1980s – whether measured in diplomatic exchanges, official visits or conferences – and these have been markedly more cooperative than conflictual. Conflict, however, remains an ever-present possibility and India's relations with Sri Lanka and Nepal deteriorated appreciably in the last two years of Rajiv's rule, though those with Pakistan briefly improved until rising political conflict in the Kashmir again led to a worsening. SAARC may help to assuage or ameliorate some fears India's neighbours have of her hegemonical tendencies, but it cannot entirely remove them. They are inherent in the inequalities of power and of India's enormously greater potential.[34]

India's expanding space

India today is a large and complex political jigsaw, many of whose component pieces have had their sizes and shapes changed, notably in the mid-1950s but on other specific occasions too,[35] especially in the vast north-east corner of what used to be called almost entirely Assam but is now made up of the 'seven-sister' states.[36] In the 1990s and beyond, even more than in the late 1980s, or in earlier years, it will be necessary to know about regions and localities in order to understand the tones and texture of nationalism within India. Locality and intra-state politics will also have to be seen and related to the whole nation–state polity in which they are encapsulated. Indeed, at no previous period in its long and complicated history have such diverse regions and vast populaces found themselves drawn so irresistibly into new orbits of political and economic activity, into new spheres of contending political influence, and by national and social ideologies which widen the expectations and ambitions of some but leave many others bewildered, confused and uncertain.

Independent India started with two major and related strategic weaknesses when compared with the subcontinent in the heyday of the British Raj. Partition and the launching of two successor states to the Raj almost inevitably made India and Pakistan rivals, even antagonists, from the start, with competing claims regarding such matters as the stores, equipment and sterling balances accumulated during British days, as well as the dispute over Kashmir and the insecurities felt by millions of recently created refugees in both countries. Whereas the British had treated the subcontinent as a strategic unity and sought to maintain inner and outer land frontiers as security belts around its imperial and quasi-imperial estates, the inception of Pakistan meant that India had to be preoccupied with a potential security threat on land and possibly simultaneously on her western and eastern flanks well south of the Himalayas, the traditional defensive glacis.[37] Furthermore, from 1805 onwards, the British had by their naval power in effect treated the Indian Ocean as a British lake, since they had a maritime preponderance. India had virtually no navy of any size and capacity in the 1940s and it was not to begin to build one up seriously until the 1970s. It thus only became a major naval power in the late 1980s.

It needs to be remembered too, as India's strategic planners certainly do, that India's national territory and maritime approaches include the Andaman and Nicobar Islands to the east and the Lakshadweeps in the west. The Andamans make a broken chain of islands in the eastern part of the Bay of Bengal commanding the northern entrance to and exit from the Straits of Malacca (one of the great maritime arteries and 'choke points' of the world's system) about 800 miles to the east and south-east of Madras. The Lakshadweeps are a group of very small islands which lie between 100 and 200 miles off the south-west coast of India.

The armed forces

Before 1947 the armed forces in India were instruments of the Raj serving to help maintain British imperial rule or paramountcy throughout the subcontinent and also being employed for British imperial policing and peacekeeping tasks in and around the Indian Ocean. In the two world wars of the twentieth century the contribution of Indian forces to Britain's war efforts was considerable and consequential. After 1947 those who had served the Raj before independence were, in the eyes of some nationalists, tinged with the memory of having been collaborators with the British (rather as those who joined the renegade self-styled Indian National Army, led by Subhash Chandra Bose, which had collaborated with the Japanese in World War Two, were regarded by some as brave patriots and by others as contemptible traitors). From 1947 until 1962 India's armed forces were relatively neglected and preoccupied with Pakistan. The Chinese attack in 1962 rapidly changed all that. Henceforth India's armed forces were, and are, regarded as vital auxiliaries of the nation's integrity, security and reputation.

The chances of a successful coup in India mounted by the military have perhaps increased in recent years, but not by much. The two most powerful reasons why a coup is unlikely to be seriously mounted, still less to succeed, remain valid. First, because India is such a vast and complex country, even a well-planned and efficiently executed take-over plot carried out in New Delhi would still not guarantee that the would-be coup makers could command support and exercise authority in Bombay, Calcutta, Madras and elsewhere in the country. Put simply, there are formidable functional difficulties in the way of a successful military take-over. Secondly, there is an ingrained professionalism of training and tradition throughout the upper reaches of India's armed forces which predisposes the officer corps to accept and prefer civilian rule in the nation's government. Some commentators would add a third consideration inhibiting a possible military take-over: the well-tried and working commitment of most Indians to a civil, indeed democratic, polity, demonstrated at many general elections since 1947 and especially in the widespread opposition to Mrs Gandhi's Emergency between 1975 and 1977. Even so, it is also said, plausibly, by some commentators that this entrenched disposition of India's armed forces to respect a civilian system and ethos of government and administration has been undermined in recent years by two unwelcome trends: the increasing use of the army in internal law-and-order operations (to quell civil unrest and communal violence – unwelcome tasks for any army) and the alienation of some Sikhs from serving in the armed forces (where, as previously noted, their presence and influence has been greatly in excess of their relatively small proportion of India's total population).

Nation-building

'Nations, it may be, have fashioned their Governments, but the Governments have paid them back in the same coin.' Dennis Austin took these mordant lines from Joseph Conrad as the epigram for his classic *Politics in Ghana 1946–1960*, first published in 1964; but they are equally relevant and applicable to the condition of India since independence and its prospects for the 1990s.

There are many tensions currently troubling India – of class and caste, region and religion. From Punjab to Assam, Kashmir to Karnataka or Tamil Nadu, the national repercussions of foreign connections and perturbations or the internationalisation of internally focused violence are obtrusive and protean. The complex interaction of these various levels needs to be studied and understood, each in its ever-changing, specific context, difficult though this is.

Elsewhere, Dennis Austin recalls, perhaps to endorse, William Butler Yeats's dictum that 'State and Nation are the work of the intellect and when you consider what comes before and after them, they are, as Victor Hugo says of something or other, not worth the blade of grass God gives for the nest of the linnet'.[38] Jawaharlal Nehru, and perhaps Mahatma Gandhi, would have appreciated this vaguely pantheistic outburst. Austin does not fail to note that Yeats, that most quixotically lyrical poet of Irish nationalism, actually devoted a great deal of his life to the ever-demanding causes of state and nation-building – causes, which, it should be added, are seldom easily or comfortably congruent, and certainly not for the India of today, or tomorrow, as has been indicated in this essay. Yeats also translated some of Rabindranath Tagore's Bengali poetry into English and it is ironical, to say the least, that Tagore's poetry should provide the words for the national anthems of not just one, but two South Asian nations, Bangladesh as well as India. Nevertheless, the fact is that millions of Indians have now been drawn into the vortices of state and nation-building by the times in which they live. For most of them, the winds of chance and change are in their lifetimes irresistible and inescapable.

Notes

1 So far as I know, there are no extended studies which focus specifically on India as a post-colonial state. But for instructive general discussion, see Hamza Alavi, 'The state in post-colonial societies: Pakistan and Bangladesh', *New Left Review*, No. 74, July-August 1972, pp. 59–81; G. van Benthem van den Bergh, *Is a Marxist Theory of the State Possible?*, Institute of Social Studies, The Hague, The Netherlands, Occasional Papers, No. 61, February 1977, 36 pp; Dennis Austin, 'What happened to the colonial state?', *The Round Table*, No. 295, July 1985, pp. 206–16, has some interesting general things to say, and the same author offers ruminations on contemporary India in 'Revisiting Delhi', *The Round Table*, No. 308, October 1988, pp. 373–86.

2 One of the most significant and, to some, surprising legacies has been the continued cultural hegemony of the English-speaking, English-language educated élites at the top echelons of Ministries, and mandarin posts within India's hierarchically ordered government and bureaucratic system. For more general treatments of this complex matter of British legacies to India, see M. and T. Zinkin, *Britain and India: Requiem for an Empire*, Chatto and Windus, London, 1964; Michael Lipton and John Firn, *Britain and India since 1960: the Erosion of a Relationship*, London, 1975; and chapters by Ainslie Embree, James Manor, Myron Weiner and others in *Transfer and Transformation: Political Institutions in the New Commonwealth*, edited by Peter Lyon and James Manor, Leicester University Press, Leicester, 1983.

3 For some discussion of this theme, see Peter Lyon, 'New states and international order' in *The Bases of International Order*, Oxford University Press, London, 1973, and various essays in *The Expansion of International Society*, edited by Hedley Bull and Adam Watson, Clarendon Press, Oxford, 1984, especially Gopal Krishna, 'India and the international order: retreat from idealism'.

4 See Tariq Ali, *An Indian Dynasty: The Story of the Nehru–Gandhi Family*, Putnams, New York, 1985.

5 See Jawaharlal Nehru, *Independence and After*, Government of India Publications, New Delhi, 1949.

6 See Judith Brown, *Gandhi and Civil Disobedience: The Mahatma in Indian Politics, 1928–34*, Cambridge University Press, Cambridge, 1977.

7 See R. J. Moore, *Making the New Commonwealth*, Clarendon Press, Oxford, 1987.

8 The literature on the Kashmir issue is already immense and growing each year. But see Peter Lyon, 'Kashmir', *International Relations*, Vol. 3 (2), October 1966, pp. 111–28; Alastair Lamb, *Crisis in Kashmir, 1947–1966*, Routledge & Kegan Paul, London, 1966.

9 See V. P. Menon, *The Story of the Integration of the Indian States*, Longman, London, 1956.

10 There are many biographies of Nehru. The two best are by Michael Brecher, *Nehru: A Political Biography*, Oxford University Press, London, 1959, and the authorised biography, drawing on much unpublished material, in 3 volumes by S. Gopal, *Jawaharlal Nehru: A Biography*, Cape, London, 1979. Nehru's own writings and speeches are, of course, an indispensable source. A convenient introduction to his speeches on foreign policy is J. Nehru, *India's Foreign Policy*, Government of India Publications, New Delhi, 1961. For a demonstration of India as a pioneer of non-alignment, see Peter Lyon, *Neutralism*, Leicester University Press, Leicester, 1963.

11 See S. Gopal, *Jawaharlal Nehru: a Biography: Vol. 2 1947–1956*, Cape, London, 1979.

12 For a classical account, critical of India, see Neville Maxwell, *India's China War*, Cape, London, 1970. For an extended review of this book, see Peter Lyon, 'Tones of injury and pride', *South Asian Review*, April 1971, pp. 237–42. Maxwell's designation of the conflict as 'India's China war' skilfully challenged official Indian versions which represented their country as the innocent victim of China's expansionism, whereas he, and the Chinese government, maintained that China was merely countering India's forward policy and was attempting to perpetuate initially dubious and then dishonest British boundary claims.

13 W. H. Morris-Jones, *Parliament in India*, Longman, London, 1957.

14 Selig Harrison, *India: The Most Dangerous Decades*, Princeton University Press, Princeton, NJ, 1960.

15 See Peter Lyon, 'Strategy and South Asia: twenty-five years on', *International Journal*, Vol. 27 (3), Summer 1972.

16 See J. Bandyopadhyaya, *The Making of India's Foreign Policy*, Allied Publishers Private Ltd, Calcutta, 2nd ed., 1979, pp. 321–7, for a brief summary of 'the Shastri era'. The author makes the point that Shastri, in picking Sardar Swaran Singh as the first full-time Foreign Minister of independent India (for Nehru had held the portfolio

coterminously with being Prime Minister), had chosen someone who was not only an unknown figure in foreign affairs, but had also not previously evinced either any grasp of or serious interest in the subject. Bandyopadhyaya nevertheless maintains that 'Shastri and Singh quietly replaced the high rhetoric and global sweep of Indian diplomacy as well as the personalized style of decision-making during the Nehru era by pragmatism, bilateralism, and institution building' (p. 325).

17 See ibid., pp. 327–41. Bandyopadhyaya remarks, *inter alia*, that one characteristic feature of Mrs Gandhi's foreign policy administration was her frequent change of Foreign Ministers. During this period of slightly less than eleven years of her Prime Ministership, 1966–77, she had five Foreign Ministers as well as holding the portfolio herself from 1967 to 1969. See also Zahir Masani, *Indira Gandhi: a Biography*, Oxford University Press, Delhi, 1978, and Surjit Mansingh, *India's Search for Power*, Sage Publications Ltd, New Delhi, 1984.

18 See W. H. Morris-Jones, 'Whose emergency – India's or Indira's?', *The World Today*, November 1976.

19 For background, see Peter Hardy, *The Muslims of British India*, Cambridge University Press, London, 1972. See also Theodore P. Wright Jr, 'Indian Muslims, the Bangladesh secession and the Indo-Pakistan War of 1971' in Giri Raj Gupta (ed.), *Contributions to Indian Sociology*, Vikas Publishing House, Delhi, 1977.

20 There is an extensive literature on Soviet-Indian relations. For some contrasting aspects of this theme, see C. van Hollen, 'The tilt policy revisited: Nixon-Kissinger geopolitics and South Asia', *Asian Survey*, Vol. XX (4), April 1980, pp. 339–61; Robert Litwak, 'The Soviet Union in India's security perspective', in T. George, R. Litwak and S. Chubin (eds.), *Security in Southern Asia: India and the Great Powers*, Gower, Aldershot, for the International Institute for Strategic Studies, 1984, pp. 69–145; Peter Lyon, 'The Soviet Union and South Asia in the 1980s', in *Soviet Interests in the Third World*, ed. Robert Cassen, Sage Publications for the Royal Institute of International Affairs, London, 1985, pp. 32– 45; and Peter J. S. Duncan, *The Soviet Union and India*, Routledge, London, for the Royal Institute of International Affairs, 1989.

21 For one succinct survey to 1983, see Shahram Chubin, 'The place of India in US foreign policy' in George, Litwak and Chubin (eds.), *Security in Southern Asia*, pp. 147–234.

22 There is still no authoritative account of India's foreign policy during the Janata government, 1977–9. But, for aspects of this theme and the fall of the government, see Arun Gandhi, *The Morarji Papers: Fall of the Janata Government*, Vision Books, New Delhi, 1983.

23 See, in addition to ibid., David E. Albright, 'The USSR and the Third World in the 1980s', *Problems of Communism*, Vol. 38 (2–3), March-June 1989, pp. 50–70.

24 See Surjit Mansingh and Steven I. Levine, 'China and India: moving beyond confrontation', in ibid., pp. 30–49.

25 For regionalist trends in South Asia as they affect India and also a detailed year-by-year account of India's foreign policy, see *Yearbook on India's Foreign Policy*, edited, since 1982–3, by Satish Kumar, Sage Publications, New Delhi and London.

26 There is no authoritative study of India's post-1947 army comparable to Stephen Cohen's study of that army to 1947, or the same author's study of the Pakistan army. But, for a useful comparative essay on this theme, see Stephen P. Cohen, *The Military and Politics in India, Pakistan and Bangladesh*, Urbana-Champaign, Illinois, 1972, mimeo.

27 See Robin Jeffrey, *What's Happening to India? Punjab, Ethnic Conflict, Mrs Gandhi's Death and the Test for Federalism*, Macmillan, London, 1986.

28 On this theme, see James Manor, 'Anomie in Indian politics', *Economic and Political Weekly*, Bombay, May 1983, and the same author's 'The electoral process amid awakening and decay: reflections on the Indian general election of 1980' in Lyon and Manor (eds.), *Transfer and Transformation*.

29 There is, as yet, no book-length, worthwhile survey of these years, but see Mark Tully and Zaheer Masani, *From Raj to Rajiv: Forty Years of Independent India*, BBC Publications, London, 1988. See also Barrington Moore Jr, *Social Origins of Dictatorship and Democracy*, Allen-Lane, London, 1966, especially Ch. VI, pp. 314–410, for some discussion of the Indian experience in a wide, comparative perspective.

30 On this theme, see Nitya Narayan Banerjee, *Hindu Polity: Positive and Perverted*, Hindutva Publications, New Delhi, 1988. The electoral successes of the Bharatiya Janata Party (BJP) in the November 1989 general election were widely construed by commentators as evidence of the growing strength of Hindu fundamentalism.

31 For the ICS, see the classic account by Philip Woodruff (pseud. for Mason), *The Men Who Ruled India*, Cape, London, 2 vols., 1954. See also David C. Potter, *India's Political Administrators, 1919–1983*, Clarendon Press, Oxford, 1986.

32 The changing styles and modes of analysis of India's political economy are conveyed in the following books:

(i) A. H. Hanson, *The Process of Planning: A Study of India's Five-Year Plans 1950–1964*, Oxford University Press for the Royal Institute of International Affairs, London, 1966 looks at the Indian planning process over the period of the first three five-year plans from the perspective of a student of politics and public administration.

(ii) Francine R. Frankel: *India's Green Revolution: Economic Gains and Political Costs*, Princeton University Press, Princeton, NJ, 1971; *India's Political Economy 1947–75: The Gradual Revolution*, Princeton University Press, Princeton, NJ, 1978. These are studies by an American political scientist of the significance and impact of agribusiness on modern India.

(iii) Lloyd I. and Susanne Hoeber Rudolph, *In Pursuit of Lakshmi: The Political Economy of the Indian State*, University of Chicago Press, Chicago and London, 1987. Lakshmi is the Hindu goddess of wealth, but there is in fact very little explicitly about this goddess in this wide-ranging scholarly book. For extensive discussion of its analysis, in five contrasting essays, see 'The state of political economy in India: the work of Lloyd and Susanne Rudolph', *The Journal of Commonwealth and Comparative Politics*, Vol. 26 (3), November 1988 with essays by W. H. Morris-Jones, Ashotosh Varshney, T. J. Byres, the Rudolphs themselves and Subrata K. Mitra.

33 Clive Crook, 'The Third World: a survey', *The Economist*, 23 September 1989, p. 4.

34 See Peter Lyon, 'India as a core state' in Martin Edmonds and Ned Sabrovsky (eds.), *Foreign Policies of Core Powers*, Prentice Hall, New York, 1990.

35 The story is complex. The Constitution, which came into force on 26 January 1950, provided for nine Part A States (Assam, Bihar, Bombay, Madhya Pradesh, Madras, Orissa, Punjab, Uttar Pradesh, and West Bengal) which corresponded to the previous governors' provinces; eight Part B States (Hyderabad, Jammu and Kashmir, Madhya Bharat, Mysore, Patalia-East Punjab (PEPSU), Rajasthan, Saurashtra, and Travancore-Cochin) which corresponded to Indian states or unions of states; ten Part C States (Ajmer, Bhopal, Bilaspur, Coorg, Delhi, Himachal Pradesh, Kutch, Manipur, Tripura, and Vindhya Pradesh) which corresponded to the chief commissioners' provinces; and Part D Territories and other areas (e.g., Andaman and Nicobar Islands). Part A States (under governors) and Part B States (under rajpramukhs) had provincial autonomy with a ministry and elected assembly. Part C States (under chief commissioners) were the direct responsibility of the Union Government, although Kutch, Manipur, and Tripura had legislatures with limited powers. Andhra was formed as a Part A State on its separation from Madras in 1953. Bilaspur was merged with Himachal Pradesh in 1954.

The States Reorganisation Act, 1956, abolished the distinction between Parts A, B and C States and established two categories for the units of the Indian Union, to be called States and Territories. The following were the main territorial changes: the Telugu districts of Hyderabad were merged with Andhra; Mysore absorbed the whole Kannada-speaking area (including Coorg, the greater part of four districts of Bombay, three districts of Hyderabad, and one district of Madras); Bhopal, Vindhya Pradesh and Madhya Bharat were merged with Madhya Pradesh, which ceded eight Marathi-speaking districts to Bombay; the new state of Kerala, comprising the majority of Malayalam-speaking peoples, was formed from Travancore-Cochin with a small area from Madras; Patalia-East Punjab was included in Punjab, Kutch and Saurashtra in Bombay, and Ajmer in Rajasthan; Hyderabad ceased to exist.

On 1 May 1960 Bombay State was divided into two parts: seventeen districts (including Saurashtra and Kutch) in the north and west became the new state of Gujarat; the remainder was renamed the state of Maharashtra.

In August 1961 the former Portuguese territories of Dadra and Nagar Haveli became a Union territory. The Portuguese territory of Goa and the smaller territories of Daman and Diu, occupied by India in December 1961, were constituted a Union territory in March 1962. In August 1962 the former French territories of Pondicherry, Karikal, Mahé, and Yanaon were formally transferred to India and became Union territory. In September 1962 the Naga Hills Tuensang Area was constituted a separate state under the name of Nagaland. On 1 November 1966, under the Punjab Reorganisation Act 1966, a new state of Haryana and a new Union Territory of Chandigarh were created from parts of Punjab (India). On 26 January 1971 Himachal Pradesh became a state. In 1972 the North East Frontier Agency and Mizo hill district were made Union territories (as Arunachal Pradesh and Mizoram), and Manipur, Meghalaya and Tripura full states. Sikkim became a state in 1975. Statehood for Mizoram was passed by parliament in July 1986, for Arunachal Pradesh in December 1986 and for Goa in May 1987.

36 K. Subrahmanyam, *India's North East Frontier Region*, The Institute for the Study of Conflict, London, 1988.

37 See, further, Peter Lyon, 'Strategy and South Asia', *International Journal*, 1972.

38 See Dennis Austin, *Politics in Africa*, Manchester University Press, Manchester, 1978, p. 160. In his notes for this and an allied passage, Austin quotes Yeats in terms which surely apply to such different, anglicised Indians as Jawaharlal Nehru, Nirad Chaudhuri, and in-

numerable others: 'I know . . . that I owe my soul to Shakespeare, to Spenser and to Blake, perhaps to William Morris, and to the English language in which I think, speak and write, that everything I love has come to me through English; my hatred tortures me with love, my love with hate.' William Butler Yeats, 'A general introduction for my work' in A. Norman Jaffares (ed.), *Yeats: Selected Criticism*, Macmillan, London, 1973, p. 265, cited by Austin, p. 192, n. 14.

3 *Anirudha Gupta*

Paradise lost: the fall of Sri Lanka

In 1947, as Ceylon approached independence, Britain looked with pride at its own accomplishment there as a colonial power. Ceylon, in every sense, had been a model colony – it had a large literate population, a per capita income which was the highest in Asia (until Japan overtook it), a sterling reserve of 1,260 million rupees and, above all, a crop of able politicians and administrators who believed that they could attain self-government in a leisurely, gentlemanly, way. They eschewed what they saw as Gandhi's rabble-rousing agitational methods in India, shunned communal politics of the type which led to India's partition, and kept their distance from the masses almost as an article of faith. Ceylon was indeed 'a paradise in contrast to India' – and there could be hardly any reason to disbelieve Lord Soulbury when he told the House of Lords in 1947 that, 'with such natural resources and with leaders of proven experience, I feel that Ceylon can face the future under the highest auspices'.[1]

That was forty years ago: yet barely a decade passed before Soulbury's prophetic utterances were overtaken by a surge of Sinhala nationalism. 'Sinhala Now' was the cry which swept S. W. R. D. Bandaranaike's Sri Lanka Freedom Party (SLFP) into power in 1956 with the support of the Buddhist church and Sinhala peasantry. Elite politics suddenly caved in – and, almost as in a chain reaction, relations between majority Sinhala and minority Tamil snapped. By the middle of the 1950s, Ceylon had witnessed revolutionary changes in two opposite directions: first, subversion of the élite and entry of the non-English speaking masses into politics; and second, a growing divide between Sinhala and Tamil.

The opposites, perhaps, fed each other: the 'Sinhala now' call pushed Sir John Kolelawala's leadership in the United National Party (UNP) on to the defensive; in no time he and his senior colleagues in the party turned round to placate the Sinhalese demand for 'paramountcy of majority interest'[2] in a race for power with Bandaranaike's SLFP and other allied parties. This pushed the Tamils into a corner: instead of working for a viable federal structure which the old party, the Tamil Congress, had upheld, they now faced the threat of extinction as a minority in the evolving Sinhala polity. The Tamil Congress and the Federal Party joined hands to press for a separate Tamil homeland – the Tamil *eelam*.

What followed thereafter was the unfolding of tragedy: the first race riots in 1958, great communal protests in 1977, 1983, 1986 and, finally, outright civil war between Sinhala and Tamil peoples in the northern and eastern provinces. 'Youth power' in both communities raised its ugly head: gun replaced ballot, as party leaders, civil servants and government men were hacked to pieces.[3] By 1985–6 Ceylon, now Sri Lanka, had turned into a virtual inferno. Facing near collapse under the unending weight of violence, anarchy and terrorism, the UNP government of J. R. Jayewardene signed an accord with Rajiv Gandhi's government in India to invite some 50,000 Indian soldiers to disarm the Tamil terrorists and, in return, work for the merger of the two Tamil majority provinces into one, with an elected legislature and some measure of devolved power.[4] As we shall see, this effort was not successful. But, long before India's intervention came to dominate the Sri Lankan tragedy, its basic course – as is the way with tragedies – had been determined.

What went wrong with Sri Lanka? Why did the 'paradise' lose its innocence? Why did the first generation of Sinhala nationalists fail to consolidate itself into a unifying élite 'rather like Professor Plumb's consolidating classes of Restoration England: class modifying ethnicity, ethnicity tempering classes?'[5] A succession of British advisers and administrators had worked ceaselessly for such an élite to emerge – from Lord Donoughmore with his committee system and adult franchise (1931–47) to Lord Soulbury who put the final touches to Ceylon's Westminster model constitution in 1947. Did nobody see any chinks in such efforts? Was there no

Cassandra around as colonial Ceylon was hammered into shape for independence as 'the best job Englishman has done anywhere in the world, almost better than in his own country'?[6]

The constitutional framework

Doubters existed but they came from strange quarters. Reflecting earlier British fears, the élite leadership of the Ceylon Congress was apprehensive of Lord Donoughmore's radical commitment to introduce adult franchise in the 1930s. Instead, they called for a limited suffrage and warned that, if the franchise went a grade lower, 'there will be a class of voters whose votes might be at the disposal of the highest bidders'.[7] What the Congress leaders wanted was responsible and not representative government: hence they opposed mass participation in politics. With the benefit of hindsight one could see that their fears were genuine. They survived largely because of the committee formula which contained party politics from bursting the seams till 1947. What would have happened had the committee system been replaced by a cabinet government, say, in 1930 instead of 1947? Would it have hastened the breakdown of Ceylon and brought the Sinhala–Tamil issue to the fore even before independence was granted? This was a point raised by other sceptics. During the debate on the Ceylon Independence Bill in the House of Commons, Captain L. D. Gammans, a spokesman for colonial affairs for the Conservative opposition, had this to say:

> The second danger which Ceylon faces is one which the right Hon. Gentleman, the Secretary of State for the Colonies, has not mentioned except very slightly today. It is that Ceylon is not a single racial unit. There are two races in Ceylon; the Sinhalese and Jaffna Tamils, who are in the northern part of the island, and number 1,500,000 out of a total of 6,500,000. They differ from the Sinhalese in race, language, religion, and, to a large extent, in background. They are extremely capable and intelligent people . . .

He then delivered a sombre verdict, warning that 'where there is a racial minority in the country the danger is that it may become a permanent political minority'. 'Ceylon's evolution on a democratic basis', he went on, 'was bound to fail.'[8]

Had the British perceived the connection between class and

ethnicity in Ceylon (where the newly enfranchised working class was dominated by the Sinhalese majority) they might have shown more care to safeguard the Tamil minorities in the Independence Constitution, or even perhaps considered granting an ethnically ascertained sub-state of Tamil provinces in a federation of independent Ceylon. That some guarantees to the minorities were considered important enough can be seen in the entrenched clauses of Article 29(2) of the constitution. They stated that Parliament was not competent to pass laws that

(a) prohibit or restrict the free exercise of any religion; or

(b) make persons of any community or religion liable to disabilities or restrictions to which persons of other communities or religions are not made liable; or

(c) confer on persons of any community or religion any privilege or advantage which is not conferred on persons of other communities or religions; or

(d) alter the constitution of any religious body except with the consent of the governing authority of that body.[9]

However, the constitution as a whole was subject to amendment by a majority vote of not less than two-thirds of the members of the Ceylon House (including those not present). As it happened, the Independence Constitution was replaced by the 1972 Constitution which *inter alia* also abolished the entrenched clauses regarding the minorities. But, even before 1972, the official Language Act of 1956, passed by a simple majority in Parliament, directly clashed with the entrenched provisions of Article 29(2). By this act Sinhala entry into administration, civil posts, colleges and universities was officially advanced and ensured at the cost of the Tamils. The result was the race riots of 1958.[10]

Could it be said, therefore, that much of the trouble the Tamils faced in later years was due to the weak structuring of the Independence Constitution? This seems surprising, especially in view of the weighting the Colonial Office always gave to minorities at the time of the transfer of power to a colony. Perhaps the framers of the Soulbury Constitution hoped that the entrenched provisions concerning the minorities would never be altered after Ceylon gained independence? Indeed, when a case involving these provisions came up for consideration before the Privy Council in 1964, Lord Pearce formulated his *obiter dictum* in these words: '[Article 29(2)] represents the solemn balance of rights between the citizens of

Ceylon, the fundamental conditions on which *inter se* they accepted the Constitution: and these are therefore unalterable under the Constitution.'[11] But the judgement itself, according to M. L. Marasinghe, 'signalled the commencement of a process towards replacing the Soulbury Constitution with an autochthonous model' – and the 1972 Constitution was a product of this autochthony.[12] Its results were disastrous: had it incorporated – instead of subsuming – Article 29(2), it could have largely prevented the Tamil-speaking people from becoming a permanent minority.[13]

Democratic commitment

And yet, in trying to trace the sources of Sinhala–Tamil conflict, we are perhaps overlooking one important aspect, namely that at no point since 1947 have the rulers of Sri Lanka moved deliberately away from the constitutional, democratic path. Elections were held regularly – 1952, 1956, twice in 1960 (March and July), 1965, 1970 and 1977 and again in 1989. Even when the UNP's massive victory in the 1977 elections led to the enactment of another constitution replacing the cabinet system by a Presidential one, a referendum was held in December 1982 to obtain an extension of the life of Parliament for a period of another six years. The move was controversial, but nevertheless had both legal and constitutional validity.[14] Notwithstanding the spread of violence in the late 1980s, with Indian troops locked in combat with the Tamil Tigers in the north, and the Janatha Vimukthi Peramuna (JVP or People's Liberation Front, an extreme Sinhalese nationalist movement) murderously engaged in killing its enemies in the south, the Sri Lankans did not wholly abandon the parliamentary path. Under the Rajiv–Jayewardene accord of July 1987, it was agreed to set up provincial ministries in nine provinces (the north and east to be joined into one), for which again – even in the face of the SLFP boycott led by Mrs Bandaranaike and threats of violence from the JVP and the Tigers – elections were held in 1988. Although it is certain that in some constituencies voters were intimidated and the ballot rigged, this did not invalidate the elections. It was only in the northern province that no contest could be held as few candidates were willing to risk their lives to defy the Tigers; but this was more than made up when over 70 per cent of voters turned up in the eastern province elections in December 1988.

Perhaps it was because Jayewardene's government showed a firm determination to go ahead with these elections that the contest for Presidential office generated widespread enthusiasm. Once more, after a gap of ten years, the UNP and the SLFP were locked in an electoral battle, with an independent candidate thrown in between to stake his claim. Ranasinghe Premadasa, the UNP's candidate, won by a big margin and this set the stage for the general elections to Parliament in February 1989. Despite great violence – as many as thirteen candidates and nearly 300 political activists lost their lives in the four weeks preceding the elections – the voter turnout was 63·3 per cent, higher than the 56 per cent recorded in the Presidential poll in December. Voting was low in the south mainly due to threats by the JVP to shoot those who voted; yet the UNP won a majority of seats in the two districts where the JVP was said to have been the most active. The election results reaffirmed the comparative strength of the parties, with the UNP capturing 125 of the 225 seats, followed by Mrs Bandaranaike's SLFP with 67. In the north-east province, the Tamil United Liberation Front (TULF) alliance won ten seats, while a militant Tamil group, the Eelam Revolutionary Organisation of Students (EROS), captured thirteen seats.[15]

A more remarkable illustration of the democratic commitment of Sri Lankan politicians since independence is that even the extremist parties, including the JVP, the Trotskyites and Communists, came round at one point or other to participating in elections. After their failed attempt at insurrection, the JVP cadres turned from violence to parliamentary politics in 1977. They contested the local District Development Council elections in 1981, polled around 10–23 per cent of the votes in different districts and actually won a total of thirteen seats.[16] The JVP leader, Rohaval Wigeweera (himself later to be a victim of the vicious cycle of violence – he was assassinated in December 1989), even stood as a Presidential candidate in 1977 and, although he got only 7·1 per cent of the total votes polled, in certain Sinhala areas his returns were impressive.

It does not appear either that the Tamil–Sinhala ethnic violence, or the terror created by the JVP after the landing of foreign troops on the island's soil – which in fact provided fodder to Sinhala nationalist passions exploited by the JVP – has yet distracted the mass of Sri Lankans from the democratic path. Elections have become a hazardous undertaking, but that is perhaps as much the case in India, the Philippines or even Jamaica. The undertaking itself has not resulted in a total breakdown of Sri Lankan society.

The character of electoral politics

This suggests that we need to take a closer look at the character of Sri Lanka's evolving electoral politics since 1947. What do we see here? The leaders of the old Ceylon National Congress (transformed in 1947 into the UNP) were largely drawn from the middle-class, Cambridge-educated, professional and property-owning families. Led by two outstanding political figures, Dudley Senanaike and John Kolelawala, they disclaimed communal politics and treated with contempt the rumbling Sinhala renaissance movement led by the Buddhist clergy. They held their ground for a time, but were increasingly moving against the current of local opinion. In the 1956 elections, the coalition Mahajana Eksath Peramuna (MEP), with Solomon Bandaranaike's SLFP at the centre and supported by the Lanka Sama Samaja Pakshaya (LSSP), the Communist Party (CP) and the Buddhists, swept the polls. From a majority of fifty-four, the UNP was left with only eight seats. The MEP combine formed a government with over 60 per cent of the seats in Parliament. Five years later, in March 1960, there was a hung Parliament which forced a second election in July and returned the United Front (UF) of SLFP and left parties. In 1965, the UF lost to the UNP which formed a rather shaky government only to lose again in a decisive manner in the 1970 elections. The UF's overwhelming majority in Parliament (116 out of 179) made it possible to turn Sri Lanka into a Republic with a new constitution. But seven years later, in 1977, the UNP returned to power winning 139 of 166 seats. This was more than the two-thirds the UNP needed to frame a new constitution with an executive President and the postponement of elections for the next ten years.[17]

Several points emerge from this bland recital of the election results. Most notable is the fact that, in spite of their altering fortunes, the two major parties – the UNP and the SLFP – retained more or less their traditional size of votes: the UNP around 30–38 per cent and the SLFP between 28 and 35 per cent. Except in 1956, when the UNP's élite leadership was virtually thrown overboard by the 'Sinhala now' movement, it should be noted that, electorally, the UNP drew its largest support as a single party between 1960 and 1977. Yet precisely because it preferred to stay alone (with perhaps a few small allies), the SLFP's electoral alliance with the left parties (LSSP and CP) enabled it to wrest a disproportionately large number of seats in Parliament. Alliance with Bandaranaike's SLFP, on the other hand, helped the left parties to win not only a steady number of seats (in 1970 the LSSP nearly doubled the seats it had won in 1965), but also greater respectability by their induction into various Bandaranaike ministries.

Thus, notwithstanding fluctuations in their electoral fortunes, the Sinhala-based parties showed every sign of securing stability by turning their votes into sizeable pockets of political support. It was only in 1977 that the UNP defeated the combined opposition on its own and, for the first time, as Jeyaratnam Wilson puts it, 'the winning party in a general election in Sri Lanka secured an absolute majority of the votes cast'.[18] But this was possible because by then the main left allies of the SLFP had left the United Front. It is remarkable that, with 30 per cent of votes, the SLFP could win only eight seats when, with a slightly larger measure of support (33 per cent), it had annexed no fewer then seventy-five seats (out of 151) in the July 1960 elections.

In other words, in the process of electoral competition a sort of stabilised party system had emerged – the UNP representing an essentially conservative tendency, and the SLFP and its smaller allies a somewhat radical but generally pro-Sinhala stream in Sri Lankan politics. The point is that, despite great pressures to which it sometimes succumbed (as on the issue of making Sinhala the official language in 1956), the UNP kept a liberal and secular approach towards ethnic minorities. Despite opposition, Jayewardene's leadership could induct some Tamils into the party and thus obtain a measure of electoral support in Tamil-dominated areas in the 1970 and 1977 elections. In contrast, the SLFP and its left allies made no pretence of keeping contact with Tamils.[19]

What about Tamil parties? Here we find another interesting feature. Throughout the period after 1956, the electoral contest in Tamil areas was mainly between the Tamil Congress (TC) and the Federal Party (FP). Between them, these two parties divided the seventeen constituencies located in the north-east provinces. In 1970, the FP nearly destroyed the TC on the basis of its campaign to save the 'Tamil race'.[20] Yet race had not yet become a major issue for Tamils; all they wanted was to close the doors against further incursions of Sinhala influence into their areas. In other words, they sought to achieve internal autonomy as far as their own affairs were concerned. This did not mean they wanted to opt out wholly from Sri Lankan politics: during the period 1965–70, the Tamil leaders worked in close association with the UNP government with a view to extracting concessions from Colombo for Tamils. Even after the general election of 1977, when Tamil parties combined to form the TULF, they did not show any indication of disengaging from national politics. On the contrary, as the second largest party (with eighteen MPs), the TULF eagerly looked forward to playing an important role in Parliament.[21] But the new constitution, with its Presidential executive and its entrenched clauses proclaiming the inviolability of Sri Lanka as a unitary state and Buddhism as the 'foremost' religion, frustrated the TULF's intentions. Instead of a policy of 'hands off Tamils', it now called for the establishment of a separate Tamil state. The stage was set for direct confrontation with Colombo.

By the end of the 1970s, then, Sri Lanka's political system was heading for a major crisis – a crisis of voluntary withdrawal on the part of an entrenched minority from what it perceived to be the *Volksdom* of the majority community. The system had, on the other hand, succeeded in absorbing an essentially peasant-based social revolt in the 1950s. S. W. R. D. Bandaranaike's MRP, supported by the Buddhists, spearheaded an unprecedented Sinhala upsurge against men of 'wealth and class', the English-speaking 6 per cent who held over 90 per cent of government jobs. Culturally, it represented a revivalist movement to free Sinhala culture and tradition from alien values and practices;[22] but in more practical terms it sought to remove the barriers founded on unequal economic and educational attainments *within* Sinhala society. The call for *Swabhasa* (the Sinhala language) to replace English thus aimed at bridging the gulf between the masses and a handful of élites. Solomon Bandaranaike was not, therefore, very insincere when he said, while moving the bill to make Sinhala the official language, that 'by giving the due and rightful place to the Sinhala language as the official language of the country, we have tried to eliminate the wide gap that existed between the government and the governed, between the élite and the masses'.[23]

So, a class revolution had succeeded, not by resorting to mass uprising but by a skilful use of the ballot box to bring the traditional, deeply religious, Sinhala peasantry on to the central stage of Sri Lankan politics. It was perhaps unintended that this Sinhala movement should have had so profound a negative impact on the Tamils who feared ethnic extinction against the onrush of Sinhala chauvinism. Basically, the 'Sinhala now' movement was not anti-Tamil, though eventually it proved to be so as it involved the all-important issue of economic openings for the Sinhalese. The advocates of *Swabhasa* were not anxious to drive the English-educated Sinhalese from the public service only to turn it over to the Tamils. Hence there came, in rapid succession, new laws to promote the Sinhala-speaking majority in business, education and public employment by progressively limiting the 'quota' for Tamils.

Ethnic rivalry was therefore an unintended fall-out of the *Swabhasa* movement. Bandaranaike admitted as much when he wrote: 'Our minds were really fixed at that time on the question of English vs *Swabhasa*. We did not bring our minds to bear, may be it was a fault on our part, on the question of Sinhala vs Tamil.'[24] Yet it was soon to become the largest single issue in Sri Lankan politics. Class had given way, only to be replaced by ethnicity. Were the two issues linked? Does a move towards egalitarianism inevitably create other fissures in a society based on culture, religion and tradition? The answer is not clear: but by the end of the 1970s, the Tamils had lost faith in Sri Lankan politicians of all hues and shades. The elderly leaders of the TULF, who had given the initial call for a separate homeland, were overthrown by their own youthful followers – angry, frustrated and ready to use any means to realise their goal. Exactly a decade after the appearance of 'youth power' had nearly toppled Bandaranaike's government, it had taken over the Jaffna peninsula. The war against Colombo had begun in real earnest: the gun had replaced the ballot for Tamils.

Conclusion

Could all this have been avoided? Perhaps so, perhaps not, what is evident is that another factor intervened critically in the Sinhala –

Tamil conflict – Sri Lanka's proximity to India. This fact of geography worked in curiously opposite ways – the closeness of India, especially Tamil Nadu, with its more than 50 million Tamils, made the Sinhalese suffer from an acute minority complex. Even with a majority of over 74 per cent of the Sri Lankan population, they dwelt on the fearful prospect of being overwhelmed and swept by a Tamil tide from across the Palk Strait. For their part, the Jaffna-Tamils utilised such proximity to build closer ties with political groups in Tamil Nadu. By 1980–3 almost every Tamil militant organisation had established its base or links in India. Parallel to Pan-Sinhala Buddhism, Tamils too had begun dreaming about a greater *eelam* uniting all Tamil-speaking peoples of India and Sri Lanka. In the world-view of both the communities, India loomed large.

What could have been the shape of Sri Lankan politics if these considerations had not played a major role? First, Tamils would have found little external support to back – and build – their struggle for a Tamil state. Second, they might have accepted eventually what Colombo was willing to give them by way of a settlement. Or, rejecting such overtures, they might have migrated in large numbers – as the Indians did in Fiji after General Rabuka's coup in 1987. Or, simply accepting fate, they might have returned to their traditional role of keeping a measure of their autonomy within the unitary state of Sri Lanka. All this was not possible because India became increasingly – though unwillingly? – involved in Sri Lanka's ethnic crisis.

The Tamil–Sinhala conflict was thus catapulted into an international dispute. It was beyond Colombo's means to resolve the crisis internally. Tragically the task has also defeated India, whose government agreed to withdraw its 'peace-keeping' force during 1990. Cleavages based on class can perhaps be mediated, if not wholly resolved; but when the process of mediation itself leads to cleavages based on language or ethnicity, the task of reconciliation or compromise becomes immeasurably more complex. How much one wishes that Sri Lanka had no strongly entrenched minorities, or that such minorities were not linked by language, history and religion with the peoples of another country. But perhaps even paradise is not free from conflict: certainly it is not in the Buddhist or Hindu vision in which the gods are continually at war with each other!

Notes

1 Quoted in Sir Charles Jeffries, *Ceylon: the Path to Independence*, Pall Mall Press, London, 1962, p. 126.
2 I am paraphrasing here Lord Devonshire's famous declaration on the 'paramountcy of majority African interest' in East Africa in 1923.
3 For a swift account, see Dennis Austin and Anirudha Gupta, *Lions and Tigers: The Crisis in Sri Lanka*, Centre for Security and Conflict Studies, London, 1988.
4 For the Accord and its legal implications, see M. L. Marasinghe, 'Ethnic politics and constitutional reform: the Indo-Sri Lankan Accord', *International and Comparative Law Quarterly*, Vol. 37, Part 3, July 1988, pp. 551–87.
5 Both the ideas and the rhetoric are borrowed from Dennis Austin's essay, 'What happened to the Colonial State? Hegel, Mann and the Tables of the Law', *The Round Table*, No. 295, 1985, pp. 206–16.
6 The words of Ceylon's first Governor-General, Oliver Goonetilleke, quoted in Calvin A. Woodward, *The Growth of a Party System in Ceylon*, Brown University Press, Providence, RI, 1969, p. 3.
7 Quoted in K. M. de Silva, *A History of Sri Lanka*, C. Hurst & Co., London, 1981, p. 419.
8 Quoted in Marasinghe, *op. cit.*, p. 558.
9 Ibid., p. 556.
10 Ibid., p. 561.
11 Quoted in ibid., p. 556.
12 Ibid., p. 561.
13 Ibid.
14 See K. M. de Silva, *Managing Ethnic Tensions in Multi-ethnic Societies: Sri Lanka 1880–1985*, University Press of America, Boston Way, Lanham, 1986, pp. 334–7.
15 Speaking after his party's victory, President Premadasa said that those outside the mainstream of politics should realise that the people had rejected violence and warned that any attempt at sabotage would be treated as an act of treachery. *The Times*, London, 17 February 1989.
16 For an interesting discussion of the JVP, see Swaroop Rani Dubey, *One Day Revolution in Sri Lanka*, Aalekh Publishers, Jaipur, 1988.
17 See Marasinghe, *op. cit.*
18 Jeyaratnam Wilson, 'General elections in Sri Lanka 1947–1977' in K. M. de Silva (ed.), *Universal Franchise 1931–81: The Sri Lankan Experience*, Department of Information, Colombo, July 1981, p. 101.
19 For details, see Jeyaratnam Wilson, *Electoral Politics in an Emergent State: The Ceylon General Election of May 1970*, Cambridge University Press, Cambridge, 1975; and K. M. de Silva, *History of Sri Lanka*.

20 Wilson, *op. cit.*, p. 177.

21 In fact, the TULF also put up its own candidate (G. Ponnambalam) to contest the 1977 Presidential election.

22 Robert N. Kearney, *Communalism and Language in the Politics of Ceylon*, Duke University Press, Durham, NC, 1967, p. 48.

23 Quoted in Kearney, *op. cit.*, p. 80.

24 S. W. R. D. Bandaranaike, *Towards a New Era*, Government Press, Colombo, 1961, p. 388.

4 *Richard Rathbone*

Politics in Ghana and politics in Ghana

Twenty-five years after the publication of Dennis Austin's *Politics in Ghana, 1946–60,*[1] it is all too easy to take it for granted in the way in which one no longer notices parts of a familiar landscape. It has somehow always been on the library shelf, monumental, authoritative and the last word on that period of Ghana's history. Perversely, while the reviews were almost universally complimentary, few suggested how very important the study was. In the general atmosphere of excitement which typified African Studies in the 1960s, excellence was always welcome but somehow expected. Virtually every new publication in the field added a massive amount of sheer information to a growing, hungry audience eager to know more and more about a newsworthy and rapidly changing continent.

But *Politics in Ghana* was unusual in a variety of ways. First, it was and is a product of more than just good scholarship. Whilst it was clearly the work of an unusually gifted scholar, it betrayed a distinctive distaste for the excesses of contemporary political science. It deployed little theory. There were few references to the trend-setting social science scholarship of the day; the author made no use of the complex neologisms, the social science 'newspeak' of that period. Dennis Austin consistently appeared to be more interested in an accessible style than in persuading his readers that he had read and understood everything that was coming out of Chicago or Ann Arbor. The resulting text was never pompous or stilted. Indeed its apparently relaxed but carefully crafted style implicitly suggested that long, fancy words and tortuous theoretical constructs very frequently concealed imprecision, poor data or cowardly conformism.

Secondly, it was very frequently an engagingly irreverent book. Austin enjoyed the jokes like a good Ghanaian would; he treasured the frequent ironies of that great concentration of hypocrisies and cant that all political arenas are. More than most of the other observers he could spot tongues in cheeks and weasel-words at great distances. Compared with, for example, David Apter's or Thomas Hodgkin's grave approaches,[2] there was throughout an intense but amused scepticism. But that scepticism was seldom cynical, never snide but rather an affectionate matter. Interviewing politicians, for example, was, for both parties, it seemed, something of a game rather than a pale imitation of the gravity of the confessional. This emerged from the third distinctive feature of the book. Unlike any of the other great pioneer studies, Austin's was an extremely intimate book. Austin knew Ghana in a way that, despite their great contributions, Martin Kilson did not know Sierra Leone, Jim Coleman Nigeria or Aristide Zolberg the Ivory Coast. More than any other contemporary expatriate political scientist, Austin came closer to a biography than to cold, hard political science.

All of this made the book immensely readable. Many of us have read it many times and it never ceases to read well. Its accessibility as well as its content have ensured that it continues to be frequently cited. It is a book that has, over time, become a hallowed primary source. But some of its great merits are more equivocally welcome. *Politics in Ghana* is such an intimate book that it is as much about the author as it is about his subject. This is most immediately obvious in the final sixty pages of the volume. The profound love of Ghana and Ghanaians and the projection of the excitement of those times which make the first 360 pages so engaging was real enough; that could not have been faked. But the final section, the eighth chapter entitled 'Independence and the new republic', reflects the fading of hope. The bounce disappears, the ironies are more bitter than amused. Unlike so many of the works of the founding fathers, Austin's great work ends on a note of great pessimism, a pessimism born of the harassment and even arrest of friends, the gradual decline of institutions whose vitality he had enjoyed, and above all the decline in the expression of robust, open opinion in a vigorous oral culture. Those last, hard pages were written by a disappointed liberal but perhaps more importantly by a very warm, disappointed liberal. It is easy to suggest that scholarship should be almost definitionally dispassionate and *disengagée*. The immense success of *Politics in Ghana* owes much to Austin's refusal to conform to such a purist demand. Scholarship without conviction is dull indeed.

All political science has at root some pretension to prediction. Austin's final chapter explicitly looked not only at what happened after 1957 but at what would happen after he got the manuscript off to Oxford University Press. In fact, it is rather an odd chapter. Unlike the earlier chapters it makes little attempt to provide a strictly narrative account of what happened after 1957. It is a more selective, thematic chapter than any other in the volume after the introduction. For those who continued to be enthused by the Convention People's Party and its leader Kwame Nkrumah, it was the resolute concentration in those concluding pages on the growing authoritarianism of the ruling party and its leader that led some critics on the left and within Ghana to regard Austin as essentially reactionary. But the 1960s had seen the beginnings of the widespread habit of epithet-hurling without reflection. What those angered by Austin's long, slow demolition of the pretensions of CPP rule ignored was the very apparent pain with which those paragraphs were penned.

It is worth thinking about how good the predictions proved to be. Austin's initial work was, after all, the product of an extremely long-term project. Data had been carefully collected over very many years. The understanding of the processes and the individuals concerned had emerged not from an all-too-brief, poorly funded research visit spent with one eye on the diary and another on the rate of decline of the research grant. Austin had been immersed in the field and had understood just how privileged his access was. Even those modern African political scientists who assuredly share by dint of domicile the inherent intimacy of long-term propinquity, very rarely enjoy the luxury of apparently relatively easy and informal access to politicians and to their documentation. Politics in Africa has changed since the 1950s; it is a hard and dangerous vocation and its practitioners are seldom relaxed enough to shoot the breeze with academic researchers, however charming they might be. Leaving Austin's undoubted skills as a researcher and his lively intelligence aside, it seems sadly unlikely that a work as ambitious and as immediately successful as *Politics in Ghana* will be emulated in the near future.

To turn specifically to that final chapter, Austin was, as we all must be, a child of his times. The frequent reiteration of the problematic of 'nation building' in the new states took its toll on his analysis. That last chapter opens with a variety of questions, the second of which worries about the strength of 'national ties'. By 1957 the country was, he wrote, 'dangerously divided'. The evidence for this was an independence constitution which had bowed to the reality of a local political culture in which there was 'excessive concern for local issues'.[3] This had thrown up regional parties in the previous four years and was shortly to give rise to a protest movement amongst the Ga, Ga Shifimo Kpee, whose course is nicely analysed later in the final chapter. This apprehension was not merely a research conclusion. It was a fear shared by the Convention People's Party. That fear is most apparent in a body of legislation which began with the Avoidance of Discrimination Act of December 1957. This act outlawed parties which based their appeal on ethnic, regional or religious grounds.

There are problems with Austin's treatment of this question. By the time he came to write the final chapter, there was abundant evidence of the Party's authoritarian use of its Parliamentary majority. The analysis of the Party's approach to the divisive politics of the opposition reflects the author's distaste for what he clearly regarded as the serious overbearing misuse of power. He quotes, with anger, Nkrumah's comment in his *Autobiography*, that the fragility of new states might require the temporary expedient of 'emergency measures of a totalitarian kind'. There can be no denying that such measures emerged with frightening frequency in the nine years after independence and even more often in the twenty-four years since the ousting of the First Republic. But it seemed that by the time the author had come to reflect on the meaning of the processes he had so admirably charted and analysed, he rather felt that all authoritarian measures, like all happy families in *Anna Karenina*, were essentially alike.

When it comes specifically to the outlawing of political expressions of regionalism or ethnicity in Ghana, it is difficult to share Austin's view. Firstly, the last quarter-century of Ghana's history seems to refute the initial apprehension. Regional distinctions undoubtedly exist in modern Ghana. Regional imbalances are apparent not merely in an obvious economic sense with the littoral being consistently better endowed than the deeper hinterland and especially the north, but also in the lack of access people further and further from the capital have to decision-making. Few can read the Ghanaian press, or, better still, listen to Ghanaian political gossip, without picking up a frequent theme of claim and counter-claim about ethnic favouritism or exclusion. Ghanaians were and are conscious of each other's origins and foam at the mouth when it is believed that such form the organising principle behind the allocation of office or resources. Political parties and, in the periods of military rule, influential factions have had, in some cases, ethnic identities. There are, after all, few political cultures in the world where none of this is the case.

But in the midst of a history of material decline of the most dramatic sort in recent years, especially in the early 1980s, Ghana has steadfastly held together. While there is absolutely no evidence to suggest that the hounding of regional/ethnic politics after independence was responsible for this subsequent relative cohesion, it is not absurd to see the firm rejection of the formal expression of political forms as a significant and creative contribution to Ghanaian political culture. We know that Nkrumah had strong personal feelings about ethnicity and about breaking down internal distinctions which there is no particular reason to be cynical about. His continued commitment to boarding at secondary schools for example, despite the obvious bourgeois provenance of this system, owed a great deal to his belief that the best and brightest from all corners of Ghana would lose their suspicions about 'strangers' in the hurly-burly of shared education and recreation. But since 1966, whilst some politicians have undoubtedly played regional and ethnic cards in seeking support and in shaping alliances, the intelligentsia at least have retained a latent fear of the divisive possibilities of such politics. It is interesting to note for example that, whilst Ghanaians were and are extremely well seized of debates and changes in Nigeria, the notion of a unitary Ghana has never been seriously challenged since 1957.

In brief, then, we can never know whether Austin's apprehensions about the strength of Ghana's 'national ties' were warranted. We cannot know this not least because of the outlawing of a brand of politics which sought to weaken those ties. The role of that legal intervention in making national unity an increasingly well-accepted element in public life is again impossible to judge. But however untestable these relationships might prove, it is at least possible to question the inclusion of this aspect of post-1957 legislation within a wider, and more obviously pernicious, body of 'measures of a totalitarian kind'.

There is not a great deal more comfort to be drawn from Austin's treatment of the CPP government's undoubtedly cavalier abandonment of many aspects of the 1957 Constitution. Here again it is possible to argue that the disappointments of the early 1960s coloured his judgement. Austin's portrayal of this cumbersome package deal is a clear one. The Independence Constitution was at best 'the seal of an agreed settlement between the parties' and at worst 'the price of reconciliation'. He goes on to argue that had the spirit and letter of that agreement been honoured it would have proved capable of 'providing both an efficient and a tolerant form of parliamentary rule'.[4] This proved an impossible course, he argues, for three reasons. Firstly, Nkrumah could not abide open criticism of his rule; secondly, the CPP chose to identify itself with the state to the detriment of democracy; and lastly, the opposition was rash in its conduct. There is no doubt that this is a decent bit of analysis. What is missing is a reflection on or recapitulation of the nature of that constitution and the circumstances of its genesis. That reconsideration would perhaps reverse the running order of the trio of causes for the failure of the constitution.

The 1957 Constitution was a rushed job. It was a kind of legal first-aid. The drafting was done in a hurry, and was done against a backdrop of a series of manoeuvres which, since late 1954, had scarcely been the acts of a parliamentary opposition. One could certainly argue that these actions were those of desperate men who were fully aware of the draconian probabilities of the years to come and would stop at nothing to prevent the otherwise inevitable destruction of parliamentary democracy at the hand of the Convention People's Party. That argument would, on the other hand, appear to dignify the undignified. The National Liberation Movement's campaigns had been steadfastly undemocratic. In an opportunistic fashion, they had played their game on the not entirely absurd assumption that a Conservative government in Britain was uncomfortable with a radical like Nkrumah as bedfellow. Their campaigns sought to tempt Nkrumah towards a violent response to their own violence in the hope that such apparently high-handed actions would excite further British disillusion with the Ghanaian nationalist government. The NLM's own violence was palpable.

While, by bloody modern standards, their terrorism was mild, it included street violence, intimidation and incessant incitement to disregard law and order. In addition to a quite clear programme of what we should today call 'destabilisation', they also sought to undo the nationalist work of fifty years, namely, to create national unity. By siting much of their action outside the parliamentary process, reconciliation proved an unbelievably difficult task for the government of the day.

To regard the outcome of the literally flying visit of Lennox-Boyd (which just, but only just, got Ghana through to independence in March 1957) as an 'agreed settlement' between the parties seems to be a strikingly apolitical judgement. The Constitution, a messy, cumbrous thing, was presented as a gun against Nkrumah's head. He and his party had not long past won a third election that was not scheduled in the run-up to independence and which they did not want to contest. The 1957 Constitution was not a reconciliation constitution. It was a necessary evil to be endured, entered into extremely unwillingly by a party which had every reason to feel intense resentment about the circumstances of its drafting. Those circumstances were almost entirely created by an extra-parliamentary opposition which had had, and then had essentially lost, its chances at the ballot box in 1956. The opposition had, moreover, rejected a package not very different from the 1957 Constitution which had been pulled together in the *Report of the Constitutional Adviser*, chaired by Sir Frederick Bourne and published in 1955. It is interesting to note that in dealing with that earlier episode Austin sees the failure of Bourne's recommendations as being bound up in the fact that they were 'an administrative answer for what was essentially a political problem'.[5] The same epitaph would have served as well for the independence constitution.

In the event that Nkrumah and the Party might have had serious reservations about *that* specific opposition is hardly to be wondered at. That distaste for *any* opposition became a more general principle must undoubtedly be seen in the light of this searing, proximate experience. Moreover, the suggestion that the constitution would have led to efficiency is entirely questionable. By any test, Ghana was a small country with a low national income. There was no way that Dennis Austin could, in the early 1960s, have predicted the almost universal contemporary fear and loathing of over-large bureaucracies, the endless and uneconomic replication of functions, and the apparently endless opportunity for corruption that overblown and rococo administrative systems provide. There is little doubt that had the 1957 Constitution been endured rather than discarded by the CPP government it would hardly have become a by-word for efficiency. And its very genesis foreclosed upon the possibility of its becoming a foundation stone for a 'tolerant form of parliamentary rule'.

While one can thus lock horns with Austin's treatment of this issue, there is little doubt that he was entirely on the right course in seeing little immediate chance for a tolerant parliamentary system emerging in Ghana. It took some courage implicitly to insist on multi-party democracy as a safeguard of civil and political rights in Africa at the time he wrote the book. As he was writing, a group of scholars, in revolt against the normative and some would say Eurocentric or perhaps western-centric ideals of pluralism, were girding their loins to challenge the older verities.[6] African states could, they were to argue, be democratic without the luxury of multi-party systems. By what right did scholarship deny this possibility? It was a nice argument, but one with which Austin was clearly uncomfortable. With a limited number of exceptions, a quarter of a century of African political history has hardly endorsed the theory. Very importantly, Ghanaians themselves have enthusiastically welcomed the rare windows of opportunity for relatively free political choice. But their country's brief periods of civilian rule since the first *coup d'état* in 1966 have betrayed them in cruel fashion. Professor Busia and his Progress Party's rule from 1969 to early 1972 was hardly more tolerant of opposition than Nkrumah and the CPP had been. Dr Hilla Limann's People's National Party which ruled Ghana extremely ineffectively from 1979 to the last day of 1981 hardly presented Ghanaians with an encouraging spectacle of an efficiently working democracy. Nor can one take issue seriously with other elements of Austin's general critique of the Ghanaian slippery slope as seen from the early 1960s. The judiciary has had its independence challenged forcefully again and again, and in one dreadful incident judges have paid for their individuality with their lives. The independence of the civil service similarly has been, as Austin predicted, significantly eroded.

At the root of Austin's trenchant and persuasive critique there is a terror of the unbridled excesses of sheer power. This is a fear shared by all decent people and for the liberal pioneers in African studies it had been honed by perceptions of Hitler's Germany, Stalin's Russia and, in some parts of Africa, by the worst excesses of colonial rule itself. Africa has itself in the post-independence years not gone short of frightening brands of unaccountable personal rule in the hands of unscrupulous and cruel men. But these episodes are exceptional. It could be argued, and perhaps should be argued, that Austin overstated, not Nkrumah's pretensions, but his, and his successors', capacity to consummate them. Those who claimed that Nkrumah's Republic was a police state must have known little about either Ghana or real police states. If it was a police state, then it was a strikingly ineffective one.

Nkrumah, and the issue is indeed very much personalised in Austin's treatment of the question, is portrayed as inherently dangerous.[7] And he is so portrayed not least because of the serial onslaught on elements within the country which might ordinarily have been expected to check such an apparent monopoly of authority. This assumption is not made without qualification. Austin sees CPP government as essentially self-destructive. By 1964 it had isolated itself and, by tinkering, and worse, with the civil service, the judiciary and the police, it had reduced its capacity to govern. Indeed, almost alone amongst the early scholars of African politics, Austin rehearses the possibility of a military intervention, though his prescience is somewhat weakened by tucking this *apperçu* away in the book's last footnote. Nonetheless, the focus is on the misuse of power and its effects rather than upon the lack of power and its no less threatening possibilities.

This is perhaps best explained by the single most serious omission in this otherwise staggeringly impressive book. Austin never really gets to grips with Ghana's economy in the course of its 421 pages. It is certainly true that in the first chapter he admirably delineates some of the proximate economic roots of the widespread disaffection which fuelled the success of the nationalists after 1940. But from there, until the final chapter, the theme is largely ignored. In the opening shots of the final chapter he surveys the economy in less than a page and later devotes two pages to what he describes as 'economic difficulties'.[8] But a full half of that account is taken up with a consideration of the 1961 Sekondi-Takoradi strike which he very properly sites not merely within an economic framework but also within the broader situation of the erosion of the power of organised labour. It is perhaps in this marginalisation of the economy that the book's predictive possibilities were the weakest.

In part, this omission emerges from Austin's de-emphasis of the history of the state as opposed to the infinitely more exciting history of political processes within that state. There is little doubt that the contemporary fascination with the state and with political economy has resulted in a series of successors to Austin's study which are, by comparison, bloodless and, to put it crudely, rather thin on good stories. There are compelling reasons for standing against the depersonalisation of politics. And much the best of these is surely that the kind of account Austin presented us with was far closer to the view of the process that Ghanaians expressed. Those who worked close on Austin's heels in the Ghana of the 1960s will readily confirm that Ghanaians talked about and practised politics in rather the way he wrote about it. Most of the press in Ghana at the time was not much given to structural analysis, and even the regulars at George Attoh's bar were happiest with gossip, often scandalous gossip, rather than analyses of the implications of state marketing or the operation of the National Bank.

All the same, *Politics in Ghana* ill prepares its reader for Ghana's vertiginous descent into penury and the political implications of that poverty. It sensitises its readers no better to the sequence of broken-backed regimes that followed upon the already weakened CPP regime's comeuppance in 1966. Part of the reason for this hangs on a reluctance throughout the book to tangle with the immensely difficult question of what politics in Ghana were really about. They were, the book is clear, about power. But power to do what? There was, of course, no single answer to that profound question. At different times and in different places there were a dizzying variety of answers. In the end much of this fascinating and frenetic competition was about who was to run, and some would say who was to profit from running, the state.

But withal there is little sense in the course of the book of the ways in which the Ghanaian state had changed, both in its last years of being the Gold Coast and its first years as an independent state. The reality is that, since the foundation of the CPP in 1949, the entire nature of the Ghanaian state had been transformed. Before World War II, the colonial state was, for the most part, transparently thin, undermanned, poorly financed and ineffective.

It remains a travesty to describe, for example, its Micawberish accountancy as an economic policy. Many possible initiatives proved unsustainable because of lack of funds, personnel and as often because of local political opposition. Technically the state was the largest employer of wage labour but it was only so because of the relative lack of an industrial sector and because it was virtually impossible to quantify the rural work force. The government's statistics were poor, often inaccurate and only reliable when they were, for structural reasons, compiled sequentially as for excise purposes. But by 1950 the state had commandeered many significant areas of marketing and purchasing. Because revenue was rising following the war-inspired commodity boom it was also directing sizeable volumes of expenditure through the new mechanism of central planning. Between 1950 and 1960 government expenditure had increased by 200 per cent. At the end of that period government interventionism had been enhanced by its not insignificant control of banking.

Although these processes had been infused with politics – it was, for example, not unimportant that Nkrumah had, throughout the 1950s, retained the development portfolio in successive governments – it is fair to say that much of this important change had occurred outside the political arena proper. Either in general or in particular these significant changes were not the subject of intense or even glancing political concern. Much of this development was, after all, uncontentious. Most Ghanaians welcomed the considerable expansion of the infrastructure, the advances made in the health and education services, just as they were all nationalist enough to cheer Ghana's expensive but enjoyable leadership of the emerging bloc of independent African nations.

The results of these changes were legion. Ghana's population was growing apace and more and more of it was to be found in the country's expanding towns. Some, but not all, of that urban expansion could be explained by the growing tendency of the state to rely upon taxation of rural production through the operation of marketing boards and more general forms of price fixing. More importantly, much of the social overhead capital, and some pretty antisocial overhead capital like expenditure on the military, was drawn from this source. In some senses the die was already cast by 1964. The state, no abstract thing but rather a huge network of people employed directly or indirectly by the government or dependent upon those who were, had in effect only two sources of revenue to fund its voracious appetite. Firstly, it taxed farmers and did so increasingly severely. Ghanaians had not invented this method of appropriation. Such confiscation, as Peter Bauer argued at the time, was implicit in the creation of the marketing boards[9] and this source lay behind the disposable surplus from which the first colonial Five Year Plan was largely financed. Secondly, and as time passed by, the state financed its shortfalls on current account by international borrowing. Micawber had been decisively abandoned before the Union Jack was taken down.

In the midst of these significant transformations, what was one to make of concepts like opposition? How was an opposition, even had it been permitted to prosper, going to reflect these immensely important changes? How, more importantly, would it have challenged them? What would an opposition have consisted of? It would hardly have been to the left of a government which by the mid-1960s was addicted to central planning and the rhetoric, if not the practice, of socialism. It could, and indeed would, have been to the right of centre. When the military displaced Dr Nkrumah, it, of course, proscribed the CPP and acquired an influential body of civilian advisers who were in many senses the old, pre-independence opposition having their turn. Neither they, nor their successors, made any serious attempt to reverse the growth of the state sector and the methods of financing it. The victims of government policy both under the CPP and then under all successor regimes until very, very recently were unlikely to have comprised that opposition for they were the scattered, largely unorganised, increasingly exploited and impoverished rural producers of Ghana.

With hindsight, it is clear that every regime in Ghana since 1957, and, as is argued here, since the mid-1940s, has espoused this heavily urban-biased economic strategy. Significantly it was a policy which became all the more onerous for the immediate victims and then for Ghanaians more generally as the world price for Ghana's single most important export, cocoa, declined. Despite episodic recoveries in the world price, like that of 1972–4, the overall scenario has been one of cumulative disaster. Poor returns on rural investment led to decline in rural production which in turn, obviously enough, led to an appalling decline in Ghana's foreign exchange reserves. What is significant about this corrosive developmental path is that, whilst it spelt doom for everyone in the medium term, it was until recently a largely unchallenged policy by the vast majority of Ghanaian politicians, civil or military, who were for the most part dependent in one way or another upon the persistence of this cumulatively damaging strategy.[10] It in no way impairs the courage of Flight-Lieutenant Rawlings's regime to suggest that the Ghanaian 'establishment', a much-changed constituency since Austin wrote about them, needed to experience what touching bottom really meant before beginning the painful task of restructuring the economy. That the long-resisted recipes of the IMF and the World Bank have been adopted by a regime in many ways more radical than any Ghana has enjoyed in its history suggests not least a long-overdue recognition of the central significance of the economy in Ghanaian politics. This is not to say that Ghanaian politicians of the past were unaware of its centrality. The argument would rather insist that previous regimes lacked the combination of power and commitment to carry through root-and-branch reform. Powerlessness has been a striking companion of all of Ghana's post-independence administrations. The Rawlings government's distinctive, if rather apocalyptic, ally in its new determination has been the damage economic decline has done to the resistant capacity of the numerous interest groups in Ghana. Ironically, when few have any real interest in the status quo, the possibilities of real change open up.

With hindsight, then, it is possible to see even more clearly the strengths and weaknesses of Austin's vitally important work. The weaknesses have a great deal to do with the strengths. The immense attraction of the book lies in its humanity. It is an intensely personal book. Unusually for its time, it presented the reader with a closer view of the actors' models of process than any of the other great country studies. But there was a price to be paid for this. The actors' models were, after all, far from being objective. The intense personalisation of politics reflected the nature of real competition. But at the same time it neatly veiled the unconscious complicity of those political actors in processes which were ultimately very damaging for ordinary, and ultimately for extraordinary, Ghanaians. Austin's intense warmth and identity with the personnel of Ghanaian politics could only have followed those contours, for a book about what Ghanaian politics was *not* about would have been a bizarre project in 1964. In sum, *Politics in Ghana*, this magnificent feast of a book, presents us with what is still the central dilemma of modern political analysis in Africa. Austin got closer than almost any other contemporary scholar to what politics felt like in Ghana. His robust account was more akin to the worlds evoked in the best of African political fiction. Austin's book is, to his eternal credit, closer to Chinuah Achebe than to David Easton. And that intimacy is all the more vital in a new era in which the majority of students of African politics will find it virtually impossible to spend time in Africa.

But the close-up lens can deny us sight of objects of importance in the wider frame. At the end of the day there seems to be an almost unbridgeable gulf between the aridity of the more obviously structural analysis, and the more obviously culturally sensitive *engagée* and readable account. The first tells us perhaps why things happen, but we rely on the second to tell us how they happen. The sheer excellence of Austin's pioneer study has overshadowed Ghanaian studies in a remarkable way. It made Ghanaian politics more accessible to an outside world than the politics of any other African state, and in some ways was partly responsible for the scholarly attraction of Ghana over the years. Many younger 'Ghana hands' owe their initial enthusiasm to a first reading of *Politics in Ghana*. This is no slight plaudit. The sheer force of Austin's intellectual personality expressed in those pages remains remarkable. But for reasons which seem implicit in the scholarly approach adopted, it is a book which only partly prepared its readership for the travails which befell Ghana in the 1970s and 1980s.

Notes

1 Dennis Austin, *Politics in Ghana, 1946–60*, Oxford University Press, Oxford, 1964.
2 See, for example, David Apter, *The Gold Coast in Transition*, Princeton University Press, Princeton, 1955, and Thomas Hodgkin, *Nationalism in Colonial Africa*, Frederick Muller, London, 1956.
3 Austin, *op. cit.*, p. 363.
4 Ibid., p. 370.
5 Ibid., p. 303.
6 See, amongst many other examples, Ruth Schachter Morgenthau, *Political Parties in French-speaking West Africa*, Oxford University Press, Oxford, 1964.
7 Austin, *op. cit.*, p. 416.
8 Ibid., pp. 400–2.

9 Peter Bauer, *West African Trade*, Cambridge University Press, Cambridge, 1954.

10 See Naomi Chazan, *An Anatomy of Ghanaian Politics: Managing Political Recession 1969–82*, Westview Press, Boulder, Colo., 1983, and Richard Jeffries, 'Rawlings and the political economy of underdevelopment in Ghana', *African Affairs*, Vol. 81, No. 324, 1982, pp. 307–17.

5 *Sam C. Nolutshungu*

Fragments of a democracy: reflections on class and politics in Nigeria

Independent politics in Nigeria began with the promise of democracy and economic progress. These notions became deeply anchored in the language of politics and of public life generally, even when the reality often provoked the deepest scepticism about the likelihood of any significant advance of either 'development' or democracy. Nearly three decades after independence, a military regime prepares for a return to civilian rule in 1992, amid a persistent crisis of external indebtedness, economic stagnation, widespread unemployment and an unprecedented depth of division about its resolution. This provides a suitable moment for reflection on democracy and the effect of 'development' on its prospects in Nigeria.

In the post-colonial situation the problem of democracy is confronted simultaneously with that of state formation. There is the inherited colonial state but without the underpinning of imperial power and prestige, and with its legitimacy limited because of its colonial character and its lack of a secure basis in popular acceptance. The central problem of statehood is that of authority: the capacity of the state, and of those who gain control of it, to secure compliance and obedience without constant recourse to physical coercion or the threat of it. That of democracy is consent. It is the problem of extending the submission to authority to a relationship between state and people which bases authority in some observable way (as through free and fair electoral procedures) upon 'the will of the people'. Democracy involves, therefore, the reciprocal recognition of a system of rights and obligations between rulers and ruled, among the rulers, and among the ruled, which are embodied in institutions and procedures broadly recognised to function according to it, and in such a way as to uphold it.

The authority of the new rulers and the authority of the state were clearly not the same thing. While the inheritors might derive some of their authority from the very fact of their occupancy of positions in an established state, they also had other claims to eminence (e.g., birth and education) which made possible between them and the people certain empowering relations – of leaders and followers, patrons and clients, as well as masters and underlings. On the other hand, their own authority might reinforce or undermine the legitimacy of the inherited state. The reciprocal reliance of state and élite implied the need for the élite to be solicitous of the prestige and authority of the state, and in pursuing their own welfare to seek that of the state as well. Such a defence of the state in its own right, and as an important source of the authority of those who rule through it, is the substance of *political responsibility* and political authority cannot be consolidated without it.

The problem here is not only the classic one of the tension between authority and consent but their complementarity and simultaneous necessity: the need to consolidate authority in order to make possible democracy, and the apparent impossibility of legitimating power without democracy (or some measure of it).

Élite conflict

Nigeria obtained its independence under a democratic federal constitution. The three regions of East, West and North had different histories both under colonialism and before it, and there were significant differences in the ways in which their élites had related to the colonial political economy – to the colonial state, the expatriate capitalist companies, and the mass of the peasantry and the emergent urban proletariat. The southern élites, for example, had a history of tension with the colonial administration and the expatriate companies which contrasted with the smoother collaboration between the northern ruling strata – the *sarauta* – and the colonial presence. This, together with the northern leadership's preference for a slower advance towards independence (for which they felt less well prepared than their southern rivals), was about the extent of 'ideological cleavage'. It did not involve any important differences over the social and economic character of the post-colonial order, even though a certain radicalism was more readily accommodated in the discourse of the southern parties, the Action Group, led by Chief Obafemi Awolowo, and the National Council of Nigeria and the Cameroons led by Dr Nnamdi Azikiwe. In addition, both these parties benefited from the support of labour unions which were completely lacking from the elements making up the northern party of Sir Abubakar Tafawa Balewa, the Nigerian Peoples Congress. The Northern Elements Progressive Union of Aminu Kano (drawing its support from the *talakawa* – the commoners – of Kano and Kaduna) embodied this popular strain in the North, but was far too weak to challenge the others for national leadership.[1]

The historical differences between regional élites, and their different relations with the popular classes within their regions, were in no way central to the political differences among them. Indeed, one of the most remarkable features of political construction in Nigeria was the effective suppression of these historical differences from mainstream politics and their relegation to vague ideological references in party propaganda, or to the care of small minority parties.

If the political élites did not represent different classes, they did not reflect contending notions of democracy either. To be sure, there were widespread reservations about the adequacy of the federal constitution, differences between regions over the rights of women (in the Islamic North they had no vote), and about the urgency of educational and social modernisation. But democracy was taken as given, as the context within which competition was to be undertaken rather than the issue of contestation. It was not championed or challenged with respect to its content of rights, but it was the mechanism through which political power would be gained or distributed, and with it economic power and status.

Although democratic politics lasted a bare four years, from 1960 to 1964 (being finally overthrown in a bloody coup in 1966), these features of post-colonial politics would leave a permanent imprint on Nigerian politics: on popular images of politics and the state, and therefore on the possibility of alternative forms of mobilisation and interest representation.[2] Politics would retain a regionalist and ethnic bias, dominated by élites with very similar class attributes and identical class trajectories.

The élites concerned were, essentially, political leaderships – creators and leaders of nationalist parties poised to succeed to the departing colonial administration. Associated with them were administrators and businessmen, élites, too, in their contexts, who could be greatly affected by the outcome of political competition but some of whom could also survive and prosper regardless of it. This was the era of Balewa, Awolowo and Azikiwe, personalities whose very names evoked powerful images of regionalist and 'tribalist' politics among African contemporaries. It was, therefore, a time of intense regional rivalry, but it was also the era of the political parties: juggernauts that crowded the political space, suppressing alternative modes of political assertion and debate.[3]

Parties were conscious and deliberate creations, rather like 'regions', only more so. They were contrived for political advantage rather than as the expression of primordial identities and sensibilities. They existed to contest other parties at the federal level, most obviously, but, equally, to dominate and define the political space at the local and regional level. The formation of these parties, from the top down, in response to the opportunity created by the imminent departure of colonial rule rather than on the basis of preexistent grass-roots organisations and interest groups, was itself a highly competitive matter. It necessitated an aggressive definition and bounding by each prospective leadership of its own territory upon the received template of the region which could, in the approximate way familiar from colonial rule, be given a cultural and ethnic significance as well.[4] The internal political geography of colonialism had always expressed itself as simultaneously a 'cultural' geography, always emphasising the distinctness of peoples, their cultures and needs. In this regard, ethnic and regional identity owed much of their political significance to the political practice of parties called into existence to succeed to a regionalised state whose operational ideology was 'tribalist' – that is to say, confronted its subjects as tribesmen, indissociable from their native territories. British colonialism contained no concept of *citizenship* for natives.

To inherit the colonial state was not, however, to inherit the alliances through which it had ruled. There were rivalries over the succession, not only as between parties, but also within regions, between elements with different, contestable, claims to rule. Regional and ethnic consolidation was an attempt to establish dominance over potential challengers, traditional as well as new, *within* the regions themselves, and the means involved bribery and physical intimidation. Sir Ahmadu Bello, the Sardauna of Sokoto, had to maintain his colonially fostered dominance over the potentially fissiparous North in order to rule Nigeria: in retrospect, we know that, in failing to rule Nigeria, he also failed to unite the North or to secure the dominance of Sokoto over it. The same can be said, with appropriate modification, of the regional and federal strategies of the parties in each region.

The élites had developed along the contours of the colonial states. Formed in the regions, their privileged domain was the region. Their lasting achievement was in sanctifying this mere artifice into an inevitability. Yet it did not take long for their domains to disassemble all but irreversibly, when, in the course of the Civil War, Gowon decided to break them up into twelve states. Himself a Tiv, Gowon had accurately judged the feelings of 'minorities' in the North and in the East where the creation of states won them over decisively to the federal cause and lost Ojukwu the war. Subsequently, more states would be established with equally obstinate, and no less specious claims to naturalness and inevitability, but also with their own 'minorities' equally desirous of states of their own.

Rivalry concerned political power, but political power with great economic importance given the inherited political economy under which the state at both the regional and federal levels was a principal (later to become *the* main) 'theatre of accumulation'.[5] It could give monopolies in trade, and would progressively decree, and largely finance, the accession of Nigerians to key positions in the state sector through 'Africanisation' and the indigenisation of foreign-owned companies.

Colonialism, in transferring power, and the political élites in assuming it, colluded in the structuring of political choices, consciousness and institutions along 'regional' and 'ethnic' lines, foreclosing the alternative of class politics. Nigeria entered independence and has continued for nearly three decades without a socialist discourse of any practical importance (beyond a denatured, *military*, 'social democracy')[6] and without effective political organisation and representation of the labouring classes.[7]

Within each élite there were competing criteria of access to status and power. The quest for supremacy and authority was essentially the struggle over the reconciliation and hierarchic ordering of competing claims to authority and privilege. Some were traditional leaders both historically and by virtue of positions in the system of native administration (and there were conflicts even within this sub-system); others were bureaucrats in a modern sense; others still were private businessmen and professionals with varying links with foreign businesses (which represented, in their own right, a distinct political interest that was both more influential politically and economically than the indigenous bourgeoisie); yet others owed their pre-eminence to politics itself through the political machines produced by the nationalist movement. Given the voting power of the masses, alliances with leaders of the working class became an additional asset in the claim to political ascendancy. Each élite sought to incorporate or to suppress such spokesmen – the 'anticommunism' of the period might be understood, at least in part, in such a light. In very many cases, individuals combined these attributes either through their own multiple memberships or through family networks. Yet, because the mix was different in each individual case, and from region to region, the strategies of exploiting such attributes and of securing the optimal hierarchy[8] were different.

Although there were much-advertised differences between the élites,[9] radicals of any kind were a marginal, if potentially disruptive minority everywhere, and rarely able to transcend regional identities. Every party made appeals to 'tradition' and few leaders were beyond assuming a chiefly title. The difference lay much more in the articulation of tradition to modernity, conservatism and radicalism, in political strategies, a matter dictated by the different historical class contexts in the regions: e.g., as between those (in the South) that had significant working-class and salaried middle-class populations and those (in the North) that did not, those where the political unification of the élite had to some degree been achieved around more or less centralising traditional structures (the North), and the more fragmented ones (the South).

Neither leaders nor followers allowed their political affiliations and coalitions to be determined by ideological or policy questions, and the reason was simple: these were infinitely less substantial than the regional structures to be consolidated and the need to win through them the control of state power within the region and at the centre. 'Democracy' was reduced to mere electoral competition for the control of the state's resources: reinforced opportunism.

If one could, loosely, speak of a feudal dominant class in reference to the *sarauta* of the North – as many are apt to do – then that class had been reduced, under colonial capitalism, to roles that were unmistakeably petty bourgeois, all the pomp and circumstance of imperially-fostered tradition notwithstanding. Although they had arrived there by a different route, they were, essentially, of the same 'political class' as their southern counterparts who, in the event, did not lack their own 'feudal' and 'traditional' trappings that were no less *folkorique* but which could be brought out whenever the need arose. In any event, such a 'feudal class' could hold on to its advantages only by transforming itself into a bourgeoisie under the wing of colonial capital in a subaltern role, or in succession to it by the gaining of state power – in other words, by the *same* process open to the rest of the aspirant regional bourgeoisies that constituted the 'political class'. They, too, had their possibilities of *embourgeoisement* constrained by a kind of colonial mercantilism, by discrimination in favour of foreigners, and by the underdevelopment of the domestic economy induced in part, at least, by the effects of colonial trading monopolies and extortionate taxation.[10] The sources of political competition and bitter strife lay, essentially, in the *similarity* of situation and intention rather than in a *difference* of class identity, though naturally, different 'feudalisms' dictated different intra-regional strategies and conflicts and limited the possibilities of the trans-regional rationalisation or reconciliation of class interests.[11]

Power was therefore transferred to a petty bourgeoisie aspiring to become a bourgeoisie but which, like all petty bourgeoisies, was constituted of elements that were differentially articulated to other classes and strata in society. As happened quite often in Africa, entry into a petty bourgeois position within the capitalist colonial political economy was in some cases via an inherited, pre-colonial, aristocratic status, far loftier in social esteem among the indigenous population, than the new petty bourgeois situation itself which might, nevertheless, open up possibilities for greater economic advancement. The elevated status had to be redeemed from the degradation of political subordination and economic subjection in the new, imposed, political economy by being exchanged for a new material situation to which the surest route was political – via the conquest of state power. The winners were those who could retain the political force of inherited status while acquiring economic advantage in the new. Yet, since the exchange was contested, and there were other routes into the petty bourgeoisie and the emergent bourgeoisie – e.g., through trade, western education, and collaboration (sometimes against hereditary eminences) with the coloniser – there was an implicit threat to inherited status and a latent conflict of meritocratic and aristocratic claims to social dominance and political leadership. The appeal to tradition was addressed as much to such conflict within the 'native' cultural domain of an élite, as it was aimed against other regions. 'Outsiders' within the region – like Igbos in the North and West – not only posed a threat of competition for positions in the state and economy, but they provided a concrete representation of the external, foreign, danger against which what was 'native', 'authentic' and 'traditional' was, one-sidedly, projected by the aspirant élites. 'Traditionalists' and modernisers alike could promise to protect 'their' people against the encroachment and domination of 'foreigners' defined in ethnic, religious or merely geographic terms.

Given the history of the country, of its colonial administration, and its uneven economic development, it would be strange, indeed, if regional and cultural differences were not important, or if they did not give rise to suspicions that needed to be allayed. What is not self-evident is that they should have become the focus of politics and the basis of 'democratic' political mobilisation.

Federalism had a regional and ethnic meaning: the states did not exist to be federated but had to be created – and the process of creation remains unfinished thirty years on – around ethnic groups. Once enshrined in constitutions and reinforced by practice, an ideological preference might begin to sound like a truism, making it difficult for competing principles to gain wide support. There may even be a temptation to assimilate them into the territorial-ethnic view via ideological redescriptions of the principle of ethnicity, as the terminology of the 'national question' on the Nigerian left now seems to do.[12]

That this is the preferred mode of thinking and action is clearly no proof that it is, in some sense, unavoidable or even sensible: all it establishes is that it is, or has been, for those who dominate the political debate and define the choices, the most advantageous and the most convenient, and that there is, here, a convergence of élite interests. An alternative emphasis might call for different leaders, social hierarchies and alliances.

Strategically, there is a catastrophic fatalism about ethnic politics as there is about racial and religious intransigence. Once one party opts for 'tribalism' or ethnic chauvinism, it becomes rational for any would-be rival to define and consolidate an ethnic base too, at least as a minimum fall-back position (which, of course, quickly becomes much more than that). For the parties in competition this may collectively be the worst option, judged by its actual outcomes, yet each fears more that the rival may triumph at its own expense, by using ethnic strategies while it abstains from such divisive mobilisation. The prisoner's dilemma applies also at the level of individual choice: to renounce an ethnic consciousness for a more cosmopolitan one foregoes the advantages of membership (and, perhaps, leadership) of an ethnic political grouping that is bound to form within one's region, whatever one does. In exchange, one has only the uncertain possibility of gainful co-operation within issue-based or ideological coalitions that may never materialise or succeed, nationally or within one's own state. And the reasoning works by anticipation as well as reactively: and, therefore, there can be a genuine simultaneity of strategic choice as in the theoretical game situation. The rationality of the catastrophic choice is determined by the character of the state at the inception of competitive politics: one that defines and confronts the polity – or, as under colonialism, its subjects – in terms of ethnic collectivities, by and large, regionally bounded.[13]

There are features of Nigerian social geography which undoubtedly facilitated ethnic politics. Nigerian political parties were characteristically constructed around individuals whose ultimate base was their home village. Typically these were notable individuals either by virtue of birth or by financial and educational achievement. The core of political organisation was the coalition of the individual with kinsmen and friends, extended by association with other similar coalitions which could then be augmented by the conquest and politicisation of functional organisations (voluntary associations as well as state apparatuses in the extended sense). Within these organisations individuals might have established positions of importance or influence, at the very least with those members having a similar origin or a proximate one, independently of the political coalitions.

In a largely unorganised political field, the selection of notables as democratic office seekers was very much a matter of self-selection (and still remains in large measure so) and the principle of coalition-formation was the mutual recognition of the self-selections and their postulated domains. It is perfectly logical under such an arrangement that there should be a constant division and subdivision of domains (as of lands) but since mere territory is of little affective or ideological force without the metaphysic of common 'cultural' identity, each claimed new domain or state or region becomes easily correlative with a 'people', 'ethnic group' or 'nationality'.[14] Besides, common or proximate origin, backed by a common language, was a plausible basis for an affective social, i.e. *collective* identity, given the low level of socio-geographical integration of populations.[15]

The second experiment with democracy, in 1979–83, was preceded by a great deal of soul-searching among political opinion-makers which was reflected in lengthy constitutional debates as well as post-mortems on the first democracy. A constitution was devised that was intended to minimise the violence and the bitterness of political competition, avoid winner-takes-all outcomes in elections, and force political parties to have a minimum of cross-ethnic support and to share and alternate the top political positions – the Presidency and the Vice-Presidency – between different regions. The principle that all positions in public life should be so distributed among 'regions' and ethnic groups as to reflect the 'federal character' of the country expressed an increased opposition to 'tribalism' – ethnic and regional chauvinism and favouritism. However, it also endorsed the view that Nigerians confronted each other in public life as representatives of ethnic groups, regions and states, and added a further feature: that the share-out of satisfactions and the positions of power – not policy in any other sense – was the central focus of political concern.[16]

It is the case that the Second Republic had far less of the 'tribalist' demagoguery and regional chauvinism of the First than might originally have been feared. President Shagari tried to produce a broadly based government and was ready to show due consideration to such opponents as Chief Awolowo. The experience of the Civil War and the events that had preceded it and the years of exclusion from politics of the civilian leaders that had followed all had a sobering effect. Furthermore, the large regions no longer existed in constitutional fact though they clearly continued to do in the minds of many people. However, the creation of states did give some autonomy and therefore unpredictability to sub-regional forces that could, if they chose, shop around among regional and extra-regional parties for allies. In the years that had passed since the First Republic many of the members of the regional élites had acquired substantial economic interests outside their regions which could best be furthered by a broader political outlook. The focus of politics, and of economic appropriation through it, had shifted decisively to the federal level, in large part because of the immense resources controlled by the federal government in the era of oil wealth.

Yet the parties were in a very high degree continuations of those of the First Republic. With the approach of the 1983 election, the ruling party experienced intense internal tensions over the issue of ethnic rotation and alternation of high office: regionalism and ethnicity came out into the open. But, as in the First, political violence in the Second Republic was predominantly between parties *within* regions – suggesting that party spirit defined a *political* cleavage that could not be reduced to ethnic identity and sentiment. It would have been too much to expect the new leaders to renounce the already existing regional bases of mobilisation which some of them had helped to set up and consolidate in the first place. Although Nigeria's need for new parties, more democratic in every sense than the earlier ones had been, was as evident, and as great, as its need for a new constitution, the task had been shunned by the makers of the Second Republic. The banning of political activity until shortly before the civilian rule elections had disadvantaged anyone who might have sought to create a new political movement or popularise a new kind of politics. It was economical to work on well-tried lines, as it was easier for leaders and coalitions with substantial private funds to buy the support of individuals with cash or to offer them lucrative 'prebends' if the party won, rather than to go through the laborious process of developing policies and representative structures.

There were other constraints. Some, inherent in 'nurture capitalism' now carried to excess, were in the political culture.[17] The centrality of winning elections, the absence of a constructive political teleology such as that of class or of significant ideological cleavage of any kind, doomed virtually all actors to short-sighted, short-cut methods to office. The decisive importance of holding power lay in the immediate control it gave over the direct allocation of the resources of the state. In the Second Republic, vital issues like trade and foreign exchange policy mattered far less to most politicians and their supporters than *who* obtained the trading permits and *who* obtained the foreign exchange. Every discussion of policy issues, economic or otherwise, was quickly side-tracked into a question of *who* gains, rather than who *ought* to benefit.

This is, clearly, more than the issue of corruption – favouritism and misappropriation – that intrudes in policy-making that is otherwise guided by clear civic norms. It is a logical outcome of the terms of political differentiation, a product of the mode of political mobilisation. There is no doubting the fact that it was *one* of the ways that people expected the state to be used however much they might decry it when it worked to their disadvantage, or when its catastrophic economic effects duly ensued.

State power was used to grant or return personal favours whether the context of these obligations was familial, ethnic, or regional or sub-regional. Parties aggregated what were essentially *personal* political projects, given the weakness of opposed class organisations or even a pluralism of organised competing interests. Indeed, the 'de-legitimation' of old-style regional 'tribalism' may have encouraged 'atomisation'.[18] There was no better illustration of the personalism of politics and of the arbitrariness and ethnic opportunism with which it is directly associated than the attempted incorporation by the NPN of Gowon and Ojukwu, simultaneously, after both had been pardoned for their quite different misdeeds.[19]

Corruption in the Second Republic demonstrated and contributed to a larger problem: that of the authority of the state. Effective control of virtually every tier of government became impossible: neither the governments nor the bureaucracies could be made to function as they should, and the sporadic attempts to investigate or check corruption resulted in farce (e.g., government buildings being set alight, in most cases, with total impunity, to destroy incriminating documents). If no level of government could control the ones below, the state, or the idea of government itself, had very limited restraining power on politicians and office-holders. Political responsibility, in the sense previously defined, was conspicuously lacking and nowhere more so than in the economic sphere: the state's wealth was not only misappropriated, it was also misspent.

Although civilian rule survived for only five years, the events of the election period, as well as the appetites for 'tribalist' log-rolling and machine politics it had whetted, contributed to a revival of ethnic suspicion which was to become painfully evident, subsequently, under the military regime of General Buhari.

The Second Republic fell to a coup that in short order went down before another led by Ibrahim Babangida who promptly committed himself to return the country to civilian rule but not without some cleansing and political adjustment. His concept of democracy is not without interest.

Like his predecessors, Babangida banned politics until the transition was imminent. Like them he called for a new constitution and established a 567-strong Constituent Assembly – partly elected by an electoral college made up of the local governments (themselves elected some months before in a no-party election), and partly nominated. He, too, discountenanced political activity by the trade unions (favouring a democracy without class, in reality, *working-class* politics). He, too, insisted that the parties that would eventually be formed should have no 'religious, ethnic or sectional undertones' though the acrimonious debates in the Constituent Assembly over the place of the Sharia law suggested that this might be difficult to realise.[20]

To make a clean sweep, Babangida decided to ban all the former politicians from coming back into politics and even (vainly) sought to prevent the new ones from consorting with them.[21] He undertook to prevent men of means from 'hijacking' political parties from their inception. There would only be two political parties and they would be given identical office accommodation in the federal capital and the local government areas. In an equally novel departure, he made a point of excluding from constitution-making, as well as from eventual political office, all 'extremists'.

The constitution would have to treat as unchangeable what Babangida characterised as the 'accepted ingredients of the country's political order': federalism, presidentialism, a secular state and 'the respect and observance of fundamental human rights' including the freedom of the press.[22] The Constituent Assembly was debarred from altering the number of states in the federation (totalling twenty-one at the time).[23] In a further move to weaken the states relative to the central government – the increase in the number of states decreed by his military predecessors had the same effect – Babangida required that local governments be made autonomous of the states while urging a 'strong federal government'. Yet when he called on the Assembly to look into the division of powers among the three levels of government and to relate that to revenue allocation, he did not have in mind the separation of powers – executive, legislative and judicial – nor any restraint of the federal executive based on rights. Indeed, his own administration was characterised by continuing tension with the judiciary, the Bar and civil rights activists.[24]

Constitution-making was, therefore, as bounded as party formation and activity. The preference for order, strong government and centralisation was a response to the problem of authority and was clearly being pursued at the expense of freedom of association and political competition. The military rulers wanted 'democracy' but they wanted it on terms dictated by themselves. The Constituent Assembly, for its part, insisted that the Constitution should ban military seizures of power and make them punishable, despite the foreseeable difficulties of ever enforcing such a provision. This provoked a sceptical response from a former military politician, General Danjuma: 'I do not think I will see any democracy in Nigeria in my life time ... Nigeria has never had a civilian government worth defending.'[25] Babangida's own utterances nevertheless reflected the broad acceptance of the principle of elected government as being indispensable for the legitimation of regimes and for the maintenance of any degree of national unity.

For the military under Babangida, 'democracy' was a formula for the return to civilian rule under conditions which the military government could accept in the light of its own notions of good government, and, no doubt, of where its interests lay. It verged on a merely administrative conception of politics with 'authority' degenerating into mere 'order' and 'discipline'. Not only was democracy to be guided by the military who had themselves been elected by no-one, but its whole nature was fundamentally misrepresented. Certainly, the Babangida regime, like all the other military governments, sought to curb the excesses of élite politics. This was the idea behind preventing the reappearance of the old politicians, in trying to ensure that parties were not 'hijacked' by men of means, and in separating local from state governments. Yet the project did not realistically confront the underlying social relationships that produced the 'disorder' and 'indiscipline' it sought to rectify.

'Bourgeois democracy'

Élite politics shaped the competition for state power and the use of it. Yet it is itself impossible to understand without regard to the state and its relation to society. The predominance of *political* élites with virtually no challenge from other points of power and influence cannot be explained satisfactorily in terms of individual leaders and their personal followers and beneficiaries, a kind of 'microeconomics' of patron-client relationships which, in any event, are more likely to be its result than its cause.

Political élites are simply people who occupy the high ground on the terrain of politics, or on sections of it: high because it has a privileged relation to the state. What else they are, or how they relate to everyone else, may help to explain why they are where they are and what they do with the positions they occupy. In these relations lie some of the fundamental problems of democratic construction.

There is hardly any need to argue for the view that democracy and constitutional government are not the gift of the state but the product of struggles which have, for the most part, a recognisable class content. Even the ideological commitment to them, which is important in its own right, is usually the residue of previous struggles: in Africa, the opposition to the imperial ruling classes and their subalterns and proconsuls, and against colonial monopolies, and so on. To a lesser extent, it was also an attempt by the new classes emerging out of colonialism to make political space for themselves in the colonial succession against the pre-emptive claims of residual pre-colonial ruling classes.

Historically, however, modern democracy arose out of struggles against a class that had state power in such a way that opposition to the state – demands for its limitation and control – became the essential means of resisting its domination and of making room for the expansion of the political influence of new class forces. In many cases that domination had already been attenuated by absolutism which gave the state – i.e., the sovereign – a considerable autonomy *vis-à-vis* the aristocracy. Its power (centralised and consolidated, and supported by the principle of sovereignty, a doctrine of state authority *par excellence*),[26] autonomy and relative isolation from the classes in civil society made possible a significant separation of political and economic struggles. This in turn both ensured that the emergent bourgeoisie would seek to resist state power to the extent of circumscribing its use and seeking to gain control of it. This was not a state which the bourgeoisie made to its own liking, or which it could unmake or remake in complete obedience to its own needs. Both the resistance to the state and the desire to gain influence over it owed to the fact that it was already there in its own right, already had authority which it could confer on those in power. The state was not neutral, or independent of class interests, but it was sufficiently distinct and apart from civil society for the struggles over its control to be separable from those involved in immediate appropriation, that is to say, in economic life. Equally important, it had a role, power, and authority, as well as a certain autonomy, precisely because of the antagonisms within and among classes.

By contrast, the post-colonial state has to democratise or be democratised in the absence of these antecedent features. In the case of Nigeria, a number of aspects appear to be crucial:

a. The state did not arise to respond to the needs of an internal class order, but to those of British colonial exploitation. It did not only raise itself above society (as in Marx's formulation) but it also decreed society into existence – deciding where 'Nigeria' began and ended – in obedience to its own needs of external domination. Likewise, there was no indigenous ruling class in control of the state against whom democratic claims could be formulated or which could sustain the state in the face of such claims.

b. The post-colonial state was not, therefore, one which could, while ultimately deriving legitimacy from an established class order, autonomise itself to a large degree in the principle of absolute sovereignty. Neither was there, by the same token, a sure basis of authority to regulate the rivalries and conflicts of the nationalist inheritors. In this central *political* respect (distinct from that of its economic importance and military potential), the state was, necessarily, weak. Both the lawlessness of the élites and the Civil War to which it inexorably led, proved it.

c. Nor was the relation of the state to economic life comparable to that which characterised both absolutism and the beginnings of bourgeois democracy: such that the state's involvement in production and trade and its taxes were essentially burdensome to the ascendant class and an obstacle to its advance and could, therefore, provide a powerful economic motive for the limitation of its role in economic life. To the contrary, this class, in all the regions, was the principal beneficiary of the state's exactions once imperial control had yielded to nationalist demands.[27]

Modern democratic discourse arose in the context of established sovereignty, within an established class order. While both can, presumably, be achieved without the replication of European history in Africa, they are generally *presupposed* in democracy rather than the result of democracy which comes at the end of struggles that might well imperil them.

At independence, there was not much of a bourgeoisie, and such as there was had no obvious need of democracy in any sense stronger than was necessary to secure immediate, specific outcomes. Democracy was required, not so much to regulate the use of the state by a dominant class, but to provide competitive access by *non-ruling* classes to its control, use and possession.

At the same time, the state was, and was expected to be, directly involved in production and trade. Apart from the Keynesian and social democratic *Zeitgeist* of the era of independence movements, this involvement partly explains the absence of any strong commitment to limitative doctrines of state power among the élites. On the contrary, the idea of ethno-regional power-sharing propounded by both the British and their successors could only favour empowerment and enlargement of the state that had to be shared.[28]

Democracy, then, has most often been seen by the key political actors and their supporters as opening up politics as a terrain of economic struggle. If the state can, indeed, be used to control and to govern, it is, nevertheless, from a class point of view, more the anarchy of the state itself which appeals: the fact that it is subject to no restraint (except, of course, the ultimate threat of mass rebellion) or, as now, externally imposed financial constraints.

It is an empirical matter whether, at any particular time, most factions will judge that their interests are best served by democracy. In Nigeria, perceptions have varied according to the rhythm of accumulation and the class struggle. In periods of military rule, it is not business organisations that clamour for a return to civilian rule; nor has the prosperous middle class decried the military coup as a means of getting rid of unwanted elected governments, even though the demand for 'civilian rule' is heard quite clearly when disillusion sets in under the military. A military counter-coup always has its partisans and beneficiaries within the upper income strata. The bourgeoisie is not of one mind about democracy any more than it is unitary in any other respect: but it singularly lacks anything that could clearly be characterised as a democratic or pro-democratic fraction. A good deal of this disposition is due to the context, one in which the bourgeoisie is still *emerging* as a class and where even the economic dominance of (private, indigenous) capital is not established, because the dominance of private capitalist production itself is largely nominal.

During the 'emergence' of a bourgeoisie, class boundaries tend to be more blurred than usual, class identities and interests being perceived not only in terms of what *is*, but also of what *might be*. By the same token, the criteria of accession to class positions, or to the economic means that guarantee access to class membership, are contested. The result is that conflict within classes in formation is as logical and, often, as intense, an expression of the contradictions of accumulation as conflict between classes. Class alliances are formed not only for the waging of inter-class conflict but also in the conduct of struggle within classes. This may render the opposition between classes, though inescapable in economic fact and determinant in 'the last analysis', of limited significance in the dispute over political positions. The general denial of class identity and interest in electoral politics and bourgeois ideology, then, acquires a particular importance, producing a politics that gives far greater weight to non-class criteria of alignment – indeed, in a very real way, an *anti-class* politics characterised by not only an obfuscation of class (or the domestication of class conflict under democracy), but its continual displacement from the field of political competition.

The tendency towards ethnic and regional politics, highly personalised, fits easily into such a context, being itself not a false consciousness of class politics but its necessary suppression. At the same time, it is a measure of the force of the *class* interest of the bourgeoisie as an ultimately conditioning reality that the emergent bourgeois factions, despite their bitter quarrels, have little desire to encourage forms of political assertion that would call into question the very fact of their 'emergence' as a bourgeoisie. Even the populist parties – like those of Awolowo and Azikiwe, twice over, but also the People's Redemption Party of Aminu Kano – were vague and enigmatic in their embrace of 'the common people'. Popular politics under these conditions is brought under the domination of politics *within* the emergent dominant class. In this sense, anti-class ideologies and strategies do not disprove the pre-eminence of economic interests – they serve it.

The politicians who took over from the British Crown had different claims to leadership but their chief distinction lay in their western education, their local or regional eminence itself often being a function of both the position which their education secured them in the colonial division of labour and of their inherited status in traditional terms (where 'tradition' had more or less been incorporated and adapted to the colonial order). Rarely were they men of great economic substance beyond what they gained directly from their political, administrative, or professional functions. Their description by contemporary political commentators as a 'political class' was very apt indeed. They were not yet a bourgeoisie but included, for the most part, elements that could better be described as petty bourgeois or 'middle class', though some had a better prospect of eventual *embourgeoisement* than others.[29]

The state was dominated by a 'class' that was inherently incapable of ruling, or of giving coherent economic direction to state and society. It sought to inherit the state, not to subdue it. Having fought the colonial 'ruling class' to a democratic outcome – at least in so far as the granting of a democratic independence constitution was, indeed, such – the political class, once independence was achieved, fought, most of the time, against itself.

The inheritor 'political class' was strategically well placed to define the terms of competition and, for some while, preserve and enlarge its advantages. It did so not by the outright suppression of rival classes, which was impossible given its own internal divisions, but by assimilation and incorporation. In 'tradition', 'region' and 'culture', colonialism had provided the ideological, administrative and political tools for the job. Those less well placed to inherit political power or unable, for various reasons, to challenge this 'class' effectively (essentially, the labouring classes, but also private indigenous businessmen) submitted to this domination, allowing their own fragmentary and little-organised struggles to be assimilated under the hegemony of 'tradition', 'tribe' and 'region'.

As for democracy, then, two observations seem warranted. First, the colonial transfer of power did not install a 'bourgeois democracy'. The bourgeoisie was almost non-existent and remained yet to be formed. The conditions for democracy of any kind did not exist and were yet to be created, like the bougeoisie itself. Second: apart from the formula 'bourgeois democracy' which assumes the commitment of the bourgeoisie to democracy, there is no reason to expect that the preference for democracy would be anything other than a historical, conjunctural, disposition on the part of the bourgeoisie.

However, the colonial transfer of power set the precedent and subsequently encouraged the expectation that democracy could be created from above by the enactment of constitutions that struck bargains among political élites – not classes – poised to succeed to the preceding (undemocratic) regime. Each 'return to civilian rule' recreates, in this way, the initial illusion of democracy.

There now exists a bourgeoisie, substantial both demographically and economically, but its economic activities are not such as to give it a coherent sense of its own collective interest which it can express in consistent organisation and with a comprehensive and coherent range of political preferences.

Industrial capital is emerging, very slowly, and is altogether dwarfed by the growth of commercial capitalism, as well as that peculiarly Nigerian version of finance capital 'contracting', linked mostly to construction. Through the system of trade controls and licenses – much reduced under the IMF-inspired Structural Adjustment Programme (SAP) – as well as on account of the general importance of the state sector and the state itself in every area of economic life, the growth of commercial capital was dependent on political patronage. In the 1970s and 1980s, faced with a mounting food deficit which could no longer be met by imports, given falling oil revenues and growing external indebtedness, the state promoted a revival of food production. With federal government subsidies and World Bank assistance, an agrarian bourgeoisie of former politicians, military men and senior bureaucrats began to emerge.

In the development of each form of capital, the state continued to play a decisive part: for industry, subsidies and protection; for commerce, trading licenses and (before SAP) a monetary and exchange policy that both favoured the consumer import trade and created opportunities for windfall profits through hoarding and speculative trading; for agriculture, capital grants and land transfers as well as subsidies; for 'contracting', everything, the business itself and the vast public works projects.

The growth of agrarian and industrial entrepreneurs could, nevertheless, have the most profound cultural and political consequences if, for once, it tied accumulation to *production* – and to the imperious rationality of productive processes and relations. That would depend on whether productive growth would not be blocked by politics and the effects of past 'development' and by the crushing burden of external obligations and dependencies.

At present, the role of the state and the terms of popular mobilisation and legitimation are limiting. Those who rule are bourgeois, but the bourgeoisie does not rule. Even to the extent that it may be conscious of the 'general interests of capitalism' it has no effective means of defining the class interest in practical political terms, or choosing a form of government appropriate to its own needs, apart from simply being the most favoured class. The central problem is, of course, the disunity fostered in politics as part of the process of its emergence as well as the inherent disorderliness of the economy itself.

The divisions of the political class are to some degree reflected in working-class politics in so far as the political alternatives open to them to support are still those offered by the élite parties. Furthermore, labour has more often been pitted against multinational companies and the state (as employer, or as initiator of policies that threaten living standard or wages), than against indigenous capital. The assertion of its interest in these instances does not present itself as beyond assimilation into some one or other bourgeois oppositional faction.

However, the conflict of class interests is real enough and has manifested itself more strongly in working-class and peasant protest as boundaries between classes and the gap in their life opportunities have become clearer. The need to control and depoliticise labour unions has been felt by all governments. Attempts in recent years include the neo-corporatist policy of the Mohammed–Obasanjo military regimes to dissolve the central labour union and reconstitute it 'from above' and the use of detention without trial and of charges of sedition against its leaders by Babangida culminating, once more, in the dissolution of the Nigerian Labour Congress and its reorganisation under state direction. The Nigerian labour movement, though resolute in its opposition to structural adjustment, remains extremely weak in terms of political organisation and its capacity to influence working conditions nationwide, forge durable alliances with other disadvantaged strata, and intervene coherently in ideological debates. It remains deeply divided over whether it should be a class force as the 'progressives' insist it should be, or merely economistic as the 'democratic' unionists demand. Both wings are confronted with the absence of any *political* movement that is particularly responsive to their specific interests whatever their brand of unionism. The capacity of peasants and small traders to assert themselves politically is no less weak. They *could* be a continuously felt force in politics in organised collaboration – even if only in issue-related, conjunctural pacts – with workers, but there is not yet any sign of this happening on any scale.[30]

Yet the resistance of the lower classes, in various forms, has considerable effect on the range of available options and forms of accumulation. For the military as well as for civilian politicians, popular disaffection and rebelliousness can be a cue to malcontents and plotters within their ranks, while it may precipitate breakdowns of law and order whose ramifications may be unpredictable.

In the 1970s and into the 1980s, there was, as well as a clear determination on the part of political leaders to avoid a repetition of the mutual provocation that precipitated the Civil War, a general unwillingness to incite or exploit communal violence. Even an emergent tendency towards religious demagoguery in certain quarters managed to be contained.[31] The pan-Nigerian nationalism boosted by the war, encouraged by the military regimes (in their own corporate interest to some extent) as well as by the vastly expanded resources controlled by the federal state, all favoured a growth of political responsibility and patriotism which managed to counterbalance both sectarianism and the incipient anarchy of the oil economy.

It remains to be seen, however, whether the material development of the bourgeoisie has advanced sufficiently far, or in such a way, as to favour both the consolidation of achieved positions rather than reckless appropriation, and the legal order and political responsibility.

Military rule creates the illusion of the ascendance of the state interest, since the soldiers' corporate interest in their own cohesion and unity translates into a preference for a cohesive, unitary and powerful state. Yet military leaders are not without wider social identities and cannot easily escape the power of the dominant mode of politics. Sectarianism remains a persistent suspicion, and corruption-free government evades the military as well as civilians, though the organisation, discipline and coercive power of the military do make some difference. However, it is well not to confuse authoritarianism with authority based on accepted norms and values – and a distribution of social power that can uphold them.

Having applauded the overthrow of the Shagari government, Nigerian public opinion has turned firmly against military rule. In opposition to the arbitrary and strong-arm methods of the Babangida regime and the suspected sectarianism of the preceding one of Buhari, several groups, notably among students, workers, journalists and lawyers, have spoken out strongly in defence of human rights and democracy. However, the deliberations of the Constituent Assembly, for some of which some of the Assemblymen felt constrained to turn up armed, inspired little confidence that anything had happened to break the mould. The issue of the Sharia law once again produced a crisis in constitution-making. The 'old' politicians appeared to be still able to exert influence, and ethnic claims revived, particularly in the form of the 'minorities-majorities' opposition.[32] The Constitution's adoption of welfare principles reflected a broadly-based repudiation of the policies of structural adjustment, but it also reaffirmed the belief in a state that spends – in the absence of democratic control, a recipe for the continuation of old abuses.

The circulation of élites

There have only been two brief periods of civilian government in all of thirty years of Nigerian independence: under Abubakar Tafawa Balewa (1960–6) and under Shehu Shagari (1979–83). Both governments demonstrated a total unwillingness to face the possibility of electoral defeat and were ready to resort to violence to hold on to power. Even though both leaders would still, in all likelihood, have won had the elections been fair, the support for the parties in the regions and states was much weaker. The first fell to a bloody coup which led directly to the Civil War. Shagari's succeeded to impose itself for a second term destined to be brief. There was no civil war the second time round, but there was an interminable series of trials for corruption ending in sentences of a length as unbelievable as the justice of the process by which the prosecution of some office-holders and not others was decided. The military regime was quickly overturned by another which in its turn faced a bloody counter-coup plot and continual suspicion of further subversion from within its own ranks. In both cases, the elections were preceded by profound and widespread discontent, a growing tendency towards coercion, and a high probability of the breakdown of public order on a massive scale. On each occasion, a military coup seemed to many to represent the only way out of an intolerable situation.

After the first breakdown, democratic politics was suppressed for fifteen years as military governments succeeded each other in power. A certain 'antipolitics' among the people, in response to the first democratic experience, seemed to accord legitimacy to military rule, while the officers themselves developed a definite taste for politics. Nevertheless, military rule continued to be presented and regarded as a temporary interlude, an 'intervention'.

Since no government has ever been removed by democratic means, popular elections or popular protest, coups have become the only means of changing governments. Yet military coups are not outside of the pattern of élite politics; they are an extension of it, while they may also pretend to a regulative function in the system as a whole. Each military intervention is not only expected to bring new policies to 'correct' and 'redeem' people and state alike but, equally important, a coup is invariably followed by a reshuffling of the best-paid positions in the state machinery and the public sector. Coups are part of a pattern of élite circulation and a crucial means for some members of the more privileged strata to accelerate their upward mobility. Military regimes always have civilian allies and collaborators who win them a certain measure of popular acceptance in addition to making military government work on a day-to-day basis – as local eminences, as 'leaders of thought', as dutiful bureaucrats, or as academics and experts who are ready to serve in a variety of roles.

The military in politics, clearly, presents a dilemma for the constitutionally minded. Some see the possibility of coups against corrupt civilians and further coups against venal military regimes as providing some protection against tyranny – a kind of system of 'checks and balances'. A few have advocated a 'dyarchy', a permanent, constitutionally guaranteed sharing of power between the military and elected politicians.[33] There is a widespread desire for a stable sharing of power among the contending factions and the military which often goes with a certain unhappiness with political competition and ideological difference. But there is also a desire for alternation in a strong sense: a 'circulation of élites' that would make every change of government not merely a cautious modification of policy, but a clear departure opening up new opportunities for those who did not do quite so well under the previous regime.[34]

It is a curious fact of Nigerian political life that, despite the long years of military rule, and the persistent scepticism about politicians, each military junta has to legitimate itself, sooner or later, by preparing for a return to civilian rule. There are various reasons why this is so. One is, simply, that the democratic spirit is well entrenched among the people and there is a widespread belief that a population of the size and complexity of Nigeria's cannot be peacefully governed without some measure of representation and consent.[35] Another is that civilian rule opens up, all at once, new economic opportunity and provides many more access points to the state. In any event more offices – and prebends – are created.

There is another reason, not entirely unrelated to the weight of public opinion in its complex diversity, but still arising more specifically from the inner logic of the circulation of élites: the 'outs' want to be 'ins' too, in their turn, and will collaborate with the 'ins' for so long as that is assured. Mere sharing of power, a mere chance to win electorally, even if elections were fair, would never suffice: the wheel must turn. Tempted by theories of élite consociation, Billy Dudley considered that the problem could be alleviated if elections did not produce 'winner-takes-all' outcomes and he helped to make a constitution along such lines. However, the problem remained of divining just how much more than nothing would satisfy the loser, or, alternatively, how much less than 'all' would please the winner.

For the military itself, the commitment to return power to civilians is a means of maintaining order within its own ranks: of discouraging further coup attempts which would threaten corporate unity and the capacity to make, relatively painlessly, the periodic 'interventions' in politics which, whatever else they do, assure the military as a whole a rather agreeable social and economic standing. Yet, by the same token, it is now an integral part of the career expectations of any ambitious young officer that he will one day hold high political office and, if he survives, retire with rank and a nest egg, no less desirable an ending than to win honours in battle or to die a hero's death. If a return to civilian rule is not intercalated, a new set of officers can only succeed their predecessors by the violent means of a coup. Babangida, the first military leader to style himself 'President', gave himself the rank of full general. It is not enough that the military should participate in the alternation of élites in political office; within the military itself the principle of 'circulation' (or taking turns, or giving every officer an opportunity, etc.) must, perforce, prevail. Gowon erred when he did not yield to it and he was undone, though *esprit de corps* ultimately prevailed and, thirteen years later, his rank was restored.

The 'circulation of élites' is neither fair nor smooth. Nor is it necessarily circular. There is always the danger of some élites being excluded altogether from the highest positions, or the circulation getting jammed, or of previous élites being thrown out violently for good. They never quite know where the next power holders will send them – to grass or to the grave. Yet many return to high politics or become its grey eminences.

Relatively bloodless though most of the changes have been since the Civil War, the process carries, at all times, grave risks of anarchy and violence, as well as repression. With every attempt by another group of officers to unseat an existing military government the state totters. Rumours of such plots abound in periods of military rule, and particularly the present, and some conspiracies made public have been bloodily rebuked.[36]

Beyond élite politics

Considering how brief has been the time lived under would-be democratic government, it could be said that with independence it was the mandarins and the imperial guard who inherited the empire. For although their power was much diminished under Babangida, senior civil servants played a decisive role in the shaping of policy under the military regimes.[37] Throughout the periods of military rule, state power was exercised by shifting alliances of the upper echelons of the military and the bureaucracy with elements from the universities (for all their divisions and periodic student revolts, the ideological state apparatus of the post-colonial state *par excellence*). The military rules, not only because of its ability to impose itself forcibly upon the populace, but due to the discredit of elected governments and the weakness of alternative social forces. It occupies a void in a state that, for its part, inhabits a space that is not filled by the power of any class.

Military rule may have been providential in certain moments of acute crisis, but it is impossible to assimilate it into a democratic view of politics. Dyarchy in the sense of the alternation of military and civilian rule might be a believable contrivance were the military itself free from internal political division and infallible in its corrective mission. But a democracy that was periodically interrupted by 'redeemers' that it believed to know the democratic interest and how to realise it would be a democracy of fools.

The neutral-sounding notion of corrective military 'intervention' may come to ring quite hollow as the soldiers are forced to make substantive choices between opposed class interests and ideologies, and between opposed political factions. Buhari's coup was seen as a means of pre-empting a junior officers' coup that would have been more radical, and the bias towards the deposed National Party of Nigeria in its policies was unmistakeable. Babangida's government, while making a point of achieving ethnic balance, has revealed a considerable measure of infighting within the military while being repressive towards unionists, radicals and critical intellectuals and students.

The regimes of Gowon, Mohammed and Obasanjo were not immune from such dangers, yet they were all helped, to some extent, by the nationalism stimulated by the war and sustained by the oil boom which made possible a pattern of state expenditure which, while it was by no means equitable, spread a sense of improvement and imminent progress quite widely across society. In particular, the urban middle and lower middle classes experienced real improvements in their situation and reciprocated by mediating as technocrats, bureaucrats and ideologists of the new nationalism between the military and the public.

The economic crisis has highlighted inequality, not only between rich and poor, but also between the petty bourgeoisie in all its diversity and the bourgeoisie. The effects of the various measures for revitalising the national economy fall unequally on society. Presented as liberalising in favouring the diminution of the role of the state in the economy seen to be in itself the cause of corruption and inefficiency, these measures have required a more authoritarian use of state power than has been seen before and might be impossible to pursue under democratic conditions. 'Deregulation' in this sense is quite another matter from empowering the people against the state.[38]

In the approach to civilian rule, the armed forces have come to be seen, increasingly, as a distinct interest, divided and divisive, as they had tended to become in the later years of Gowon's once popular regime, and to a lesser extent, at the end of Obasanjo's also. Babangida's alternation between a consultative and conciliatory approach and draconian measures against opponents betrays not only a certain partisanship between existing and latent civilian political blocs, and between classes, but also an underlying tension between 'the military' and 'the people' as perceived in populist terms.[39]

Discontent alone cannot produce democracy: otherwise, the world would be a stranger to tyranny.[40] Nor can a mere coincidence of interests. The working class, the lower strata of the middle class, middle and small peasants have a clear interest in a genuine participatory democracy as a means of defence against both civilian and military incompetence as well as economic oppression. Yet none has the organisation or the awareness of political potential to assert themselves. The organisation of a democratic political bloc demands a conscious rupture with the established modes of self-defence within and through élite politics and military rule. It may be stimulated by hardship and political repression, but its emergence is neither predestined nor the natural self-expression of any class.

The political recklessness of many party leaders in the past, the anarchy and division of the bourgeoisie, and the arbitrary seizures of power by the military depend in no small measure on the weakness and relative passivity of the masses. The impulse towards democratic legitimation and the all-too-imperfect, but nonetheless real, interludes of elected government, on the other hand, reflect a recognition on the part of the dominant strata of their own weakness and potential vulnerability to popular revolt. However, they rest on a negative condition: not an equilibrium of power between classes, but a balance of weakness.[41]

The balance of weakness is reflected in state practice. Despite the considerable economic role of the state, both the military and the civilian regimes have had to tread warily in power, being incapable of performing vital tasks of government. That was graphically illustrated by the hesitation and costly delay in implementing an economic adjustment programme (involving the predictably unpopular devaluation of the naira and a cut in subsidies, whether or not done under IMF auspices). No government since Gowon has felt strong enough to conduct a population census, and Babangida has postponed doing so to the very end of his term so that, arguably, the results may be disputed under his civilian successors. No government has been able to act resolutely and consistently against corruption and fraud even against subordinate functionaries, while economic crimes of every kind, from tax evasion to armed robbery and piracy at sea, have defied all.

It is difficult to see how Nigeria could be any nearer to democracy without the political organisation of the vast majority of the population through structures over which they have some direct control. As in most of the continent, they are caught in a circle that is truly vicious: workers, artisans, small traders and small farmers are not politically organised because there is not democracy, but there can be no democracy because the people are not organised. Only when the circle is broken can there be real advance. The independent state that was to remake all things may have done no greater harm than to feed the hope that it could break that circle or that it might even wish to. If there is a problem that is more basic than others, and is, indeed, the source of many, then it is this one. It is a problem of post-colonial societies but it is one that their political systems carried, as it were, in their genes – the heritage of the colonialism that designed them, authoritarian in its day, but also, invariably, in its retreat, a champion of élitist and paternalist notions of democracy.

Yet in nearly three decades of independence there has not been a decisive repudiation of democratic ideals, and those thirty years could, conceivably, have been much worse from the point of view of all classes of Nigerians. A return to civilian rule may just provide the opportunity for political construction in the area in which Nigeria is in greatest need of progress: that of the building of representative popular structures that can give coherent form to the demos and serve as instruments of the exploited, oppressed and misgoverned.[42]

Notes

1 Paul M. Lubeck, *Islam and Urban Labor in Northern Nigeria: The Making of a Muslim Working Class*, Cambridge University Press, Cambridge, 1986, is of particular interest here, especially Chs. 1, 3 and 7.

2 Although the Balewa government was not overthrown by the military until the coup of January 1966, democracy effectively came to an end in the constitutional crisis provoked by the General Election of 1964.

3 Cf. B J. Dudley, *Parties and Politics in Northern Nigeria*, Frank Cass, London, 1968, and *Politics and Crisis in Nigeria: Instability and Political Order*, Ibadan University Press, Ibadan, 1973, pp. 40–83; R. L. Sklar, *Nigerian Political Parties: Power in an Emergent Nation*, Princeton University Press, Princeton, NJ, 1963; and C. S. Whitaker Jr, *The Politics of Tradition, Continuity and Change in Northern Nigeria*, Princeton University Press, Princeton, NJ, 1970.

4 This was particularly true of the Nigerian People's Congress which amounted largely to a conversion of the Native Administration set up by the British into an electoral machine.

5 Cf. Michael Watts, 'Peasantry, merchant capital and the state: class in northern Nigeria 1900–1945' in P. M. Lubeck (ed.), *The African Bourgeoisie: Capitalist Development in Nigeria, Kenya and Ivory Coast*, Lynne Rienner Publishers, Boulder, Colo., 1986, Ch. 3.

6 On the political thinking of the military, see also R. Joseph, 'The principles and practices of Nigerian military government' in J. Harbeson (ed.), *The Military in African Politics*, Praeger, New York, 1987, pp. 70–91; and N. Kasfir, *Soldiers as Policymakers in Nigeria*, American Universities Fieldstaff Reports, Hanover, 1977.

7 Nigerian workers have, on various occasions, demonstrated a capacity for effective resistance and strike action as well as an ability to mobilise other less privileged strata to support them. See W. Ananaba, *The Trade Union Movement in Nigeria*, C. Hurst and Co., London, 1969; R. Cohen, *Labour and Politics in Nigeria*, Heinemann, London, 1974; A. Peace, 'The Lagos proletariat: labour aristocrats or populist militants' in R. Sandbrook and R. Cohen (eds.), *The Development of an African Working Class*, Longman, London, 1975, pp. 281–302; T. Falola and J. Ihonvbere, *The Rise and Fall of Nigeria's Second Republic, 1979–84*, Zed Press, London, 1985; and Paul M. Lubeck, *Islam and Urban Labor*.

8 I.e. one that minimised internal conflict, generated a potentially winning coalition, and for each member (subjectively) the best obtainable payoff.

9 See, among others, K. W. J. Post and M. Vickers, *Structure and Conflict in Nigeria, 1960–65*, Heinemann Educational Books, London, 1973.

10 Cf. R. Shenton, *The Development of Capitalism in Northern Nigeria*, James Currey, London, 1986.

11 None of this is to deny the importance in point of theoretical principle

of the differences in the ways in which bourgeoisies and petty bourgeoisies in different regions laid claim to the social surplus, collaborated or contended with metropolitan capital, colluded or conflicted with the colonial state. Nor is it in any way to deny the reality of cultural differences – indigenous (African) and hybrid (Afro-English) – in the respective ethnic regions. It is to suggest, however, that the effects of these may be more fruitfully sought elsewhere than in the political projects of the parties and their relation to the less privileged classes. It is to insist, moreover, that culture and class did not oppose each other but that, instead, political appropriations of culture functioned in the same way to obscure an identical class project.

12 Cf. A. R. Mustapha, 'The national question and radical politics in Nigeria', *Review of African Political Economy*, No. 37, 1986.

13 This is assuredly not a unique feature of colonial states, though there is, indeed, a privileged relationship between the racialism of colonialism and the 'tribalisation' of post-colonial politics, but may be inherent to some degree in the very character of political domination which the state always represents. It has very little to do with colonial boundaries being arbitrary, colonial states being multitribal or any mere ethnographic fact of that order, and everything to do with the techniques of domination dictating *political* (and, in more or less, corresponding ways *economic)*, rather than merely cultural differentiation of race, ethnic group, tribes and religions as an instrument of rule which by the force of domination becomes internalised in a strongly ideological sense as a 'cultural' (meaning, evidently, irreducible) identity.

14 The issue of 'Anambra South' in the run-up to the 1979 return to civilian rule is a case in point. See R. A. Joseph, *Democracy in Nigeria: The Rise and Fall of the Second Republic*, Cambridge University Press, Cambridge, 1987, pp. 96–103.

15 The disorganisation of the political field and individual self-selection (supported by face-to-face relations of support at the crucial village level) explains more than the notion of patron-client relations which suggests rather improbably that every Nigerian is a client to some patron (whose own status remains otherwise unexplained). It would be much truer to say that every supplicant *seeks* a patron (and may not find a dependable one or may find several according to his own bargaining power) and every patron finds his clients, in other words that unequal personal alliances, but *alliances*, nevertheless, emerge naturally out of a personalised politics. Many are they who are doomed to be supernumerary to any alliance that might interest a worthwhile patron.

16 I. Ofanogoro, A. Ojo, and A. Jinadu (eds.), *The Great Debate: Nigerian Viewpoints on the Draft Constitution*, Lagos, *Daily Times*, n.d., Ch. VII; and Yusufu B. Usman, *For the Liberation of Nigeria*, New Beacon Books, London, 1979, Chs. 8, 10, 11 and 12.

17 On 'nurture capitalism', see S. Schatz, *Nigerian Capitalism*, University of California Press, Berkeley, 1977, who coined the phrase to describe an earlier phase.

18 Cf. W. Kornhauser, *The Politics of Mass Society*, Free Press, New York, 1959, though this was a mass society of a kind that Kornhauser could never have foreseen.

19 See also Falola and Ihonvbere, *op. cit.*, Ch. 4.

20 *West Africa*, 10–16 October 1988.

21 *West Africa*, 19–25 September 1988.

22 All this in spite of a running conflict with the press, many of whose members had been detained and one assassinated, and an announcement by the Information Minister, Prince Tony Momoh, to the effect that the government was trying to acquire radio sets that could only receive broadcasts by the Federal Radio Corporation of Nigeria as well as state radio stations 'as a means of ensuring that information about the country was adequately disseminated'. *West Africa*, 4 April 1988.

23 *West Africa*, 23 May 1988.

24 Cf. *West Africa*, 19–25 September 1988.

25 *West Africa*, 6 June 1988 and 27 June 1988.

26 The powerful support which the doctrine derived specifically from (indigenous or indigenised) religion (itself in many ways a system of domination whatever else it might be), but also in a general way from culture, was of the first importance in the construction of state authority.

27 The contribution of absolutism to bourgeois democracy is all too often, all too easily, overlooked. Yet it is doubtful if this kind of democracy could have developed as easily as it did without that background: if it had been a mere matter of opinions and ideology, divorced from the pressing material concerns of determinate classes. Similarly, the modern democratic concern with the *distributive* functions of the state – whether to achieve equity or to accelerate 'development' – might have been a major complicating factor at the start of the process. Instead of constitutionalism and the emphasis on procedural rules and principles, bourgeois ideology and political claims might have had an overwhelming and near single-minded focus on *substantive* outcomes – as has been the case in Nigeria.

28 It is also true that the weight of British cultural influence had a part to play in this development. British constitutional theory and practice

favour far greater discretion for the state (and the ruling class) than do, e.g., American constitutional doctrines, to the point where rights sometimes appear as privileges merely conceded by Parliament or, what very nearly amounts to the same thing most of the time, the party in power.

29 For economy of exposition we have deliberately left out of discussion the economic dominance of foreign capital and the implications of dependency.

30 Cf., however, Lubeck, *Islam and Urban Labor*, on the 'leburori' and the *talakawa*.

31 Cf. *ibid.*, pp. 308–11.

32 *West Africa*, 17–23 October 1988, also 8 August 1988, 26 September–2 October 1988, 27 March–2 April 1989.

33 There are many who look to the emergence of some military saviour – a Sankara/Compaore, a Rawlings, or Mengistu? – who will create the opening for a radical transformation of society. Cf. Bjorn Beckman, 'The military as a revolutionary vanguard: a critique', *Review of African Political Economy*, No. 37, 1986.

34 The banned politicians were blamed for the rigging of the local government elections in December 1987. See *West Africa*, 22 and 29 February 1988.

35 Cf. Joseph, *op. cit.*, pp. 1–42.

36 The 'circulation of élites', in this case, has little to do with notions of democratic élitism, though clearly there are élites and there are episodes of elected civilian government.

37 The top bureaucrats enjoyed great power under Gowon, which after a major purge under Mohammed they soon began to regain only to suffer a marked dimunition in power under Babangida who has also initiated a major reorganisation of the civil service. The decline may reflect a growing confidence on the part of the military in government and less of a need to rely on the civilian bureaucracy. It may also be the product of a greater tendency for military rule to become more assertive and more dictatorial.

38 Radical deregulation runs counter to the historic role of the Nigerian state which has always had to play a large role because of the under-development of the national bourgeoisie. It has the function of creating such a class as part of its essential role of mediating between the national economy and international capital. This aspect of the post-colonial state has never been more apparent than in the management of IMF-imposed adjustment policies. Yet the large economic role of the state is necessary for the expansion of national capital, for its ideological defence (nationalism and welfare) and, therefore, for the expansion of the state's own authority. All kinds of interests

converged in the colonial era and in the succession to it, to favour the interventionist ('overregulated' state). It is very doubtful whether a minimal state role, linked to obedience to the demands of external creditors and agencies (effectively, themselves regulatory agencies of a kind – the IMF and the World Bank) is compatible with political stability. The resistance to SAP in Nigeria indicates that it may not be. Cf. C. Legum, *Africa Contemporary Record 1984–85*, Holmes and Meier, London, 1986, B545–B563; *Africa Confidential*, 18 September 1985, 1 October 1985, 4 September 1985, 2 January 1986 and 12 March 1986; Y. Bangura, 'Structural adjustment and the political question', *Review of African Political Economy*, No. 37, 1986; see also Watts, *op. cit.*; S. Schatz, *op. cit.*; and T. Forrest, 'State capital, capitalist development and class formation in Nigeria' in Lubeck (ed.), *op. cit.*

39 Cf. Tunde Obadina's rather cautious commentary in *West Africa*, 3–9 October 1988 on the class biases of the Babangida regime. See also Jibrin Ibrahim, 'The political debate and the struggle for democracy in Nigeria', *Review of African Political Economy*, No. 37, 1986; and R. Mustapha and S. Othman, 'The idea of democracy', *West Africa*, 5, 12 October and 21 December 1987.

40 Since the military is not a class, and it merely 'intervenes', disaffection with it can hardly form the basis of democratic claims that go beyond the mere 'return to civilian rule' and that are firmly based in enduring social structures (i.e., strata, classes or fractions of classes).

41 It is a situation in which both the bourgeoisie and the proletariat have a great power to disrupt any project of political and economic development while neither is sufficiently strong to force a decisive breakthrough in terms of extending its class leadership and influence over society, hence the role of the middle and lower middle class through the state – a Gramscian theme of the dynamics of retarded capitalism which, incidentally, still needs to be taken out of the context of the rise of fascism and developed more fully for the analysis of postcolonial capitalism.

42 I am very grateful to Gavin Williams for his comments on an earlier version of this article.

6 *Paul Sutton*

Constancy, change and accommodation: the distinct tradition of the Commonwealth Caribbean

The experience of independence for the majority of the inhabitants of the Commonwealth Caribbean is now a generation old. If the measure of that experience is confined solely to the political realm, its citizens, compared to many 'new' states, have an enviable record of achievement: parliamentary government is the norm, political violence, military intervention and inter-state conflict very much the exception. On the other hand, if that experience is extended to embrace the economic and the social, questions begin to emerge. Despite rises in per capita income and other associated indicators of modernity and growth, Caribbean economies remain constrained by a system in which employment opportunities are limited, production is stagnant and dependence is deepened. Social disadvantage, historically derived, also continues to be manifest in continuing inequalities of race, class, status, sex and district, in turn feeding an ever-expanding appetite to 'escape' by whatever means available, preferably by emigration to North America.

On the one side of the balance sheet, there is apparent success: on the other side, apparent failure. Yet too much should not immediately be read into such an audit. The political achievements need to be qualified critically and the social and economic deficiences leavened by recognition of many positive developments, especially in the field of culture. West Indian diversity, as ever, refuses any simple labelling and if there is tension, disquiet and unease in the region, its causes are multifaceted, deep-seated and complex. Moreover, problems do not all arise from within the region. In no other part of the post-colonial world has dependency been more marked or external factors more routinely admitted into everyday life. What is endogenous and what is exogenous is difficult to determine, almost impossibly so, with the consequence that credit or blame, if it is to be apportioned, is necessarily somewhat arbitrary.

Nevertheless, an identity has emerged and an experience evolved which may be authenticated as West Indian. It partakes of the past, contributes to the present, and maintains a boundary that preserves its distinctiveness. In political life these features are affirmed in a constancy to a departed colonial order, a liberal and generally constructive adaptation to socio-economic change, and an appreciation of and accommodation to geopolitical realities. These themes underpin the principal argument of this chapter: that politics and political life in the Commonwealth Caribbean is consolidating itself into a particular configuration, unlike those of either neighbouring Latin America or distant, but seemingly similar, sub-Saharan Africa.

Political constancy

In a discussion of the comparative politics of the Caribbean region Patrick Emmanuel has written:

> If the Commonwealth Caribbean states possess a distinctive feature it lies in the nature and relative durability of their constitutional regime – an adaptation of the British Westminster system. In almost every other of the new states, profound changes have been wrought in the constitutional systems of competitive politics inherited at independence. Military and one-party regimes, of varying ideological hues abound. In the English-speaking Caribbean, on the other hand, the Westminster constitutions, with the partial exception of Guyana and the full exception of Grenada, have remained intact; although this is by no means to suggest that the practice of politics in these states is consonant with the requirements of the 'letter and spirit of the constitution'.[1]

Fidelity to the Westminster model, the reasons for this and the degree of departure from it, are therefore the necessary starting point for any broad review of Commonwealth Caribbean politics.

In respect of the first question the matter is relatively quickly settled by reference to history. The tutelage exercised by the Colonial Office in the Caribbean was long and for the most part respected, at least by the political élites to which formal political power was eventually bequeathed. Political independence, perhaps more than anywhere else, became focused on the agitation for, and the concession of, a succession of adjustments to the constitutional order. The political horizon was thus fixed and lifted only piecemeal as the programme for political change was carefully crafted to focus upon it. Aspiring West Indian politicians for the most part both acquiesced in and helped fashion the parameters, with the consequence that when independence eventually came it was orderly, calculated and decidedly constitutionalist. At independence every Commonwealth Caribbean state therefore chose to express its personality through the Westminster–Whitehall system, suitably modified as might be expected to local context, but not changed in essence by that fact.

The same conclusion may be sustained with regard to post-independence constitutional change in the region. With the exceptions of Grenada and Guyana, reform has sought improvements within the model rather than its fundamental revision.[2] Thus it is of note that the constitutions of the Bahamas, Barbados and Jamaica remain almost as they were at independence. This is so notwithstanding a comprehensive review of the constitution of Barbados published in 1979 and a prospective review of the constitution of Jamaica during Michael Manley's second term of office, 1976–80. The independence of the smaller Commonwealth Caribbean states has been too recent to witness much in this direction, especially as considerable efforts were made at the time of independence to resolve at least foreseeable constitutional problems, such as the status of Barbuda in respect of Antigua, and Anguilla and Nevis in respect of St Kitts. This leaves Trinidad and Tobago as the state attempting the most comprehensive reform within the system; a Republic was created in 1976 (within which the Prime Minister yielded significant power of appointment to the President) and a number of new posts were established, notably an Ombudsman, a Director of Public Prosecutions and an Integrity Commission. Subsequently, a measure of self-government was also conceded to Tobago in 1980. However, none of this changed the concept of Trinidad and Tobago as a unitary state nor disturbed the formulation of the Westminster–Whitehall model. Indeed, parts were even reinforced, for example, appeals to the Judicial Committee of the Privy Council in London were retained. As Prime Minister Eric Williams was to remind his party but a year before his death: 'If the Westminster model has helped Trinidad and Tobago in not producing our own barbarities and monsters, then we need not be too perturbed about the non-uprooting of our colonial structures, remembering that colonial Trinidad and Tobago, before the PNM, was a parody and a caricature of the Westminster model.'[3] In other words, independence provided the context for perfecting, not rejecting, the inherited model.

Nevertheless, 'Westminster' has been explicitly set aside, both by the New Jewel Movement in Grenada, 1979–83, and the People's National Congress regime in Guyana from 1980 onwards. Their reasons for so doing were many and varied and in each case fundamentally different from the other, but with one presumption held in common: that the Westminster model no longer fitted the vision of the present and future society held by the political directorate. Maurice Bishop put this forcefully in his dismissal of Westminster parliamentary democracy in Grenada as 'really Westminster parliamentary hypocrisy'.[4] In its place he proposed popular democracy and a constitution embodying social and economic rights and obligations. Likewise, Forbes Burnham dismissed the 1966 Constitution of Guyana, even as later amended by him, as essentially 'unsatisfactory, untidy and unaesthetic', and managed to secure in the new constitution a section on political, economic and social rights expressive of the theory of the party and government as propagated at the time.[5] The somewhat narrow legalistic formulations of the Westminster model have therefore been comprehensively broached. But it is of note that in neither instance did the course of action recommend itself to Commonwealth Caribbean neighbours. Rather, the reverse was the case, so that over time both regimes became increasingly subject to censure and suffered a degree of isolation in the region.

The cases outlined above emphasise what in retrospect is the real basis for the continuity of the Westminster–Whitehall system throughout the region. Quite simply, it is concordant with and expressive of a deeply conservative political culture. This is not always appreciated, the region having attracted considerable attention in recent years for its alleged instability. Undeniably there has been political violence, assassination and death. Yet such processes have not been sustained nor in any way routinised except, arguably, in Guyana and Grenada. And here the very fact of their presumed existence has served warning on others as to the general unacceptability of violence as a means of political change, so reinforcing the inherited notion of a consensual and legalistic political order.

The roots of that order are again to be found in the colonial past, particularly in the reaction to chattel slavery, apprenticeship, indenture and the ordeal of 'free labour'. The denial or restrictions on liberty and mobility implied in all the above have put a premium on freedom in the Commonwealth Caribbean and have invested that freedom with a positive association to private property, especially in land, and the practice of a lively religiosity, witnessed individually or in joyous free association with others.[6] All this the Westminster system has been especially good at preserving. Its seventeenth-century foundations and eighteenth-century evolution were crucially concerned with such questions and their relevance to the region today are but confirmed by the preambulary provisions of the majority of the Commonwealth Caribbean constitutions. Moreover, as the nineteenth and twentieth centuries saw change forced upon Westminster to admit the dispossessed, by degrees, to full citizenship, so a later parallel process in the West Indies (proceeding without individual difficulty except in British Guiana) could not but confirm the merits of a system able to sustain such admirable environmental equilibrium. Accordingly, the creole élite at independence wanted no other form of government than the Westminster model, regarding it not as 'foreign derived' but as 'autochthonous'.[7]

Nothing in the last twenty-five years or so suggests that a similar choice would not be lauded today. Conservatism has come to be celebrated as virtue, its values generally appreciated and widely distributed throughout society as political 'common sense'. Regular public opinion surveys by Carl Stone in Jamaica and Selwyn Ryan in Trinidad confirm this in every respect. The Westminster–Whitehall system, as inherited and sustained, appears both immutable and omniscient. Yet the qualification of Emmanuel's opening paragraph on the need to observe the 'letter and spirit of the constitution' should not be forgotten as neither should the observation by the Constitution Commission of Trinidad and Tobago in 1974 that 'the Westminster political system has a propensity to become transformed into dictatorship when transplanted in societies without political cultures which support its operative conventions'.[8] In the early 1960s surveys of the political élite by

Bell and Moskos revealed a strong antidemocratic undercurrent[9] and there have been many examples in recent years of authoritarian practices in states other than Grenada and Guyana. At the very apex of the system it is therefore possible to cite seemingly 'arbitrary' acts undertaken by Prime Ministers for no other advantage than political expediency: the removal of Governor-Generals from office on questionable grounds in St Lucia and St Kitts-Nevis; the impugning of the integrity of the Head of the Civil Service in Trinidad and Tobago; and the setting aside of conventions and procedures regarding consultation with the Leader of the Opposition in Jamaica and St Vincent have been but among the most publicised. Lower down in the system one can only wonder at the extent to which 'office' may be quietly abused; it is but a short step from the manipulation of office for power associated with widespread, almost 'institutionalised', systems of patronage, as in Jamaica, to the temptation of office for gain. Widespread corruption has so far not been a notorious feature of Commonwealth Caribbean politics,[10] but in recent years both an escalating drugs trade and the attributes of sovereignty have tempted senior ministers to excess, proven or alleged, in the Bahamas, Antigua and the Turks and Caicos Islands. The fabric of the Westminster system can easily become unravelled in such circumstances, as events elsewhere in the former colonies of Britain so clearly show. That it has not yet done so in the Commonwealth Caribbean may be fortuitous, although of probably greater significance is the fact that redress continues to be available to the citizen through a number of channels, not least of which is the possibility of removing the government currently in power by electoral means.

Political change

Since formal independence Commonwealth Caribbean governments have held thirty-eight general elections, twelve of which have resulted in changes of government. If the record of the era of Associated Statehood is added as well, the totals become fifty-two and eighteen respectively.[11] This alone shows that within the Commonwealth Caribbean elections are clearly significant and the electoral process important as a mechanism of regime change. Only the Bahamas (independent since 1973) and Guyana (independent since 1966) have not been affected, the former having seen the government reconfirmed three times in free and fair elections since then, while the latter very much constitutes a special case. Many reasons may be advanced for this survival of the electoral process, beginning with the British colonial legacy, which bequeathed a better chance, especially for the smaller countries, of the maintenance of a liberal democratic tradition than existed in other former European colonies. But of particular note in the Commonwealth Caribbean are the ways in which competitive party politics evolved to give both meaning to elections as the basis of periodic political change, and substance to the parliamentary process as the representation of interest.

Three factors have been of key significance in establishing and maintaining electoral politics. The first is the relatively early granting, before independence, of universal suffrage as the basis of the electoral system: Jamaica in 1944, Trinidad in 1946, Barbados and the eastern Caribbean in 1951, Guyana in 1953, Belize in 1954 and the Bahamas in 1962. A socialisation into, and a familiarisation with, the electoral game has in consequence been the norm for the majority. A sense of citizenship has evolved to give expression to this, represented in high levels of voter registration and high turnout at general elections, usually over 50 per cent. The exceptions, notably Trinidad in 1971, Jamaica in 1983 and Guyana since 1980, are to be viewed precisely as such and to be explained by unusual and particular circumstances.[12]

The second is the emergence and institutionalisation of 'mass' political parties and competitive party systems. The People's National Party in Jamaica celebrated the fiftieth anniversary of its founding in 1988 and the great majority of governing or leading opposition parties have origins in the 1950s. For many the prospects of being returned to office in the foreseeable future are good. Indeed, the evolution of party systems is precisely in this direction. One-party dominance, as witnessed in the long periods of government of the People's United Party in Belize, the St Kitts Labour Party and the People's National Movement in Trinidad, has been broken in recent years by the emergence of 'new' parties contesting and winning office. At the same time, the 'winnowing' effect of the first-past-the-post electoral system has operated to squeeze minor parties and limit the growth of multiple-party systems as a persistent probability. The gradual consolidation of two-party systems as the acceptable and working norm in the region is thus to be expected, especially in the absence of strident or credible demands for the reform of the electoral method.

Following on from this is the third factor of the alternation of parties in government. The pattern has been set by the twin-term governments of Jamaica (since 1944 the PNP and the Jamaica Labour Party have each held office for two terms before being replaced by the other) and by the example of Barbados (where since 1951 the cycle has been two-to-three general elections won, two-to-three lost). Other examples are to be readily found in Grenada, St Lucia and St Vincent. Only in the cases of the Bahamas and Guyana do the prospects of opposition victory at the polls look poor. Accordingly, opposition politicians almost everywhere and in nearly every instance have much to lose by the careless advocacy of extra-parliamentary action and correspondingly much to gain by the cultivation of a reputation for 'responsible' dissent. The distance from 'Westminster'-type electoral politics, once studiously cultivated by radicals and would-be revolutionaries, has been replaced of late by an engagement in elections and associated processes whenever deemed appropriate.

Citizens in Commonwealth Caribbean countries are thus presented at election time with choice: rarely is it a choice of ideology or policy, more often it is a question of personality, political leader and political élite. These can and do differ quite markedly from each other both in style and social base. Lloyd Best, drawing on Archie Singham's seminal study, *The Hero and the Crowd in a Colonial Polity*,[13] early distinguished three types of leaders: 'Sunday School Doctors', produced in the mature plantation colonies where there was no escape for potential leaders from organising labour, where the education came chiefly from Sunday School and the rhetoric was Biblical (e.g. Vere Bird in Antigua, Eric Gairy in Grenada and Robert Bradshaw in St Kitts); 'Public School Doctors', arising from a local ruling class which emerged after the end of slavery imbued with the values of their English counterparts (e.g. Norman Manley and now Michael Manley, Grantley Adams and then 'Tom' Adams); and 'Grammar School Doctors', emerging in the new plantation colonies where education, rather than property, has become the medium of advancement (e.g. Eric Williams in Trinidad and Forbes Burnham in Guyana).[14] To these it is now possible to add a fourth: the 'Managerial Doctor'. An update of the third sub-type, the incumbent draws on US educational models, promotes economic success as the basis of achievement, and trades upon western international support as a sign of acceptability. Such leaders assiduously cultivate a reputation for managerial efficiency and offer themselves to the electorate as better able to 'manage dependency'[15] than any of their rivals. 'Tom' Adams in Barbados, Eugenia Charles in Dominica and Edward Seaga in Jamaica are prototypical. Many others are aspirant, especially since such leadership responds to the needs of the new social classes spawned by the accelerating, if still only partial, economic and social modernisation of the last twenty-five years. At present it is therefore possible to witness a growing emulation of such a style by heads of government as different from one another as Erskine Sandiford in Barbados, Kennedy Simmonds in St Kitts-Nevis, A. N. R. Robinson in Trinidad and Tobago and, most significantly of all, Michael Manley in the Jamaican general election of February 1989. The manipulative success of these individuals in recent years stands in stark contrast to the relative failure of the ideologically strident leaders of 'official' communist parties to attract much more than fringe support, such as Cheddi Jagan, leader of the long-established People's Progressive Party in Guyana, and Trevor Munroe, leader of the Workers' Party of Jamaica.

The main conclusion arising from this is that the institutionalisation of political parties and of styles of leadership in the region relate directly to the practice of electoral democracy. The commitment to winning elections at all costs, as Eddie Greene pointed out some years ago, inexorably leads away from ideological or radical politics and towards consolidation of the social order. It also explains, in good part, the failure of independent candidates, the decline of third parties and the longevity of regimes able to command patronage to the advantage of their supporters.[16] Elections circulate élites but do little to encourage sustained political participation outside of the hectic period of the hustings themselves. For this to be a reality the institutionalised representation of interests is required. Parliamentary procedures and consultative processes as developed in the Commonwealth Caribbean provide symbol and substance for both, thereby ensuring that a measure of focused pluralism pervades and structures political life in much of the region.

The most obvious manifestation of pluralism in politics is the existence of an appointed Upper House (the 'dignified element') in a majority of the parliaments. Even where a senate does not exist in its own right (Dominica, Guyana, St Kitts-Nevis and St Vincent), appointed 'senators' or 'representatives' sit alongside elected members in a single chamber. Since both government and opposition play a part in selection, the 'nominated' element clearly reflects the partisan division at the time. However, in filling such offices there is, explicitly or by convention, a recognition of the need for 'independent' voices to be heard. By common consent, those regarded as having an importance above others are religious organisations (especially the major Christian denominations); business, manufacturing and commodity associations (especially the chambers of commerce) and trade unions.

The 'quasi-fusion of unions and parties' has long been seen as a 'peculiar' feature of 'historical and constitutional development in the region'.[17] Everywhere, except Trinidad and Tobago, trade unions and political parties grew alongside and with each other, and the political leaders who took their countries to independence almost invariably had served as union leaders or spokesmen in the cause of labour. To recognise this, however, is not to ascribe to trade unions any decisive or preponderant weight in the political process. Indeed, the 1960s, arguably the period of their greatest power, also witnessed the elaboration of industrial relations legislation throughout the area, designed in good measure to curb or canalise it. Accordingly, the power of organised labour has been proportionately diminished, whilst that of the political directorate has been enhanced. Or, more accurately, the trade unions have been co-opted into government through representation on innumerable committees and rendered dependent, in many instances, on favour by government for the privileges and opportunities that come their way. The independent power of trade unions has thus been reduced to that of a pressure group advocating for the most part limited economistic demands on behalf of a significant, but by no means expanding, percentage of the workforce.

Not so the various private capitalist interests. Except in the cases of Grenada under Bishop, Guyana under Burnham and Jamaica under Manley in the 1970s, the power and prestige of business, manufacturing and commodity associations has been maintained, even advanced. Of particular significance has been the role of the various chambers of commerce, now collectively represented by the Caribbean Association of Industry and Commerce. Recently reinvigorated and headquartered in Barbados since 1980, this organisation has courted powerful external interests, notably but not exclusively in the USA, and has generally advanced the profile of business in the region as the major producer of wealth. The suspicion with which commercial interests were held at the time of independence by the nationalist political élites[18] has given way of late to general approval and to levels of support extending well beyond the traditional provision of tax incentives for industrial and tourist development. Whilst business empires have collapsed in the region, it is noticeable that they have done so generally for internal reasons such as managerial or liquidity failures. Wholesale nationalisation of local private capital (as opposed to transnational capital) has not occurred. Jamaican enterprise thus continues to be dominated by the fabled 'twenty-one families', Trinidad business by the French creole élite, and Barbadian commerce by the more adaptable elements of the old plantocracy. More to the point, not only do their leading figures advise government, but they also occupy ministerial office and not infrequently represent the nation on important missions abroad.

Parallel developments can be seen in the political influence of religious organisations. Whereas, for example, the Catholic church could be pilloried in Trinidad in 1970 as a symbol of 'white oppression', today in Guyana it has become a focus for sustained and popular opposition to the PNC regime. Similarly, while the major Protestant denominations – Anglican, Baptist, Methodist and Presbyterian – have in the not-too-distant past been regarded as apologists of the established order, now they are seen as more critical of it, prepared to agitate and organise around specific issues and even to maintain a controversial regional voice in the widely circulated monthly church newspaper, *Caribbean Contact*. Not that its message is all that revolutionary: social justice, reasoned dissent and the primacy of spiritual values are its staple fare, and where political engagement is advocated it is always within the constitutional order rather than subversive of it.[19] Church and state are in this sense complementary. Meanwhile, the revival of religious faith and practice presently witnessed in the region is to be found at all levels of society. Folk sects – Pentecostal, Rastafarian and Seventh Day Adventist – continue to attract large numbers of adherents, as do the non-Christian religions of Hinduism and Islam. Indeed, conversion to the latter by growing numbers of West Indians of

African descent is currently one of the more interesting and potentially politically charged undercurrents manifest in the region today.

The co-optation of labour, the prestige of business and the revival of religion point once again toward conservative influence as uppermost. Yet Commonwealth Caribbean politics in the age of independence has never been a zero-sum game. The state is not an impartial referee, but neither is it, except in Guyana and possibly Antigua, the exclusive province of any particular group. A professional civil service, an independent judiciary and a competitive media act nearly everywhere to support a pluralistic political order and to encourage accommodation as the favoured means by which political conflict can be resolved. Only when such an avenue is closed does public opinion and interest group activity spill out into the streets and coalesce to force the dismissal of unpopular governments – as in Dominica in 1979–80 and St Lucia 1981–2 – or to support their overthrow, as in the coup/insurrection in Grenada in March 1979. The situation in Guyana again presently constitutes the exception that proves the rule.

Political change in the Commonwealth Caribbean is inherently piecemeal and instinctively peaceful. The region may often give the impression of instability and crisis, but as Maingot has compellingly argued:

> This results from their intrinsic democracy and social and political pluralism. Without the gray and deadening quiet of the one-party system, or the militarized dictatorships with their censored and regimented systems, the West Indies appear as systems perpetually in inner conflict and tension. But it is precisely this dynamic tension and conflict which finds in the parliamentary system the ideal mechanism of ensuring both change and stability. The very manipulation and amendment of the constitutions which (some see) as the basis of the political instability or crisis are, in fact, solutions characteristic of the parliamentary system. They reflect the flexibility and responsiveness that is built into the constitutional political system.[20]

The argument thus returns once more to the Westminster–Whitehall model. Violence is not necessarily dysfunctional to the effective application of this system (as Jamaican politics has shown over the last twenty years), but it is very much secondary to pragmatism, bargaining and studied consensus as a means of engineering change. In turn, this rests on a general willingness to abide by the rules of the game (the analogy with cricket is far from spurious)[21] and on effective and relatively impartial public administration. There is a real danger in much of this that government becomes synonymous with administration – a charge to which many West Indian office holders would readily plead 'guilty' – and that politics, in turn, becomes focused simply on entering government – a charge that again could be levelled and sustained against most West Indian politicians. But on balance the system works tolerably well for politician and people alike and, of no small measure of importance, it also works well enough for the metropolitan powers which continue to sustain an interest in the region.

Geopolitical accommodation

In the global configuration of powers all Commonwealth Caribbean states may be regarded as small. Rather than implying that they have to eschew foreign affairs, this actually requires an attention to the international environment greater than that routinely demanded of larger powers. Reinforcing this has been an acute awareness of their dependent position in the global pattern of international relations. Whether it be trade, or investment in goods, services, people or ideas, Commonwealth Caribbean countries have come to accept, albeit reluctantly, a subordinate position in international exchange, involving an acceptance of the international system as given and their position within it as peripheral. Finally, and of growing importance in recent years, has been geography. The anomalous position of the Commonwealth Caribbean, being within the Americas but not of it, has come to be challenged. So that additional to the long-established links with Canada has come accelerated intercourse with the US and openings toward Latin America. In this new and dynamic setting the Commonwealth Caribbean has had not only to accommodate the realities of hemispheric power, but also to recognise the intrusive and profoundly divisive effects of superpower competition. The 'age of innocence' for the diplomats of the Commonwealth Caribbean is decidedly over and, with its passing, new temptations, as well as new options, have appeared on the agenda.

The context is therefore simultaneously one of adjustment to the old order and accommodation to the new. Relations with Britain are illustrative of the theme. Independence did not sever connections, but over the years ties have become somewhat attenuated – in the view of the Foreign Affairs Committee of the House of Commons, which investigated this at length in 1981–2, somewhat too much so. The Committee called on the British government 'to reaffirm its commitment to the area'[22] – a plea to which the Foreign and Commonwealth Office has eventually responded, although not on the scale or in the direction anticipated. Canada, likewise, has seen its connections revised. The special place the Commonwealth Caribbean once occupied in Canadian trade and investment has diminished. At the same time, the flow of people – tourists and migrants – has increased, as has the flow of aid. Canadian commitments to the region therefore remain and indeed have been enhanced in recent years by explicit governmental provision and recognition of the constructive role this can play in development. This is welcomed by the Commonwealth Caribbean, as is the continued British presence (expressed, in part, since 1975, through the trade and aid provisions of the Lomé conventions). Neither Canada nor Europe, however, can or are meant in any way to substitute for US leadership. The exercise of this in the Commonwealth Caribbean is now the foremost aspect of geopolitical reality before the region.

The US first decisively entered West Indian calculations in international affairs with the bases-for-destroyers deal in 1940. This signalled that the security of the West Indies could no longer be guaranteed by Britain and that, in turn, the security of the US rested on a military presence within the region.[23] By contrast, for the West Indies, beset with poverty, the US represented economic opportunity – at first chiefly via migration, but later to include investment, trade and aid. A duality has therefore developed in which US concerns for security, pursued largely and until lately through an 'economy of force' approach, were matched by a Commonwealth Caribbean concern for 'benefits', economic and psychological.

The relationship, if not equal, has nevertheless become increasingly symbiotic, and in its current phase exhibits what Gordon Lewis has described as an 'imperialist ideology and mentality' and a 'dependent colonial ideology and mentality'.[24] The former rests on the principle that 'might is right', and has very much been the leitmotiv of the Reagan Administration. The latter expresses the conservative, not to say reactionary, tradition in the region, and is represented by the ascendancy of the new middle class. Of this group Lewis has this to say:

> They have accepted political independence only reluctantly, never with enthusiasm, in part because they mistrust their own ability to govern their own country and in part because they fear that independence will pave the way to dangerous social policies. In everything dealing with regional and foreign affairs they value more than anything else metropolitan ties as safeguards against revolution, especially through contamination by way of Haiti or Cuba. It is in this area, more than any other, that their dependency complex is most pronounced.

> That last point is vital. The West Indian middle-class groups, when in power as ruling élites, unequivocally identify their local class-national interests with what they perceive as the most friendly and powerful metropolitan power available. That power, of course, used to be Britain. But with the disappearance of the British Empire the colonial loyalty has shifted to the United States. The old anglophilism is still there. But it is now more and more replaced by a new pro-Americanism. The new postindependence élites identify American interests as their own. They regard American goodwill as crucial and basic, and accept for granted the permanency of American concerns in the region . . . They remain, of course, loyal members of the Commonwealth, and Britain is still regarded with affection. But British governments are seen as being too weak or unwilling to play the old protective role. It is in that sense that the old British colonial loyalty is replaced by the new American neocolonial loyalty.[25]

The reward for such loyalty, as exemplified by support and participation in the invasion of Grenada, has been privileged access to the US market and increased aid, including military assistance, for Jamaica and the eastern Caribbean. Not everyone has seen such developments as necessarily advantageous. One of the most influential and eloquent to raise a note of dissent has been the Guyanese-born Commonwealth Secretary General, Shridath Ramphal. Reviewing the options before the Commonwealth Caribbean in 1985, he warned against adoption of a *realpolitik* of short-term interest orchestrated by the US, arguing that 'there is a difference between making an accommodation with power and welcoming dominion'. 'Reality, pragmatism', he went on, 'may justify the former. They can never require the latter.'[26] The distinction is a fine one. But the West Indies has enough capacity and technical skill in its diplomatic services to draw it; whether, individually or collectively, the various leaders have the political will to carry it forward is another matter. Unilateral denunciations and bilateral dealings have been more to the fore in recent times than effective and judicious diplomacy for which the region acquired a well deserved reputation in global fora in the 1970s.[27]

The question is acute largely because the record of regional co-operation has been inconclusive. The Commonwealth Caribbean, as a scattering of separate states, was born out of the failure of the West Indies Federation in 1962. Attempts at regional co-operation since then, notably the creation of the Caribbean Free Trade Association in 1968 and then the Caribbean Community and Common Market in 1973, have kept hopes of economic integration alive; in parallel fashion, fairly regular meetings of the Heads of Government of the Commonwealth Caribbean have promoted and maintained a West Indian political identity within diverse international agencies such as the ACP grouping, the Commonwealth, the Non-Aligned Movement, the OAS and UNCTAD. Against this, however, there have been fissiparous tendencies at work rooted in ideological division and external definition: Cuba, Grenada and the Caribbean Basin Initiative have all featured prominently in this context, threatening at various times the integrity of the regional movement as a whole. That it has not collapsed is remarkable, and is due in part to the real institutional strengths the region possesses, especially in the areas of functional co-operation. There is also a sense in which none of the present political leadership in the region wishes to see the integration movement fail. But neither do any one or several of them wish to see it succeed at their expense. Summing up the experience of the regional movement several years ago, Payne coined the concept of 'regionalisation' which he defined as 'a method of international cooperation which enables the advantages of decision-making at the regional level to be reconciled with the preservation of the institutions of the nation state'.[28] This qualification of any 'deepening' of integration holds today; within the region as a whole, or indeed any part of it, hopes for political integration, i.e. federation, remain only a remote possibility.

The weight of the geopolitical environment on the policy calculations of Commonwealth Caribbean countries is reflected, above all, in their almost universal adoption of a politics of 'acquiescent adaptation' as the most appropriate orientation toward international affairs.[29] As elaborated by Rosenau, this specifies that a state will not so much seek to alter the extra-societal environment by policy output as to endeavour to keep its essential economic, social and political structures within acceptable limits by making them consistent with the demands and changes emanating from that environment.[30] In other words, it will seek to accommodate domestic arrangements to foreign considerations. Regionally, as already noted, it is the other way around, but with respect to the dominant metropolitan connections, the observation very much holds. Sovereignty, for Commonwealth Caribbean states, is closely circumscribed. But it does not have to be surrendered. Sensitive management strategies (as contrasted with ideological denunciations) can be fashioned within such a framework to enhance local decision-making. The most obvious are those extending national ownership in the economy, either by state acquisition of existing transnational company assets or through private/public participation in joint-venture schemes. Other available mechanisms are fiscal control, exchange rate policy and legal prohibition. The platform from which these are most frequently announced and opened for comment is the annual budget speech. Anyone familiar with the Commonwealth Caribbean will recognise this as one of the most important set-pieces of the political year (the other being the address by the political leader to the annual convention of his/her political party). No wonder, then, that Prime Ministers are also often Finance Ministers, and that the speech provides opportunities for wide-ranging debate, including that on international affairs.

The importance of the budget speech attests to the significance of political economy as the principal concern of both domestic and foreign policy. To almost a determining degree performance in this area has been the single most important variable affecting the standing of governments and their chances of re-election. Political power rests to a great extent on state power, and especially on effective manipulation of the institutions and agencies through which national (and transnational) economic processes can be guided and regulated. The proliferation of such bodies, the ethos surrounding them, and the employment they create, must be considered one of the more important developments of independence – indeed, to be especially characteristic of government in the Commonwealth Caribbean in the 1960s and 1970s. Initially, the agenda was very much to establish viability – political and economic; now it has been adjusted to admit security issues as well. The international environment in which the Commonwealth Caribbean operates is thus not only more complex than before, but is also perceived as more threatening. Militarisation has been a natural response by some of the more vulnerable eastern Caribbean states,[31] but for most, this option is still seen as inconsistent with the open and democratic political temper that is the hallmark of the region.

A distinct tradition?

In a recent essay[32] and monograph[33] Carl Stone has sought to determine the political configuration of Central America and the Caribbean. Although there are many points of comparison, and occasionally of convergence, between as well as within the two regions, the predominant theme to emerge from his analysis is that of contrast. The Caribbean is seen as essentially stable contrasted to Central American instability: the non-Hispanic Caribbean as heir to strong centralised colonial administrations in contrast to the weak authoritarian tradition of state power among Hispanic countries: and the Commonwealth Caribbean as exhibiting, typically, a political profile of liberal democracy (democratic–pluralist) in contrast to the authoritarian and populist–statist (leftist–socialist) regimes to be expected among the non-English speaking states of the region. None of this, of course, implies that the Commonwealth Caribbean will necessarily continue along such a path. Both Grenada and Guyana have witnessed regime transformation away from the regional norm. But it does point out that Latin America, the Spanish speaking islands and the Luso-Hispanic mainland, are politically distant from the region and likely to remain so for some time to come.

Similar conclusions apply in the case of African states. With them, the Commonwealth Caribbean shares a history of colonialism, a search for national identity, a desire for economic diversification and a need to fashion effective and credible political institutions. But, unlike them, the Commonwealth Caribbean was better placed at independence to undertake such tasks, so that the post-independence experience has largely been a process of departure. The move from pluralism to centralisation of power in the hands of a single party has been resisted; power has been personalised, but leaders have not been deified; military coups have been averted; the unchecked growth of bureaucratic power has been contained and subjected to judicial review; socialism has been espoused, but to a lesser extent than capitalism; and regional co-operation has been sustained, albeit with difficulty.[34] Additional points of emphasis and contrast could easily be made. But the evidence is overwhelming – African politics is distinct from Commonwealth Caribbean politics. Bearing in mind the very different geopolitical environment in which the two regions operate, the difference is likely to become even more marked in the future.

Is there, then, a West Indian identity? Sir Arthur Lewis, a former Vice-Chancellor of the University of the West Indies (UWI) and a former Professor at Manchester University (among much else), has talked of West Indians being different, particularly from Africans, and as being a particularly adaptable and cosmopolitan people.[35] Alister McIntyre, the current Vice-Chancellor of UWI and former Deputy-Director of UNCTAD (among much else), has also identified a distinctive political legacy of pragmatism, bridge-building, commitment to democratic values and 'an unambiguous preference for dialogue and negotiation over the use of force'.[36] Certainly, the political culture of the Commonwealth Caribbean is unique. It shares attributes of the First World and the Third World, with the political institutions and the behaviour of its political élite strongly shaped by both. Similarly influenced also are its political economy and, increasingly, its foreign policy. None of this makes for easy living. The problems of the economic and social order identified at the beginning of this chapter are very real and not open to obvious or easy solutions. Their cumulative effect may yet overwhelm the region. However, the history of the Caribbean is in many ways a history of survival: retentions, adaptations and innovations mark its passage and highlight its contradictions. In the Commonwealth Caribbean all are to be found in abundance. Out of constancy, change and accommodation may come chaos – but more likely is the consolidation of a political culture of resourcefulness, an institutionalised and more-or-less responsive political order, and an original and creative political theory and practice.

Notes

1 Patrick Emmanuel, 'Approaches to the comparative study of Caribbean politics: some comments', *Social and Economic Studies*, Vol. 30, No. 3, 1981, pp. 125–6.

2 For details, see Sir Fred Philips, *West Indian Constitutions: Post Independence Reform*, Oceana Publications Inc., New York, 1985.

3 Dr Eric Williams, *Forged from the Love of Liberty: Selected Speeches of Dr Eric Williams*, comp. Paul Sutton, Longman Caribbean, Trinidad, 1981, p. 425.

4 Maurice Bishop, *Maurice Bishop Speaks: The Grenada Revolution 1979–1983*, ed. Bruce Marcus and Michael Taber, Pathfinder Press, New York, 1983, pp. 187–8, 301–2. A substantial critique had been advanced earlier in the New Jewel Movement's Manifesto of 1973. This claimed: 'Firstly, parties divide the people into warring camps. Secondly, the system places power in the hands of a small ruling clique. That clique victimises and terrorises members of the other party. Thirdly, the ruling élite seizes control of all avenues of public information, for example, the radio station, and uses them for its own ends. Finally, and most importantly, it fails to involve the people except for a few seconds in every five years when they make an "X" on a ballot paper.' p. 153.

5 Philips, *West Indian Constitutions*, p. 57.

6 See, in particular, Anthony P. Maingot, 'The Caribbean: the structure of modern conservative societies' in J. K. Black (ed.), *Latin America, Its Problems and Its Promises: a Multidisciplinary Introduction*, Westview Press, Boulder, Colo., and London, 1984, pp. 362–78. He also attributes conservatism to the fundamentally matriarchal and matrilocal nature of Caribbean societies.

7 An early and valuable discussion of this question is Trevor Munroe, *The Politics of Constitutional Decolonisation: Jamaica, 1944–62*, Institute of Social and Economic Research, University of the West Indies, Jamaica, 1972, pp. 175–8.

8 Constitution Commission of Trinidad and Tobago, *Report of the Constitution Commission*, Government of Trinidad and Tobago, 22 January 1974, paragraph 35.

9 See, in particular, Charles Moskos and Wendell Bell, 'Attitudes toward democracy' in W. Bell (ed.), *The Democratic Revolution in the West Indies*, Schenkman, Cambridge, Mass., 1967, pp. 68–85.

10 Only in the Bahamas and Trinidad and Tobago is there specific legislation dealing with corruption and immorality in public life. Elsewhere charges would need to be brought under the common law offence of 'misbehaviour in public office'. In recent years ministers and officials have been prosecuted under this provision in St Vincent,

Antigua and Trinidad. See Donald Trotman, 'Some aspects of human rights abuse as a threat to democracy' in The Bustamante Institute of Public and International Affairs, *Threats to Democracy in the Caribbean*, Report of a Seminar held in St Vincent, 31 July–1 August 1986, pp. 27–33.

11 Calculated to 30 May 1989.

12 In Trinidad and Jamaica the major opposition parties deliberately organised boycotts of the elections; in Guyana electoral fraud by the People's National Congress government has been a growing feature since 1968.

13 A. W. Singham, *The Hero and the Crowd in a Colonial Polity*, Yale University Press, New Haven, CT, 1968. Of more than passing interest is that the subject of study in this case was Eric Gairy and the political system that of Grenada. It was also originally presented as a Ph. D. thesis to Manchester University – the first of a distinguished series on the government and politics of the Commonwealth Caribbean.

14 *The Express*, Trinidad, 31 May 1969. Lloyd Best has recently elaborated upon this in his 'West Indian society 150 years after abolition: a re-examination of some classic theories' in J. Hayward (ed.), *Out of Slavery: Abolition and After*, Frank Cass, London, 1985, pp. 148–52.

15 The management of dependency emerges as the common distinguishing characteristic of the political economy of the Commonwealth Caribbean in the 1970s. See, in particular, Anthony Payne and Paul Sutton (eds.), *Dependency under Challenge: The Political Economy of the Commonwealth Caribbean*, Manchester University Press, Manchester, 1984.

16 J. E. Greene, 'Institutionalization of party systems' in Vaughan A. Lewis (ed.), *Size, Self-Determination and International Relations: The Caribbean*, Institute of Social and Economic Research, University of the West Indies, Jamaica, 1976, pp. 203–26, especially pp. 221–4.

17 Elisabeth Wallace, *The British Caribbean: From the Decline of Colonialism to the End of Federation*, University of Toronto Press, Toronto, 1977, p. 75.

18 The opposition of prosperous planters and merchants to political independence in the early 1960s is reported throughout Bell (ed.), *The Democratic Revolution in the West Indies*. It is repeated in muted form in the 1970s for the Associated States. See A. E. Thorndike, 'Associated statehood and the eastern Caribbean: the search for independence', paper presented to the Political Studies Association Conference, Sheffield, April 1979.

19 Attitudes toward the Grenada Revolution provide a good example. At first, the various established churches, including the dominant Catholic Church, were supportive of the PRG. As the revolution unfolded

and 'heavy manners', i.e. selective detention without trial, became more widespread, they began to qualify support and eventually to distance themselves from the regime, with the Catholic Church and the fundamentalist sects moving into active opposition.

20 Anthony P. Maingot, 'Comment' on Vaughan A. Lewis, 'Political change and crisis in the English-speaking Caribbean' in A. Adelman and R. Reading (eds.), *Confrontation in the Caribbean Basin*, University of Pittsburgh Center for Latin American Studies, Pittsburgh, 1984, p. 119.

21 The fact that one of the Commonwealth Caribbean's foremost revolutionary intellectuals, C. L. R. James, and one of its most distinguished politicians, Michael Manley, should both write authoritatively about cricket is evidence in itself. Nevertheless, the place of cricket in contemporary Caribbean politics is yet to be fully determined. See C. L. R. James, *Beyond a Boundary*, Stanley Paul, London, 1963; and Michael Manley, *History of West Indies Cricket*, André Deutsch, London, 1988.

22 House of Commons, *Fifth Report of the Foreign Affairs Committee of the House of Commons: Caribbean and Central America*, HMSO, London, 1982, p. lxiii.

23 In 1941 the Lend-Lease Agreement between the US and Britain allowed the US to lease rent-free for ninety-nine years naval and air bases in Antigua, the Bahamas, Bermuda, British Guiana, Jamaica, St Lucia and Trinidad in exchange for fifty aged destroyers needed by Britain for the war effort. With this deal, the US assumed unprecedented military superiority in the region.

24 Gordon K. Lewis, *Grenada: The Jewel Despoiled*, The Johns Hopkins University Press, Baltimore and London, 1987.

25 Ibid., pp. 137–8.

26 Shridath Ramphal, 'Options for the Caribbean: the lure of realpolitik', Institute of International Relations, *Distinguished Lecturer Series*, Institute of International Relations, UWI, Trinidad, 1985, p. 23.

27 For a recent discussion of foreign policy, see Jacqueline Braveboy-Wagner, *The Caribbean in World Affairs: the Foreign Policies of the English-speaking States*, Westview Press, Boulder, Colo., 1989.

28 A. J. Payne, *The Politics of the Caribbean Community 1961–1979: Regional Integration amongst New States*, Manchester University Press, Manchester, 1980, p. 286.

29 The exceptions are Grenada under Bishop, and in part Jamaica under Michael Manley and Guyana under Forbes Burnham. See the various contributions in J. Heine and L. Manigat (eds.), *The Caribbean in World Politics: Cross Currents and Cleavages*, Holmes and Meier, New York and London, 1988.

30 J. N. Rosenau, *The Adaptation of National Societies: A Theory of Political System Behaviour and Transformation*, The McCaleb Seiber Publishing Co., New York, 1970.

31 In October 1982 a 'Memorandum of Understanding Relating to Security and Military Co-operation' was signed by Antigua, Barbados, Dominica, St Lucia and St Vincent (St Kitts-Nevis acceded on independence in September 1983) establishing a framework for military security co-operation in the eastern Caribbean. Subsequent to the invasion of Grenada, considerable efforts have been directed toward enhancing the security capabilities of these states and Grenada through programmes of external assistance providing for paramilitary and police training, improved coastguard provision, and logistic support. For details see Humberto Garcia Muniz, *Boots, Boots, Boots: Intervention, Regional Security and Militarization in the Caribbean 1979–1986*, Caribbean Project for Justice and Peace, Militarism Series 2, Puerto Rico, June 1986.

32 Carl Stone, 'A political profile of the Caribbean' in R. Price and S. Mintz (eds.), *Caribbean Contours*, The Johns Hopkins University Press, Baltimore and London, 1985, pp. 13–53.

33 Carl Stone, *Power in the Caribbean Basin: A Comparative Study of Political Economy*, Institute for the Study of Human Issues, Philadelphia, 1986.

34 See, for example, the discussion of African politics in William Tordoff, *Government and Politics in Africa*, Macmillan, London, 1984, especially Ch. 1.

35 W. Arthur Lewis, 'On being different' in D. Lowenthal and L. Comitas (eds.), *The Aftermath of Sovereignty: West Indian Perspectives*, Anchor Books, New York, 1973, pp. 293–302.

36 Alister McIntyre, 'The Caribbean after Grenada: four challenges facing the regional movement', Institute of International Relations, *Distinguished Lecturer Series*, Institute of International Relations, UWI, Trinidad, 1984, p. 11.

7 *James Craig*

Escape from the fortress colony: the politics of economic diversification in Malta

Malta was always one of the more unusual of Britain's colonial possessions. A tiny unit twenty-six square miles in size, consisting of two small islands, plus a few islets, its position at the centre of the Mediterranean and its superb natural harbour have been the country's only significant historical resources. But, for these reasons, seagoing peoples over many centuries have visited and possessed the Maltese islands. British dominance, which began in 1800, has been merely the last phase of a long history of subordination which has given rise to Malta's classic designation as a 'fortress colony'.[1] In the formal political sense, independence was achieved in September 1964, but Britain retained military facilities on the islands until March 1979. It was only then that the country can be said to have begun to shake off its fortress past.

During those fifteen years successive Maltese governments had to face similar developmental problems – above all, how to manage the transition from being a fortress and a base for British defence needs into becoming a viable economic unit where defence expenditure was no longer of crucial importance. Even today when Malta is no longer a base for foreign military activity, the relative lack of natural resources poses important policy problems in relation to development. To achieve some room for manoeuvre, Maltese political leaders have had to use the territory's international political setting as a key resource for economic and social development.[2] The theme of the 'manoeuvrability' of a small post-colonial state is thus the focus of this chapter. In such a discussion, it is all too easy to conclude that relationships of dependency imply a problem. At least as far as the Maltese case is concerned, it can be argued that dependence on Britain and its NATO allies also provided policy opportunities. Britain was clearly more powerful in every political and economic sense, but the relationship provided successive Maltese governments with an opportunity to bargain and indeed to win important concessions on a number of fronts.

The case of Malta does provide at least one general lesson for the future of post-colonial states, namely that the application of political skills in international relations can provide tangible advantages to even a small country and that power in international politics is not just about economic strength or military might. Political leadership is very much a part of the equation.[3] Certainly, in Malta, there is no doubt that personalities have played a key part in recent political history. Borg Olivier, Prime Minister from 1962 until 1971 as leader of the Nationalist Party (PN), and Dom Mintoff, Prime Minister from 1971 until 1984 as leader of the Malta Labour Party (MLP), so dominated Maltese politics in this period of the island's history that their policy preferences were rarely challenged.

For the purposes of analysis, the period 1964–84 has been divided into two phases. 'Dependent sovereignty' can be said to characterise the Borg Olivier years, with the military rundown crisis of 1966–7 effectively encapsulating the PN strategy for Malta until the party's defeat in 1971. By contrast, 'positive neutralism' summarises the MLP approach, which is highlighted by an examination of the 1971–2 crisis and the post-1979 era. Despite the very different approaches of Borg Olivier and Mintoff, there are areas of similarity. Both sought from their different perspectives to further Maltese interests against difficult odds. The economic and social progress achieved in the 1960s and 1970s at least testifies to some successes.

Dependent sovereignty, 1964–71

On the successful completion of independence negotiations in September 1964, Malta and Britain signed a Defence and Financial Agreement, designed to facilitate economic development within the security of a British and NATO presence. The Agreement reflected much of the political thinking of the PN under the leadership of Borg Olivier with regard to Malta's future development. At first sight, Malta's policy options looked painfully curtailed by Britain's declining role in the Mediterranean area. As far back as 1959, the colonial government had recognised the need to bring together a battery of policy proposals to strengthen and expand sectors of the economy, such as tourism, light industry, and agriculture, in order to achieve diversification away from British services-related expenditure and employment. All parties concerned – Britain, the PN and the MLP – were united in the conviction that economic viability would only be achieved if Britain and its NATO allies were prepared to assist Malta and harmonise their own defence planning and Malta's interests for long-term development. The PN and the MLP disagreed fundamentally on how this was to be achieved, though a UN mission visited the islands in 1963 and stated that economic viability was likely to take fifteen to twenty-five years to achieve, a conclusion which was accepted by Britain as a realistic assessment.

The Defence and Financial Agreement negotiated by Borg Olivier and the British Commonwealth Secretary, Duncan Sandys, stated that Britain would provide a sum of £51 million over a ten-year period, 75 per cent of which was to be in the form of a grant and 25 per cent a loan at current UK interest rates.[4] These financial arrangements were to last for a five-year period and then be subject to further review in 1969. A parallel defence agreement was also signed which gave Britain considerable control over key installations and the use of property and land for military purposes.[5] Britain also agreed to train and assist generally with the development of Malta's own small defence forces.

What emerged emphasised the PN commitment to a solidly pro-western foreign and security policy. Borg Olivier had strong backing from the Cabinet and party for this position. Although a nationalist, Borg Olivier was cautious in his approach to policy. He held to the view that the aim of economic viability required the security of a British and NATO presence. He was aware that, in 1964, 13 per cent of all gainfully employed Maltese worked for British services departments and that the wages and salaries paid to Maltese employees of the services constituted 23 per cent of the total wage bill.[6] Although services expenditure was falling at a rate of £2 million per year from a peak of £22·3 million in 1961, and such falls were likely to continue, the pace of that decline was of the essence. The Defence and Financial Agreement remained the main pillar of PN thinking for the rest of the decade, even though it was fully realised that Malta had to use the ten-year period to good effect. Defence, security, and the economy were thus interwoven. The presence of British forces provided defence of an order that Malta could not provide for itself; Southern HQ of NATO provided a security network and a stage on which Malta might play a part in wider European and North American concerns; and the entire relationship could be translated into tangible economic benefits.

This may appear, on the surface, to be a curious form of nationalism. However, it will be argued later that Borg Olivier's defence of Malta's interests in his negotiations with Britain in the second half of the 1960s did not suggest he was a neo-colonial puppet. With great determination and considerable political skill, he fought to extract the best out of the increasingly retreating British. The election of a British Labour government under Harold Wilson soon after Maltese independence in 1964 proved difficult for the PN government. Wilson and his Defence Secretary, Denis Healey, were determined to extract cuts and reduce the commitments of British forces. Malta was obviously unlikely to escape the effects of this policy. Whatever the benefits of the Financial Agreement, a programme of cuts in British forces was bound to result in reduced economic activity and consequent unemployment in Malta.

Two connected themes then emerged that, in effect, set the parameters of development policy for the rest of the 1960s and the 1970s. The first, as mentioned, was how to operate the British connection to minimise the effects on Malta of Britain's Mediterranean withdrawal; the second was how to widen the NATO connection from security to economic development. This latter goal was another aspect of Borg Olivier's conservative nationalism. His leadership of the PN had seen the party scuttle its Italianate past, with the consequence that Italian language and culture had all but disappeared as a political force. This was replaced by a desire on the part of the Maltese middle and professional classes, from whom the PN obtained much of its support, to be seen as part of wider European culture. Borg Olivier spoke frequently of the island's attachment to Europe, the west and NATO. In a 1966 speech to the House of Representatives (the Maltese one-chamber parliament), he declared, for example, that Malta's place was with the west, with NATO and all they stood for. Throughout his premiership and beyond, he held consistently to this view. He believed that Maltese national interests and Europeanism were complementary; NATO, for Borg Olivier, was thus a security *and* political expression of his intellectual and emotional attachment to the western cause.

The question that has now to be asked is this: how successfully did Borg Olivier manage to weave together his defence, security, and economic policies to achieve tangible development for Malta until his narrow defeat at the hands of the MLP in 1971? The critical test was the dispute with the British government which arose in 1966–7 over proposed reductions in British forces in Malta and the consequent employment effects upon locally engaged workers. The issue came to a head after the PN government had been returned to office in 1966 at the end of an election campaign dominated by a long-running dispute between the MLP and the island's Roman Catholic bishops. Controversy surrounds the electoral benefit derived by the PN from the dispute, but the economic indicators do suggest that Borg Olivier's claims – that the economy was expanding, the tourist industry growing, and gross production rising – played at least some part in the victory.[7]

However, improved economic performance was to prove double-edged for Malta. In the middle of the election campaign, the British government published its Defence Review. This stated: 'we shall continue these responsibilities and obligations [in the Mediterranean] while making substantial economies in our contingents in Cyprus and Malta'.[8] Britain adopted the view that substantial savings could be made in defence expenditure in the Mediterranean in general and in Malta in particular, while still fulfilling the basic demands of NATO and the agreement with Malta. It also considered that Malta's growing economic prosperity meant that the financial and employment effects of a British rundown would not be devastating. For the Maltese, the issue looked very different. Here was Britain sacrificing Maltese interests on the altar of economy only two years after granting independence and signing a defence and financial agreement. Not only was Malta's defence and security put in question, but the economic gains of the last few years were likely to falter if Maltese workers were made redundant as the economies were carried out.[9]

The situation posed a real dilemma for Malta, difficult for it to handle. Mintoff's MLP asked repeatedly, and with devastating effect, what Malta was really achieving by sheltering so closely under the British and NATO umbrella. The 1964 agreement stated quite clearly that Malta would be consulted before any major changes were contemplated, but Borg Olivier denied that he had been consulted prior to the publication of the defence review. The word 'consultation' is, of course, conveniently ambiguous. In the House of Commons in Britain, it was stated that the Maltese government had been informed of that part of the review referring to Malta. But it is difficult to regard information of a decision already taken as constituting consultation. Borg Olivier's reply to the British was clearly intended to give him time in which to see his party safely back in power at the 1966 general election and to begin the type of negotiations which he regarded as his right under the Defence Agreement.

By the second half of 1966, it was clear that there were major differences between London and Valletta. Lord Beswick, the Parliamentary Under-Secretary of State for Commonwealth Affairs, visited Malta in August 1966 with proposals to put into effect the objective outlined in the Defence Review. Borg Olivier went to London for the Commonwealth Prime Ministers' Conference and had discussions with Wilson and other ministers. Borg Olivier refused to state publicly what the British government's proposals were, but he left no doubt as to his hostility. The London *Daily Telegraph*[10] reported that the British intention was to save £8 million by cutting British servicemen in Malta and discharging local personnel. It warned that Britain would have no-one to blame if the Maltese decided to abrogate the Defence Agreement, expel the troops, and sell to the highest bidder; this was a clear reference to the *Telegraph's* interpretation of the policy of Mintoff and the MLP.

There followed months of bargaining in which Borg Olivier played a critical role. At first, he tried to convince Britain that severe reductions in service personnel would harm vital strategic interests. The growing Soviet presence in the Mediterranean showed the importance of Malta for Britain and NATO. There was probably some pressure on the Wilson government from the United States and Italy to proceed gently with troop reductions in Malta; hence the willingness of the British government to continue to negotiate. Borg Olivier certainly visited the US and Italy to gain support for his position. The Secretary of State for Commonwealth Affairs, Herbert Bowden, in turn, visited Malta in January 1967 with revised proposals designed to win the support of the Maltese government. His concession was that the proposed rundown of British forces would be phased over four years instead of two, but this, he stated, was Britain's last offer.[11] With the full approval of his Cabinet, Borg Olivier accused Britain of breaking the 1964 Defence Agreement and declared that Britain could not undertake its treaty obligations to Malta with such reduced forces.

There was a period of maximum pressure on the British government in the early months of 1967. Malta was increasingly regarded as a pained innocent fighting a moving battle against overwhelming odds. Wilson's treatment of Britain's ally was even attacked by the pro-Labour weekly magazine, the *New Statesman.* This was precisely the kind of comment which the Maltese government wanted to see. It had unofficially accepted the principle of the rundown, but somehow concessions had to be extracted from Britain. To do this, leverage had to be created, and Borg Olivier was at the forefront of this process. On visits to Britain and elsewhere, he rarely missed an opportunity to use the press and television to further the Maltese case. He frequently spoke of the historic link between the two countries and utilised residual pro-Maltese feeling to try to drive a wedge between Wilson's government and public opinion.

With hindsight, it is probably fair to say that Borg Olivier knew that he had got about as much movement out of the British as he was likely to achieve, at least as far as the principle of a rundown was concerned. What he required was a settlement in circumstances that would give his government maximum political mileage. Accordingly, he mobilised every conceivable group within Malta in a wave of protest – the church, voluntary organisations, the trade unions, business, commerce and the professions. Even British residents (mostly retired servicemen) held a silent march through the streets of Valletta, protesting against British policy. The largest trade union, the General Workers Union, joined in, much to the annoyance of Mintoff and the MLP. The Maltese High Commission in London was flooded with letters from all over Britain attacking the Wilson government's treatment of Malta. Finally, the Maltese government informed Britain in late January 1967 that facilities available to British forces under the Defence Agreement could no longer be used and that it was introducing into the Maltese parliament a so-called Visiting Forces Bill to change the status of service personnel on the islands.

Eventually, on 13 March 1967, an agreement was officially announced. Britain obtained its broad aim, as enshrined in the 1966 Defence Review. The rundown was to be phased over a four-year, instead of a two-year, period, with the concession that Malta could seek a review during the rundown if Maltese unemployment was to rise dramatically. A joint mission of British and Maltese experts was to start work on a plan for job creation and the general strengthening of the Maltese economy to cope with local discharges. This latter point was considered an essential ingredient of the agreement, as a loss of 6,500 jobs by the end of the rundown period would have left Malta with an unemployment rate of 17 per cent. Britain also agreed to pay some £2 million in gratuities to discharged Maltese workers and further conceded that £3 million from the Agreement in Financial Assistance spent since the dispute started should not revert to the British Treasury, but be carried over for the use of the Maltese government.

For the better part of a year, Borg Olivier had been engaged in protracted negotiations with Britain. How is one to evaluate the final outcome? At one level, the conclusion reached by the Maltese opposition led by Dom Mintoff has a clarity that is both seductive and appealing. Malta, he argued, would always face dire economic problems when Britain changed its defence policies. Britain must therefore be told what the price was for Malta's facilities: if it was unwilling to pay, it must be told to leave and another power found which was willing to pay the required price. To the cautious Borg Olivier, this was too radical and risky. He wanted to know who would substitute for Britain and NATO if the asking price was too high. In opposition, of course, Mintoff could pose the question without having to provide a policy answer, and he tantalisingly spoke of the US and others without directly clarifying his position. There can be little doubt, though, that by the mid-1960s Mintoff was well on the way towards developing a strategy that would put a time limit on the British presence and substitute a foreign policy of non-alignment for the previous policy of support for NATO. These ideas were only evolving in 1966–7, but, in retrospect, the dispute with Britain can be seen to have represented a watershed in Mintoff's thinking which will be discussed in greater detail below.

Borg Olivier's government was assisted in selling the 1967 agreement locally by the fact that the years 1966–9 witnessed considerable economic progress in Malta. The worst fears for the future held by so many did not materialise and many sectors of the economy showed distinct signs of health. Unemployment, which stood at 8·2 per cent (7,859 persons) at the beginning of the period, fell to 3·7 per cent (3,813 persons) at the same time as emigration was also falling.[12] A boom in tourism, construction, and light industry largely accounted for the expansion and employment. A Central Bank had been created in 1968 and the Malta Development Corporation had been established shortly afterwards to provide aid and practical help for investors. Tourist arrivals in 1969 rose to 186,084, with a planned target of 250,000 by 1972. Restrictions on travel outside the sterling area imposed by Britain at this time were welcomed by the Maltese tourist trade as tourist arrivals were overwhelmingly from Britain (a situation which continues despite attempts at diversification). Financial incentives attracted light manufacturing and numbers gainfully employed rose from 86,080 in 1966 to 100,460 in 1969.[13] The construction industry operated at a high level of activity, despite criticisms of lack of implementation of planning regulations. By 1968, 9,290 persons were employed in construction and there was a dramatic rise in the number of construction firms on the islands.[14] Finally, the Joint Mission reported in July 1968 and set as a major objective the creation of 15,000 jobs by 1972. Its chairman certainly appeared reasonably happy with progress to date, particularly as the number of people discharged by the services had not been as great as predicted.[15]

To sum up, the Anglo-Maltese dispute of 1966–7 aptly illuminates many of the features of Maltese security and development policy under Borg Olivier and the PN government. Another serious dispute arose over the second phase of the Financial Agreement in 1968–9.[16] Characteristically, Borg Olivier used similar tactics to gain concessions, and the election of a British Conservative government in 1970 saw him achieve all that he had asked.

Positive neutrality, 1971–84

In June 1971, in elections marked by a poll of 92·6 per cent, Mintoff's MLP gained power by a majority of one seat and thus formed the new government. It had to confront a Maltese economy which, by that period, was in some difficulty. The boom of 1967–9 had run out of steam, unemployment was rising, and tourist arrivals were falling. Underlying the new government's approach to Malta's economic problems lay the conviction that the arrangements on finance and defence negotiated by Borg Olivier in 1964 required fundamental reappraisal. There were, in essence, two strands to Mintoff's thinking, both of which he had publicly developed in speeches throughout the 1960s. In the first place, he considered that the Borg Olivier agreements gave too much to the British, considering Malta's independent status. Malta needed to reclaim its identity from years of subservience to Britain. Mintoff was determined to assert Maltese identity and, by so doing, give the country a pride in itself. In this sense, Mintoff's nationalism was more strident and angry than the 'softer' approach of Borg Olivier and the PN. Mintoff felt strongly that the British had always patronised Malta and its people, and he was determined that Malta should be treated as a free and independent nation. Secondly, he held that the British paid far too small a sum for the facilities offered. He regarded the £5 million per year given in financial assistance to be nothing like the amount that Malta was worth to Britain and NATO – and, to add insult, 25 per cent of the sum was in the form of loans. Throughout the 1971 election campaign and before, he made perfectly clear that a fundamental renegotiation of the relationship with Britain would be the top priority for an MLP government. Despite his narrow election victory, Mintoff believed that he had a mandate for such a move. It was thus the battle over renegotiation which occupied Mintoff in the first months of his government.

At first sight it might appear that Malta had little with which to bargain. The strategic value of the island had declined, as was aptly demonstrated by the events of the 1960s; therefore, if Britain was pressed too hard, it might simply leave. Yet the significance of Malta's position in the Mediterranean had been shored up by the increasingly competitive nature of the activities of the naval forces of both superpowers. Malta was still useful (if not critical) for NATO's system of shadowing Soviet naval activity. It is certainly clear that the US and Italy were concerned to avoid a break between Britain and Malta. Both countries used their efforts to keep the two sides talking and were willing to help financially in a final settlement. This wider international involvement in the Malta question was used effectively by Mintoff.

Although the question of the level of payment that Malta enjoyed from the relationship with Britain was a major factor in Mintoff's thinking, other factors require analysis. Mintoff was extremely suspicious of British governments in their dealings with Malta and his distrust was voiced frequently and in public. To an extent, these expressions were part of a political game – 'small' Malta kicking the pants of 'great' Britain – an entertainment which his supporters loved. More seriously, though, Mintoff had come round to the view that Malta would be best served by adopting a policy of non-alignment. Therefore, if there was to be a new agreement with Britain, it must include a time limit beyond which Malta would no longer have foreign troops on its soil. Malta must also achieve a level of 'rent' (as it was termed by Mintoff) sufficient to make a substantial contribution to economic independence. A renegotiated settlement with Britain and a foreign policy of non-alignment were of a piece, for Mintoff was convinced that many leaders of non-aligned countries would be willing to help Malta build its economy by granting economic aid. Throughout the 1960s, he had established strong links with a number of countries in the non-aligned group, particularly with Libya under Colonel Gadafy. There can be little doubt that Gadafy had promised economic support for a policy of limiting Britain's presence in Malta: Mintoff's willingness to take negotiations with the Heath government to the very edge of failure was testimony to the probability that Libya would assist if the British pulled out.

Like Borg Olivier before him, Mintoff entered a period of negotiations with Britain which stretched over a number of months. A combination of threats, staged walkouts, and visits to London and Rome were used to extract a settlement which Mintoff considered acceptable to his long-term aims.[17] Press speculation was considerable as to Mintoff's demands, and a well-connected local journalist put the figure at £30 million per year as the opening bid.[18] A shot had been fired across the bows of NATO by the virtual expulsion of Admiral Birindelli, NATO's naval commander in Malta, and the transfer of Southern HQ to Naples. If NATO was in any doubt as to Mintoff's determination, this aptly demonstrated the seriousness of purpose of the new Maltese government. During the months of negotiation, Mintoff's skill and his willingness to take risks were valuable assets. In December 1971, for example, Malta set a deadline for the withdrawal of all British forces for the end of the month, because of the failure to reach agreement. This deadline was then extended and talks restarted. In the end, an agreement was signed in London on 21 March 1972. Britain was to rent facilities in Malta for a period of seven years, but on 31 March 1979 Malta was to end its long history as a 'fortress'. Britain and NATO were to meet an annual rent of £14 million payable in advance in two instalments of £7 million. This was a major economic gain for the Maltese economy, as it was an outright payment to the Maltese exchequer and contained no loan element.[19]

The departure of the British forces in March 1979 did to some extent leave Malta exposed. This can be demonstrated by examining the relationship with Libya and the question of oil exploration. The friendship with Libya was a cornerstone of Mintoff's personal political credo. But it had within it a number of potential problems, not the least of which was the distinct possibility that oil might be found on the continental shelf separating the two countries. During the 1971 general election campaign Mintoff had attacked Borg Olivier for indolence in not pushing ahead with the exploratory work. Ironically, it was not until 1980, by which time negotiations between Valletta and Tripoli had failed to produce any agreement on the division of the area, that Malta decided to go it alone and charter an oil rig to begin exploration. No sooner was the rig in place than a Libyan gunboat appeared alongside and ordered the cessation of activity. Operations were halted and relations between the two countries cooled noticeably until 1982 when the matter was finally taken to the International Court.

During 1980 and 1981 Mintoff secured Italian and Soviet guarantees for Malta's neutrality, accompanied by agreements on economic co-operation and assistance. The final years of Mintoff's premiership saw a continuation of the search for friends and economic assistance in the Arab world, China, North Korea, eastern Europe, and latterly the USSR. Yet, despite the signing of many government-to-government agreements, Malta's economic fate still lay solidly with its western trading partners. This had not been substantially altered by the years of effort to diversify, although West Germany had replaced Britain as the major recipient of Maltese exports. The problem was that Malta possessed little that the USSR desired or needed, apart from ship repairing and bulk oil storage facilities, and even these were not critical to Soviet Mediterranean policy.

Conclusion

Mintoff retired in December 1984. Just as in the final years of the Borg Olivier era, the early 1980s were economically difficult for Malta. The new Prime Minister, Dr Carmelo Mifsud Bonnici, decided to seek closer ties with Europe while maintaining the edifice of positive neutrality. Nevertheless, despite Mintoff's controversial style and the considerable doubts raised about a number of internal developments, dependent sovereignty for Malta is dead and positive neutrality is now accepted even by the opposition PN. This has been the achievement of the immediate post-colonial years in Malta. After gaining its formal independence from Britain in 1964, the country had to work for another fifteen years to give substantive meaning to that status. In that period, Borg Olivier and Dom Mintoff successively played their limited diplomatic and strategic hands with consummate skill and gained a greater control over the process of final British withdrawal than a reading of the objective realities of the situation would suggest. Like all Mediterranean peoples, the Maltese have had necessarily to forge a tradition of political opportunism which seeks to turn to advantage each turn of the historical tide in the sea. If so, it proved to be a legacy of the past which stood Malta in good stead during its first twenty years of independent statehood. The ironic lesson perhaps is that a long history of dependency on outside forces does, in time and in the end, give rise to a canny politics of diversification.

Notes

An earlier version of this chapter appeared in Colin Clarke and Tony Payne (eds.), *Politics, Security and Development in Small States*, Allen & Unwin, London, 1987, pp. 170–83.

1 H. Frendo, *Party Politics in a Fortress Colony: the Maltese Experience*, Midsea Books, Valletta, 1979.
2 P. Selwyn (ed.), *Development Policy in Small Countries*, Croom Helm, London, 1975.
3 J. A. Craig, 'The politics of economic development: the Maltese experience', *Manchester Papers on Development*, No. 8, 1983.
4 Colonial Office, *Proposed Agreement on Financial Assistance*, Cmnd. 2423, HMSO, London, 1964.
5 Colonial Office, *Proposed Agreement on Mutual Defence and Assistance*, Cmnd. 2410, HMSO, London, 1964.

6 M. Pirotta, 'The British services sector in Malta, 1946–69', unpublished BA economics dissertation, University of Malta, 1974.
7 *Times of Malta*, 6 January 1966.
8 Ministry of Defence, *The Defence Review*, Cmnd. 2910, Part 1, para. 21, HMSO, London, 1966.
9 Craig, *Manchester Papers*.
10 *Daily Telegraph*, London, 29 August 1966.
11 *Times of Malta*, 18 January 1967.
12 L. M. Cassar, 'Unemployment and the Maltese economy 1959–1969', unpublished BA economics dissertation, University of Malta, 1972.
13 Ibid.
14 L. Spiteri, 'Aspects of the property boom', mimeo, Valletta, no date.
15 *Times of Malta*, 19 July 1968.
16 Craig, *Manchester Papers*.
17 L. Davies, 'Malta versus the NATO powers 1971–2', unpublished BA history dissertation, University of Malta, 1975.
18 *Bulletin*, Valletta, 30 June 1971.
19 Davies, 'Malta versus the NATO powers'.

8 *Jack Spence*

Domestic order, regional power and international relations: the future of South Africa

In 1984, in a study of South Africa which ended, as all such analyses must, by considering the Republic's future, Dennis Austin concluded, hesitantly and cautiously, that the South African state would survive yet a while. Repression rather than reform would characterise the immediate future. But, he went on,

> if against the odds repression does fail, then much else will fail ... Down will come the whole edifice of domestic order and regional power ... In spite of what we said earlier about the advantages of wait and see, the immediate damage to Western economies ... would be substantial ... A collapsed South African state might require international rescue over a long period of recovery, and how that might be done it is impossible to foresee.[1]

Rarely have the alternatives facing western governments on the vexing issue of South Africa been so succinctly and starkly described. He adds a personal, scholarly caveat: 'There is no agreed prognosis and never likely to be one. The seismograph that can measure the scale of political unrest, and the barometer that can forecast changes in social pressure, is yet to be invented.'[2] This chapter attempts an explanation and an updating of some of these themes. It examines the interaction between South African domestic policies and its relations with the West and focuses in particular on changing perceptions and the likelihood of new initiatives in the Southern African region following the signing of the Angola–Namibia Accords in December 1988.

Historical background, 1976–88

It is clear that South Africa's domestic and external environments changed qualitatively during the period 1984–8. But to understand these changes it is important to recognise that their origins can be traced back to a series of crucial events occurring between 1974 and 1976. Before that period South Africa contrived, with some success, to prevent its domestic policies from damaging its external relations. Opposition to apartheid abroad, apart from the imposition of arms and sports embargoes, was largely rhetorical, making little impact on the government's determination to implement apartheid through the development of Bantustans or homelands for the various ethnic groups that constituted the black population. The government concentrated on cultivating close economic links with the states of Western Europe and the United States on the assumption that increasing integration into the international economy would make sanctions improbable. In the Southern African region efforts were made to establish political and economic ties with neighbouring states, while internally the black opposition was dormant and its leaders in prison or in exile.

The South African government's hostility to Soviet communism had its origins early in the post-war period. In the late 1960s and throughout the next two decades, Pretoria mounted an intensive campaign to convince both its domestic constituency and western governments that the Soviet Union was by a variety of means bent on subverting the Republic, and, by definition, western interests in South Africa: these included the conventional threat allegedly represented by the growth of a Soviet naval presence in the Indian Ocean after 1968; increased military support for the exiled African National Congress's 'armed struggle'; and a long-term strategy of resource denial designed to deprive the West of essential mineral supplies.

The debate over the Cape sea route: 1968–73

Throughout this period, the South African government repeatedly emphasised its strategic value as a 'bastion of the free world' in the struggle against communism. The need to protect the sea routes around the Cape – especially after the closure of the Suez Canal in 1967 – was frequently cited in support of the claim for the Republic's incorporation into the western alliance system. Moreover, South Africa was encouraged by the enunciation of the Nixon Doctrine in 1969 to believe that a crucial role would in due course be assigned to its military and economic capabilities for the protection of western interests in the Southern African region. Nonetheless, the Pretoria government concentrated its efforts on Britain, and in the late 1960s there were angry exchanges at Westminster about the morality and usefulness of resuming arms sales to the Republic, and the precise meaning of British obligations arising from the agreement by which Britain had access to South Africa's Simonstown naval base. The 'spirit' of the agreement was invoked by British Conservatives and South African politicians alike to justify giving South Africa status as a quasi-member of NATO.

The West, however, refused to accept South Africa's definition of the nature and scope of the Soviet threat. The arguments which proved decisive were as follows:

1 While accepting the significance of the Cape route as a vital trade artery, western military planners were sceptical about the likelihood of a Soviet blockade. The stretch of ocean between the Cape and Antarctica – unlike, by contrast, the Straits of Hormuz – was perceived as an improbable choke-point from which to harass and sink western oil tankers and merchant shipping.

2 There was also a recognition that hostile naval action against western shipping – whether in the Gulf or around the Cape – would hardly constitute a limited engagement. Such attacks would amount to a declaration of war on the West, and the scope of the resulting conflict would rapidly escalate – both geographically and in terms of the capabilities deployed by both sides. Nuclear deterrence, after all, was (and is) indivisible and designed to deter threats – whether conventional or nuclear – whenever and wherever they occur. Despite Soviet willingness to project power, whether by the use of Cuban surrogates in Angola or cruisers in the southern ocean, the Brezhnev regime understood only too well the risks involved in direct military confrontation in areas which the West regarded as vital, and clearly within its own sphere of interest. Making limited gains in disputed areas of interest was one thing; challenging western dependence on crucial sea routes was quite another! Here Soviet ideology may well come into play: a major constraint on Soviet 'adventurism' has been the perception that South Africa is part of an integrated capitalist international society; an attack on one of its outposts would – in terms of Marxist–Leninist theory – invite immediate defence by the core, represented by the USA and Western Europe. That there is nothing inevitable about such a response is neither here nor there;

what matters – to the West anyway – is the constraining impact of flawed ideological perception.

3 South Africa was in the unenviable position of a state unable to threaten 'unfaithfulness' to the West. Despite abortive attempts in the 1970s to establish a South Atlantic Treaty Organisation with, for example, Brazil and Argentina, or adopt a neutralist position in world politics, western governments have always been comforted by the likelihood that if the worst happened and a shooting war began in the southern oceans, South Africa would have little alternative but to place its ports, harbours and military facilities at its disposal. Thus the West has had the best of both worlds; a near-certain guarantee of South African availability without the political costs incurred by closer political and military co-operation.

4 There was a profound divergence between western governments and Pretoria about the significance of the Soviet naval presence in the Indian Ocean. The former acknowledged that it was part and parcel of the Soviet attempt to assert superpower status in distant waters, to gain political influence, rather than prepare the way for the initiation of direct military confrontation with the West, as South Africa's ministers have repeatedly asserted.

5 Some commentators have also pointed to Russian concern about the possible deployment of American Polaris submarines in the Indian Ocean and the need to provide the necessary deterrent capability to match in time of peace and to neutralise in time of war the strength of American seaborne nuclear forces. Michael MacGuire, for example, argued that the 'Soviet navy moved reluctantly into the Indian Ocean because it had to, and in fact was operationally ill-prepared for such a move'.[3] From the Russian point of view, the Arabian Sea might in time become an increasingly attractive area for the deployment of American Polaris submarines, especially when longer-range missiles became operational; these would provide substantial target coverage over China and the Soviet Union. Their fears in this regard were given further stimulus by the decision of the British and American governments to build, in 1967, a communications facility on Diego Garcia.[4] If this analysis is correct, then Soviet deployment in the Indian Ocean in the late 1960s and in the 1970s – far from demonstrating aggressive intent – was designed

to catch up with perceived American predominance in strategic nuclear capability at the seaborne level.[5]

The resource war thesis

Following the impact of the 1973 oil crisis on western economies, Pretoria shifted its ground. South Africa's strategic significance – it was claimed – lay in its value as a repository of certain minerals vital to western industrial and defence production. Certainly, South Africa's importance is not in doubt: its share, for example, of the world's reserve base in four key minerals is high, having 81 per cent of the platinum group of metals, 71 per cent of manganese, 84 per cent of chrome, and 47 per cent of vanadium reserves. In addition, South Africa is the second-largest producer of manganese, platinum and chrome, and leads the field in gold and vanadium. The degree of dependence of western countries on South Africa's supplies varies. The United States imports 41 per cent of its chrome from the Republic, the EEC 48 per cent, and Japan 44 per cent. For manganese, the figures are 41, 48, and 42 per cent respectively.

The proposition that the Soviet Union is committed to a long-term strategy of resource denial has featured in public statements by South African ministers and in Defence White Papers.[6] Yet it is open to the same objection that applies with respect to the alleged threat to the sea routes. The argument assumes, incorrectly, as Philip Nel has rightly asserted, 'that *because* of western dependency, the Soviets are *ipso facto* committed to exploit this dependency.'[7] What is ignored by supporters of this view is the fear of confrontation – whether by accident or design – at superpower level that deters an aggressive strike at South Africa's mineral resources.

A more sophisticated version of this strategy is expressed in the 1982 White Paper, which claims that: 'In view of the wealth of Southern Africa, the USSR strives to extend its influence to this area by assisting terrorist organizations such as SWAPO and the South African ANC, by creating unrest and exploiting the situation, and by making use of surrogate forces such as the Cubans'.[8] Hence the further assumption that a black successor regime in Pretoria would threaten continuity of supply to the West, if only out of gratitude to Moscow for military support in a successful war of liberation. This is 'worst case' thinking at its worst: a radical black regime, if the portents of Angola and Zimbabwe are any guide, would have little alternative but to sell minerals to the West to earn the revenue required for the tasks of reconstruction. In any case, the threat in the medium term is not cataclysmic upheaval, but rather sporadic disruption, a state of 'unstable equilibrium', and western governments have made efforts to stockpile resources to counter that threat.

As Phil Nel reminds us, the Soviet Union has 'advised against any attempts by their clients in the Third World to use their exports as a weapon against the receivers of those exports'.[9] Moreover, the growing involvement of the Soviet Union in the international economy, and its own dependence on imports of grain and high technology goods from the West, were major constraints on any attempt to promote resource denial. This was true enough even in the 1970s when the Brezhnev regime was pursuing a more assertive strategy in Africa.

The shift in perceptions: 1974–88

The Republic's position in the region changed dramatically with the collapse of Portuguese rule in Angola and Mozambique in 1974. The South African government intervened militarily in Angola in support of UNITA against the newly-established Marxist MPLA government, but withdrew in the face of a counter-intervention by Cuban troops despatched to defend the Luanda regime. The effect of this withdrawal on young blacks in Soweto and elsewhere was profound: in their perception the seemingly impregnable South African military machine had been forced into retreat by the military prowess of a Third World state and this encouraged blacks to challenge the South African state in the streets of Soweto in June 1976.

In effect, the crisis provoked by the nationwide disturbances of that year indicated that the government had lost its capacity to deter black opposition, although clearly it retained a powerful capability for defence once deterrence had broken down. Thus, external events in Angola and Mozambique impinged directly on South Africa's domestic order and this trend was reinforced by the granting of independence to Zimbabwe in 1980. Equally important, however, was the change in perception induced in western capitals by these developments in the mid-1970s: governments abroad began to question the time-honoured assumption that economic growth and its impact on the structure of South Africa's industrial and commercial sectors, would be sufficient to ameliorate and ultimately break down the barriers of apartheid to black advancement. Western leaders, therefore, increasingly began to recognise the need for a more self-conscious involvement in the process of change in South Africa; hence the origins of the process of 'constructive engagement' to encourage the reformist aspirations of the Vorster and subsequently the Botha governments – aspirations which in themselves amounted to a recognition that the Verwoerdian solutions of the 1960s, based on the theory and practice of grand apartheid, were no longer adequate to meet black expectations. From a western point of view peaceful constitutional change was essential if vital economic and political interests were to be safeguarded. To do nothing, to adopt a minimalist strategy, would lead to an increase in the level of violent confrontation between black and white, or, at the very least, ever-shortening intervals of calm between outbursts of Soweto-style unrest. And – so it was argued in the early 1980s – the consequence would be an acceleration of pressure on western governments to take dramatic measures before the seemingly inevitable apocalypse occurred.

The fears expressed by western policy makers in the late 1970s and early 1980s appeared justified with the outbreak of violence that began in September 1984 and continued until the imposition of a second, more stringent, State of Emergency in June 1986. During that period the black townships in both rural and urban areas became storm centres of protest as young 'comrades' attempted to make them 'ungovernable'; extensive media coverage alarmed foreign investors whose 'private' sanctions by means of disinvestment led to a renewed debate about the desirability of 'public' sanctions by international organisations. The US Congress, the EEC, and the Commonwealth – despite strong objections by western conservative governments – imposed limited sanctions packages on the Republic, the economy of which was already suffering from severe recession compounded by rising inflation and excessive public expenditure.

The reform process ground to a halt with the inevitable sticking point arising from the government's failure to tempt recognised and credible black leaders into negotiation over a new constitutional dispensation. Indeed, what was striking was the black opposition's success in occupying the ideological high ground, despite its emasculation by stringent repression and its incapacity to mobilise discontent after February 1988. In effect, organisations like the United Democratic Front were able to set the pre-negotiations agenda which included demands that the state of emergency be lifted, all political prisoners (including Nelson Mandela) be released, and the ANC allowed a role in the political process. Thus Dennis Austin's 1984 prediction that 'repression (not reform) will succeed in holding the line against violence for the immediate future ...'[10] seemed amply confirmed. Yet the two-year period after February 1988 witnessed the beginnings of a slow and tortuous programme of change on both the Namibian issue and the domestic front, the consequences of which remain – at the time of writing – unclear.

The Angola–Namibia breakthrough, 1988–9

By 1988 stalemate at home on the reform front, together with sharp divisions within the black opposition (cruelly symbolised by a bitter struggle for dominance between the United Democratic Front and Chief Gatsha Buthelezi's Inkatha movement in Natal) appeared to leave little room for great power initiatives in the Southern African region as a whole. The imposition of limited sanctions had made little, if any, impact on the Pretoria government's determination to institute reform at a time and pace of its own choosing and it was, therefore, all the more surprising when negotiations under American auspices began in May 1988 between South Africa, Angola and Cuba in search of a solution to the twin problems of Namibian independence and the Cuban military presence in Angola. Yet after ten 'public' rounds of negotiation, agreement was reached in the form of the Angola–Namibia Accords signed on 22 December 1988 in New York. What made this agreement possible was the combination of superpower midwifery – in particular, the adroit diplomacy of Chester Crocker, the United States Assistant Secretary of State for African Affairs – and the discovery of new and unexpected incentives by the local protagonists: Angola, Cuba and South Africa.

Briefly, the Accords incorporated: first, an agreement between Cuba, Angola and South Africa on a timetable for Namibian independence following the implementation of UN Security Council Resolution 435 (1978) from 1 April 1989 under the supervision of a United Nations Transition Assistance Group (UNTAG).[11] This body was to be responsible for monitoring South African withdrawal, policing the ceasefire in Namibia, and supervising the elections to a Constituent Assembly held on 1 November 1989.[12] South African troops were to be reduced from 20,000 to 15,000 by 1 November, and final withdrawal would follow a week after the elections were announced. Namibia – if the timetable was observed – would become independent in the spring of 1990. A second agreement signed by Cuba and Angola provided for the phased withdrawal of Cuban soldiers from Angola: 3,000 to leave by 1 April; the rest to follow in batches – 25,000 by 1 November 1989; 33,000 by 1 April 1990; the remainder by 1 July 1991.

The motives which led the local protagonists to sign – and, in the case of the superpowers, to sponsor the Accords – were compelling: stalemate in the battlefield in Angola followed by a series of offensives and counter-offensives by the warring parties in the 1986–7 period, culminating in the failure of South African forces and the units of the National Union for the Independence of Angola (UNITA) to dislodge a combined Cuban and Angolan government force from Cutio Cuanavale, the southernmost Angolan airbase. Cuba's willingness to upgrade its commitment to Angola by increasing its presence from 35,000 troops to 50,000 in 1987 and to risk advancing in mid-1988 to provocative deployment close to the Namibian border – all that and the superiority of newly-supplied Soviet weapons (especially Mig-23s and ground-to-air missiles) suggested the likelihood of major defeat for South Africa if the war persisted. Nor could Pretoria ignore the mounting cost of its financial commitment to Namibia and to its proxy in Angola, UNITA. Military and civil expenditure for 1988–9 was projected at some R2,000m, while the price of supporting UNITA was likely to exceed the 1987 figure of R42m. Moreover, the failure of the South African army to break the stalemate in Angola revived the influence of the Department of Foreign Affairs in the State Security Council where – in and out of season – Pik Botha, the Foreign Minister, had extolled the utility of diplomatic and economic instruments in preference to military coercion in the pursuit of the Republic's interests in the Southern African region.

Angola, too, had good reasons for wanting a negotiated outcome: the civil war has inflicted severe damage on the economy and some 85 per cent of its major source of revenue ($1·3bn to $1·8bn from oil) has been devoted to the struggle against UNITA. For Cuba –

despite the difficulties involved in absorbing some 50,000 troops into a depressed economy – Namibian independence could be interpreted as a vindication of Cuba's commitment to defending a Third World state against destabilisation by the apartheid regime. Finally, both superpowers had much to gain from a settlement: Chester Crocker's emphasis on 'linkage' between Namibian independence and Cuban withdrawal from Angola had at last been accepted by the local protagonists as the basis for negotiation. As for the Soviet Union, Gorbachev, as early as April 1986, had signalled a more conciliatory line on Southern Africa, acknowledging, as a leading Soviet academic, Dr Victor Goncharov, explained in June 1986 that: 'We should take into account the global problems and the global consequences of our behaviour in every part of the world . . . There may be changes and differences in approach to these problems . . . to behave more realistically, more flexibly, with every side participating in the [resolution of the] conflict.'[13]

A striking feature of the Accords is the relatively long lead-time required for Cuban withdrawal from Angola. By setting July 1991 as the date, the parties were implicitly acknowledging UNITA's incorporation in a 'government of national reconciliation', and while there have been rumours of negotiations between the parties to the conflict, matching the timing of a final Cuban departure to the establishment of a new political dispensation in Luanda is likely to prove difficult. It is true that the Accords provide for UN Security Council (i.e. Soviet and American collaboration) supervision of the Cuban withdrawal.[14] As Geoff Berridge has perceptively remarked: '... As in the Afghanistan negotiations, so in the Angola–Namibia talks the impression was strongly conveyed that any party seeking to undermine a settlement would incur the disfavour of the superpowers. It would be surprising if this did not facilitate the resolution of the conflict as well.'[15] But how far external actors can affect reconciliation within a war-torn state, compared with their successful role in 'facilitating' agreement between states, as in the Namibian Accord, is likely to prove the most serious test of superpower commitment to, and capability of, 'managing' the Angolan crisis to an outcome acceptable to all parties.

By contrast, the Namibian talks stayed on course not least because President Botha (whose approval was sought at every stage of the protracted negotiations) displayed a willingness to gamble on white support for his country's withdrawal from the territory. This was unexpected and uncharacteristic in view of both his oft-declared hostility to the South West African People's Organisation (SWAPO) as Moscow's tool in the 'total onslaught' against the Republic and his failure to provide imaginative leadership on this issue of domestic reform. A white blacklash on the Namibian issue was clearly discounted, if only because the mounting cost in blood and treasure was beginning to disturb his Afrikaner constituency, while the persistence of a military stalemate over the long term would play into the hands of his conservative opponents. Indeed, paradoxically, President De Klerk, like P. W. Botha whom he succeeded in September 1989, now had more to lose from a collapse of the Accords, providing the Conservatives with a potent indictment of diplomatic failure. Indeed, the Namibian issue barely figured as a topic for debate during the General Election in August/September 1989, although the government was able to claim that Cuban withdrawal from Angola and agreement by the new state to refuse bases to the exiled African National Congress (ANC) constituted major political gains for the Republic. And it was generally recognised that a Namibian government – of whatever political hue – must of necessity acknowledge South Africa's dominance in the region.

Nor did the spectre of a large UN presence in Namibia alarm Pretoria although, once deployed and engaged in monitoring the phased withdrawal of both South African and Cuban forces, UNTAG constituted a major inhibition on any South African attempt to renege on the agreements. The parallel with the withdrawal of the United Nations Emergency Force in 1967 at Egypt's insistence is hardly exact. The latter was based on territory over which Egypt had sovereign rights, whereas South Africa's jurisdiction over Namibia was never accepted by the United Nations.

Whatever the optimistic gloss put by Pretoria on the Accords, the fact remains that withdrawal from Namibia represents a victory for the cause of African nationalism in the region and Third World aspirations to end apartheid. In several respects Botha's decision to accept the bitter political logic of military stalemate in the Namibian bush and on the Angolan battlefield provided a classic illustration of the dictum that guerrillas do not have to win; it is enough to force a stalemate, the political and economic costs of which prove increasingly unacceptable to a war-weary metropole. No matter that SWAPO's 'victory' was a result of the failure of

South Africa's military forces to defeat the former's Cuban and Angolan supporters in conventional terms. A SWAPO-governed Namibia (even one forced to accommodate the interests of its political opponents) will be perceived throughout the Third World as a profound setback for the apartheid state – another link snapped in the chain of buffer states that began to break with the independence of the former Portuguese colonies in 1975 and continued with Zimbabwe's independence in 1980, serving to vindicate the liberation strategy first enunciated by Ben Bella of Algeria in the 1960s.

The Republic has attempted to make a virtue out of dire necessity: 1989 witnessed a rejuvenated Department of Foreign Affairs attempting a new regional initiative beginning with President Botha's visits to Malawi, Mozambique and Zaire in the autumn of 1988. Certainly, in the short term, Pretoria hopes to gain some relief from external pressure and in particular any increase in the scope and pace of economic sanctions. Its co-operation was, of course, required in implementing the Accords and a similar agreement ending the civil war in Mozambique still appears a tempting prospect. The achievement of regional stability involving South African co-operation with the superpowers and Britain, and a willingness to assist, for example, in Mozambique's economic and political rehabilitation, would therefore strengthen Pretoria's case that sanctions are a dangerous and irrational mechanism for promoting change, as their effect is to damage the economies of poorer, weaker neighbours as well. Britain, too, in South African eyes, has a crucial role in this context: Pik Botha's discussions with Mrs Thatcher in March 1989 may have encouraged the British Prime Minister to believe that some future initiative might be launched to help end civil conflicts in Southern Africa. If such an initiative could provide the Republic with a positive role, it would constitute a considerable gain for South Africa. This is especially true at a time (April 1990) when the South African government is pressing the west to lift sanctions as an indication of good faith in President De Klerk's efforts to promote negotiations.

Hence the optimism emanating from the Department of Foreign Affairs in mid-March 1989 about the possibility of a constructive role for the Soviet Union in Southern Africa.[16] As Neil van Heerden, Director-General of the DFA, explained: 'If the Namibia thing goes well . . . it could set the scene for a general relaxation in Southern Africa.' Hinting at the possibility of South Africa opening diplomatic relations with Moscow, he argued that 'given the new world we are living in, which is strikingly bipolar, having relations only with one of the super powers is clearly not an ideal situation'.[17] This is heady stuff, but South Africa hopes to gain much from a conciliatory approach by the Soviet Union to the region's problems, in particular from any Soviet success in persuading the ANC to abandon the 'armed struggle' as a prelude to the latter's willingness to discuss a new constitutional dispensation in the Republic. Certainly, most recent Soviet statements (at, for example, a conference of Soviet, South African, and British academics in Britain in March 1989) indicate a desire for a negotiated settlement of the apartheid issue in preference to a military solution. As Yuri Yukalov, the head of the Southern African Department of the Soviet Foreign Ministry, emphasised: 'We would prefer a political settlement and want apartheid to be dealt with by political means. Any solution through military means will be short-lived.'[18]

However, a note of caution is required here: the Soviet Union remains committed to supporting the ANC as the legitimate voice of the black majority in South Africa. Even if it is no longer prepared to emphasise the 'armed struggle' as the sole mechanism for promoting change in the Republic (if only because the Republic is not a good candidate for the application of orthodox Marxist–Leninist theories of revolution), and is willing to encourage those elements in the ANC who accept the necessity for a negotiated political settlement, it is worth noting Yukalov's statement that Moscow 'did not want to emphasise the need to *enlarge* the armed struggle'.[19] Similarly, with respect to the utility of economic sanctions, Soviet spokesmen have emphasised that they regard such measures as important for maintaining political pressure on Pretoria. No relaxation of the Soviet position is likely unless and until the South African government provides evidence of fundamental structural reform of the political system.

Moreover, the Soviet Union has emphasised that it does not regard the Angola–Namibian settlement as a model for a negotiated outcome in South Africa. At private meetings and seminars – most notably at the March 1989 conference in Britain – Soviet scholars have emphasised that they regarded the Accords as a solution to an international problem involving the conflicting interests of the local protagonists – Angola, Cuba and South Africa –

as well as those of the superpowers. But the end of apartheid, it was acknowledged, would be largely achieved by a combination of internal pressures – economic and political – and both superpowers would therefore be well advised to recognise that the process of change will not be straightforward or easily maintained in the short term. Managing crises between states is difficult enough: the notion of a superpower condominium, self-consciously attempting to manipulate the pace and scope of change within South Africa – attempting, in other words, to impose a solution – is rightly regarded with profound scepticism. At best, the superpowers, together with Britain, might be able to foster a climate – and this is the real achievement of the Angola–Namibian Accords – in which the conflicting parties within and outside the Republic see some virtue in compromising extreme positions as a prelude to negotiation.

What is improbable, and will in any case be decisively rejected by Pretoria, is any attempt by external powers to promote a Lancaster House-type solution in which South Africa finds itself having to negotiate, *à la* Ian Smith's Rhodesia, at the behest of states whose interests would not necessarily coincide with Pretoria's, and the prospect of whose 'interference' would be bitterly resented by a substantial majority of the white electorate. The Lancaster House analogy is, therefore, misplaced: South Africa is a state jealous of its sovereignty, confident that revolution is not around the corner; Rhodesia was an illegal regime, in rebellion against the Crown and ultimately the colonial responsibility of Britain. It was, in fact, forced to the conference table by the costs of a civil war and the slow erosive impact of economic sanctions. South Africa has not yet reached that point of no return.

Furthermore, a superpower bilateral attempt to 'facilitate' change in Southern Africa will face its first severe test in the Mozambique context which, as Neil von Heerden remarked, is 'a tough nut to crack'.[20] Success or failure here will determine what, if anything, can be done to deal with the 'nub of the crisis in the region – the relationship within South Africa between the black majority and the ruling white minority'.[21] South Africa clearly has an interest in undertaking an initiative on the Mozambique issue, and its offer of economic assistance is clearly designed to provide evidence of good faith in finding solutions to regional problems.

Yet the obstacles to peace in Mozambique remain formidable, just as they do in Angola where, despite the Accords, UNITA continues to play a destabilising role. After all, signature of the Angola–Namibian Accords did not mean an end to the civil war; that task was tacitly set aside to be achieved at some point in the future by a combination of incentives and pressures exerted on the warring Angolan factions by the external actors. (One source of pressure was South Africa's agreement – as emphatically stated by Pik Botha on signing the Accords – to abandon support of UNITA.) Indeed, it may be presumed that the last Cuban will only leave Angola if and when the Luanda government feels confident about the state's internal stability. Therefore, peace in Angola (achieved by either the elimination of UNITA or its absorption into the MPLA regime) is a prerequisite for the successful implementation of the Accord describing the modalities of Cuban withdrawal.

It would, therefore, be unwise to conclude that the Accords provide a neat and readily applicable model for use in a Mozambique context, let alone a South African one. The real impact of the Accords on the region's future is that their agreement has produced a mood of optimism throughout Southern Africa. Yet the task of translating that optimism into concrete achievement will require massive reserves of diplomatic skill and political commitment by all the relevant parties.

In the short term, South Africa hopes to achieve two significant objectives: firstly, an end to its diplomatic isolation by the Soviet Union and its neighbours in the region; secondly, a strengthening of western and Soviet perceptions that the Republic is a key regional actor whose co-operation is required to achieve stability and economic development and against which – from a western perspective – further economic sanctions would be undesirable.

Prospects for the future

This attempt to chart the scope and substance of South Africa's relations with the great powers suggests that the latter have always been constrained to work within very limited parameters. Short-term economic interests, together with a profound scepticism about the efficacy over the long term of more dramatic measures such as sanctions, have contrived to produce an ambivalent response whenever these interests have been threatened by periodic bouts of disorder within the Republic. Nor, despite the euphoria generated by the Angola–Namibia Accords, is there much prospect of a superpower condominium intervening successfully to compel Pretoria to do its will with respect to fundamental political change. Indeed, the notion of a condominium is based on false assumptions about the present and likely future course of international relations:

a. *détente* between the West and the Soviet Union may spring from nothing more than a desire to keep out of each other's way in regional conflicts, rather than act as a spur to detailed, day-by-day co-operation magisterially to settle those conflicts;

b. condominium, moreover, assumes a high level of trust and confidence between the great powers as well as a willingness to pool resources to recognise and manage effective intervention in regions like Southern Africa and the Middle East;

c. indeed, far from feeling confident about their capacity to manage change, the West and the Soviet Union may be more concerned with finding solutions to pressing internal problems – an attitude strengthened by their neutral perception of the sheer intractability of regional conflict and its resistance to solutions imposed from without.

This is not to argue that the South Africa issue will slip off the agendas of the great powers as their leaders concentrate their energies on domestic issues over which they can exert some degree of control. Rather, it is to acknowledge that busy statesmen are all too easily and understandably distracted by the current crisis, wherever that happens to be, to be able to think and plan meaningfully for the long term about problems like South Africa. This particular issue will continue to escape their undivided and determined attention so long as internal order is maintained and the black majority remain powerless to change their condition by force of arms.

Dennis Austin's scepticism about the likelihood of a major break in the log-jam of South African politics, whether internally achieved or externally provoked, remains as sound a reflection today as at the time it was written. For many observers, President De Klerk's decision (announced on 2 February 1990) to legalise the African National Congress and allied organisations and thus open the way to negotiations on a new constitutional dispensation, together with the release of Nelson Mandela, was just such a breakthrough. The imperatives were clear, the need to restore overseas confidence in a stagnant economy (publicly acknowledged during the 1989 election), and the long-term pressure of population growth: by the year 2000 blacks would number 36·4 million (an increase of sixteen million on the 1980 figure) – a formidable statistic which cannot but cast doubt on the capacity of the South African state to maintain the degree of social control which in the past has guaranteed white survival.

Both the government and the black opposition appear set on an irreversible course leading to the conference table, although no one supposes that the journey will be easy or straightforward given the need to satisfy a variety of constituencies that opposing protagonists are acting in good faith. And, if we assume that negotiations will take place, their protracted course may well result in renewed stalemate, given the gulf between the government's desire to 'share power without losing control' and the ANC's firm commitment to black majority rule in a unitary state.

And the prospect of failure at this critical juncture can only invite apocalyptic speculation: will sheer weight of numbers, and deprivation of jobs and food by the failure of the economy to grow in keeping with population expansion, produce an outburst of rage and violence to force the collapse of the state security system? Alternatively, will intense deprivation produce a passive black majority surrounding heavily guarded white enclaves of privilege and relative comfort? These questions are unanswerable from today's vantage point, but that does not mean for a moment that we should stop asking them.

Notes

1 D. Austin, *South Africa 1984*, Routledge & Kegan Paul, London, 1985, p. 71.

2 Ibid.

3 Michael MacGuire, 'The Russian "all at sea"', *Guardian*, 26 August 1970.

4 See J. E. Spence, *The Political and Military Framework for Investment in South Africa*, Africa Publications Trust, London, 1975, p. 25.

5 Kurt Campbell argues that the deployment of Polaris in the north-west Indian Ocean has never, in fact, occurred. 'The significance of the southern Indian Ocean to the overall strategic balance between the Super Powers remains limited and South Africa is irrelevant to the nuclear competition between the United States and the Soviet Union.' Kurt M. Campbell, *Soviet Policy towards South Africa*, Macmillan, London, 1986, p. 150.

6 See, for example, the 1984 White Paper which stated that 'one of the most important considerations of Soviet strategy towards southern Africa is the gaining of control over the subcontinent's wealth of strategic minerals and its denial to the West'. Quoted in Philip Nel, 'Does Moscow want S. A. minerals?', *Optima*, Vol. 36, No. 1, 1988, p. 34.

7 Ibid., p. 38.

8 Ibid., p. 34.

9 Ibid., p. 40.

10 Austin, *South Africa 1984*, p. 71.

11 UNTAG consists of 4,650 troops, plus another 2,850 held in reserve. The UN Security Council Resolution 435 provided for 7,500, but the Security Council insisted on paring down the number deployed despite Third World objections that South Africa would attempt to influence the outcome of the November elections to the Constituent Assembly.

12 Although SWAPO, the leading nationalist party, won 57 per cent of the vote, it did not secure the two-thirds majority required to give it exclusive control over the shaping of the new constitution. It is likely, therefore, that the discussions in the Constituent Assembly will be characterised by hard bargaining between SWAPO and the minority parties.

13 Cited in *Front File, Southern African Brief*, Vol. 3, No. 3, July 1987.

14 The task of verifying Cuban withdrawal is the responsibility of UNAVEM (UN Angolan Verification Mission) established by the Security Council on 20 December 1988.

15 G. R. Berridge, 'Diplomatic procedure and the Angola/Namibia Accords, 1988', paper presented to the 1989 Joint Conference of the British International Studies Association and the US International Studies Association, University of London.

16 John Carlin, 'South Africa feels it is moving into special times', *Independent*, 17 March 1989.

17 Ibid.

18 Richard Dowden, 'South Africa on verge of drive for peace', *Independent*, 16 March 1989. Note also the statements in the same report by Dr Anatoly Gromyko, Director of the Africa Institute in Moscow: 'There would have to be a programme of reforms submitted to nationwide discussion at which all sections of society would be represented . . . This will mean sitting down for negotiations for two, three or however many years to solve the problems.'

19 Ibid. Yukalov's emphasis.

20 Ibid., 17 March 1989.

21 Ibid. (leading article), 13 August 1988.

9 *James Mayall*

The dream of a 'quick fix': the Commonwealth Third World in the international economy

One hope that accompanied the transfer of power was that it would usher in a period of rapid social and economic progress. On the frontiers of empire, the advantages of the *Pax Britannica* were not widely appreciated by those who went in pursuit of the political kingdom. The order fashioned by the European great powers, and presided over for much of the nineteenth century by Britain, was designed with their interests in mind, not those of their colonial subjects. The new rulers intended to reverse these priorities.

Post-colonial optimism had a mixed ancestry. Lenin had concluded that the conquest of the globe by imperialism was the logical and necessary outcome of capitalist development. Imperialism was the highest but also the final stage of this development. The fatal contradictions of capitalism would be revealed by the combined effects of anticolonial nationalism and the world communist movement under Soviet leadership. Very few of the first generation of Asian, African and Caribbean leaders knew or cared much for the details of Marxist–Leninist argument, and most of them were suspicious of communism itself. But they accepted that the imperialist order had been inherently exploitative and peered into the future along a broadly socialist perspective. In their brave new world, development would be substituted for exploitation, collective security for the balance of power and international cooperation for mercantilist rivalries. Jawaharlal Nehru, the first Prime Minister of India, set the tone for Third World economic and foreign policy. Throughout his political life, according to Professor Hansen, 'Nehru dreamed of combining economic mobilisation with political conciliation, a Soviet economy with a western polity'.[1] The five-year development plan rapidly became the economic symbol of independent status just as, for the majority of ex-colonies, a non-aligned foreign policy was the political symbol.

As the transfer of power recedes into history, this vision of a new order based on principles of social and economic justice has disappeared from view. Despair is more characteristic of contemporary writing on Third World economies and societies than hope. In many countries poverty and indebtedness appear to be endemic; governments have squandered the resources inherited at independence; the privileged few grow rich at the expense of the rural majority; and in some capital cities economic activity is at so low a level that politics seems to be the only paying business in town. Yet it is not clear that the new pessimism is either more accurate or more appropriate than the old optimism.[2] Whatever the case may be in respect of constitutional development or the erosion of civil and political liberties, evidence of economic development in the post-colonial world is not only contested, but profoundly ambivalent.

It is not difficult to uncover statistical support for a pessimistic analysis. The data of despair stare out at one from the pages of the World Bank's annual *World Development Report*. Whereas in most industrial countries annual population growth is less than 1 per cent and the growth of the labour force, even in hard times, sufficient to cope with this natural increase – the figure in most Third World countries is nearly 2½ per cent and in many as high as 3½ per cent. Moreover, not only does the growth of the labour force almost everywhere fall well short of population growth, but the number of people living in cities is growing at a much faster rate than wage employment. Since those who live in towns depend on wages for their subsistence, the incidence of poverty in the Third World as a whole is increasing.

Macro-economic mapping of this kind conceals as much as it reveals. But even if one sharpens the focus, the resulting picture offers little comfort, except here and there. Urban growth has been significantly cut in Hong Kong and Singapore, but these are city–states with only small rural populations in the surrounding hinterland. By contrast, between 1960 and 1975 the proportion of the population living in cities in Ghana, Nigeria, Zambia and Jamaica, all still predominantly agricultural societies, rose respectively from 23 to 32 per cent, 18 to 29 per cent, 18 to 37 per cent and 30 to 45 per cent.[3] In no case was industrialisation remotely able to keep pace with this expansion.

Even the good news in one area often reveals failure elsewhere or a distortion in the way the evidence is presented. In most parts of the world modest improvements in the provision of public health facilities, and in female education, have led to a decline in infant mortality – in Jamaica, for example, the figures are rapidly approaching those achieved in the industrial democracies. But this is not so in Africa: after a period of declining infant mortality in the 1950s and 1960s, the absolute number of annual child deaths has risen from 4 million to 4½ million since 1970. Nearly 11,000 children under five die every day.[4] No doubt these figures are partly accounted for by the famines in Ethiopia and the Sahel in the mid-1970s and in the Horn of Africa and the Sudan since 1984 – disasters which were not wholly man-made. But then famine, as Amayrta Sen has demonstrated,[5] is avoidable: it usually springs not from a lack of availability of food, but from a lack of entitlement, i.e. purchasing power, in the stricken area. And at least in India (although not Bangladesh) the record of famine avoidance has been better since independence than under the Raj – there has been no repeat of the 1943 famine in West Bengal. There is little room for complacency or self-congratulation, however: Indians may have been relatively more successful than Africans in avoiding absolute catastrophe, but they have been less successful, Sen argues, in spreading the misery of malnutrition equitably, particularly between the sexes. In terms of access to inadequate supplies of food, Indian girls fare worse than their African sisters.

Such cataloguing of Third World economic failure may tell us more about modern consciousness than about either the process or the long-run potential for development. David Fieldhouse rightly insists that it is much too early to say whether decolonisation will turn out to have created the possibilities of modernisation and affluence, or to have ensured the continuation of poverty.[6] Indeed, one might go further and say that since we cannot know what the situation would have been had the colonial order been maintained, we shall never know the answer to this question and that it is not, therefore, a question worth asking. Nonetheless, change the angle of vision and the time-frame, and the data on Third World development will appear in a less gloomy light.

Aggregate statistics mask a wide range of variation between countries. Nonetheless, the growth rates of most Third World countries between 1950 and 1975 were high not only in comparison with their own past experience, but with the rates of the now industrialised countries during the nineteenth century. For example, per capita GNP in Africa and South Asia, the two least successful areas of the Third World in these terms, grew by 1·81 and 1·52 per cent respectively, compared with a figure of 0·96 per cent for all European countries between 1860 and 1910 and 1·6 per cent for the Scandinavian countries which recorded the highest per capita growth figures during that period.[7] The same generally favourable comparison emerges if the focus is shifted from economic growth to a range of social indicators:

> By the mid-1960s life expectancy in LDCs was 49 years, a level reached by developed areas only in 1900. In 1970 the average rate of infant mortality was 65 deaths per one thousand live births for semi-developed countries and 123/1000 for less developed countries, ranging from 19 for Hong Kong to 250 for Nepal. In 1900 the average rate of infant mortality for European countries was 166, ranging from 91 for Norway to 252 for Russia. Educational opportunity has increased more rapidly in the Third World in recent years than it did in industrialised areas during the 19th century.[8]

It may seem odd that such contrasting pictures can be constructed from the relatively uncontested data of economic performance. But the data merely reflects the questions asked. What is odd is that it should have been so widely believed that independence would lead to modernisation without the social turbulence and misery that accompanied the process in Europe during the nineteenth century. Perhaps the question to ask is not whether decolonisation retarded or accelerated the process, but why western liberals and Third World nationalists were so optimistic about the possibility. In an attempt to answer this question, three others need also to be addressed. Why, immediately after the transfer of power, did the governments of the new states elevate economic development to the forefront of their political objectives? What was the international contribution to this selection of priorities and why was it so significant? Finally, what has led to the loss of confidence in development, not as a desirable ultimate end (to be against *development* is like being against God or the family) but as an attainable political goal?

Decolonisation and legitimacy

In the Commonwealth, as over most of the Third World, dynastism did not survive the colonial era. In India and Pakistan, the princes were temporarily able to maintain privileges, including not only their palaces but a salary paid by the state. But in return they had to surrender their political authority. In much of Africa, traditional leaders continued to enjoy considerable social prestige and hence indirectly political influence, but as collaborators with the colonial power under the system of indirect rule they were often unpopular with the nationalist leadership. And, in any case, as in South Asia, the boundaries of their fiefdoms were seldom congruent with those of the post-colonial political map. Most people in the Caribbean were descendants of either slaves or indentured labour from India or the Far East. There had been a ruling settler class but never a political caste with a prescriptive right to rule.

The consequent crisis of legitimacy which has been such a recurrent feature of Third World polities was not widely foreseen (or at any rate commented on) in the run-up to independence. So long as politics had a single aim – independence – the parties which grew up to pursue it seldom had to justify their right to rule, either to themselves or to society at large. Groups and classes which, in a free state, would demonstrate that they had conflicting and often incompatible interests and perceptions, were united in their determination to rid themselves of colonial rule. Kwame Nkrumah's insistence on the benefits that would flow from seeking the political kingdom may have been a false prophecy, but it was an accurate description of the strategy adopted by anti-colonial nationalists throughout the Commonwealth Third World. Even in Zimbabwe, whose leaders had fought a long guerrilla war, power was transferred on the basis of a democratic constitution.

This method of transfer masked and postponed the challenge to the concept of legitimate authority that was latent everywhere. The sovereignty that was transferred was popular sovereignty. For this reason the basis of the successor governments' legitimacy – by what right did they rule? – was almost bound to be called in question as soon as independence was achieved. Promises are the coinage of democratic politics. In multi-party systems, politicians have to have a programme with which to purchase the votes of their constituents. Even where the habit of contested elections was not well rooted, or was quickly abandoned, political leaders had to explain why they laid claim to office – and military leaders in turn why they presumed to overthrow the existing government by force.

To claim that independence would lead to good government was not sufficient for this purpose. This was partly, perhaps, because the ideal of good government formed the essential ideology of colonial administration, so that to add nothing to the colonial recipe would have appeared too slavish to populations that had been fed the strong meat of anticolonial rhetoric. But there was another reason. Even where the nationalist movement was under the control of a propertied middle class, the struggle for power was with a foreign government, not, as in Europe a century earlier, with a landed aristocracy. The victors could not, therefore, as they could then, confine themselves to redressing the wrongs of the *ancien régime* by redistributing political office – although they certainly did that – and economic assets. When the colonial power withdrew, it merely retreated behind its own national frontiers; its political identity remained intact, and its economic power, if reduced, was still significantly more impressive than that of any of the new states.[9] It followed that if successive governments were to exercise authority in ex-colonial states they would have to promise social and economic progress. This requirement was particularly strong in Britain's ex-colonies, most of which had achieved independence as a result of a relatively orderly and peaceful process of negotiation. Such 'collaborationist' regimes could not claim to be the rightful heirs of the revolution, claiming their right to rule by virtue of survival. Leaders who had been spared baptism by terror stood in need of a more mundane justification.

Virtually all Third World successor governments espoused some variety of either socialism or developmentalism, suitably tailored to local circumstances and the nationalist preference for keeping clear of the ideological battle between the superpowers. In India, where the Congress Party originally enjoyed enormous prestige and parliamentary democracy worked reasonably well, Nehru opted for a pragmatic and relatively undoctrinaire socialism. As he said in 1949:

> It is not a question of theory, of communism or socialism or capitalism. It is a question of hard fact . . . our problem today is to raise the standard of the masses, supply them with their needs, give them the wherewithal to lead a decent life, and help them to progress and advance in life not only

in regard to material things, but in regard to cultural and spiritual things also. What will happen in the distant future I do not know, but I should like to set them on the right road and I do not care what 'ism' that helps me to set them on that road provided I do it.[10]

In Africa, where organised opposition was often regarded as treason, it was sometimes said that socialism and democracy were built into African culture and therefore did not need the institutional support of the modern democratic state. Julius Nyerere, the first President of Tanzania, put it this way: 'We have no more need of being "converted" to socialism than we have of being "taught" democracy. Both are rooted in our past, in the traditional society that produced us.'[11]

The nationalist leaders in the Commonwealth Caribbean, whose societies had been shaped by plantation capital, and who had to pursue their political ambitions without arousing the ideological fury of their powerful northern neighbour, had no doubt about the political primacy of economic development. In the larger territories, nationalist politics had developed on a class basis in the context of the economic depression of the 1930s. In a speech delivered in 1955, in which he announced his impending entry into politics, Eric Williams argued that 'the problem of jobs is . . . a number one priority in Trinidad and Tobago'. He continued with a populist plea for national mobilisation: 'It is not a question of race, religion or colour. It is not a question of labour or capital. It calls for the united effort of the entire population'.[12]

These random examples could be supplemented without difficulty from many Third World countries both in and outside of the Commonwealth. Such widespread consensus on the priorities of post-colonial government suggests an answer to the question of why the governments of the new states placed such emphasis on economic development. This answer is that there was no practical alternative, no other principle of legitimation to underpin the power and authority of new non-traditional rulers. When prescription is out, governments need programmes.

Even so this analysis is not sufficient to explain the optimism with which many Third World nationalist leaders viewed the probable outcome of their efforts. No doubt making virtue of necessity is a large part of the explanation. If one is condemned to aim high – to transform, control and improve the performance of the national economy, all at the same time – it is no good accepting at the outset that it cannot be done, or that human progress is an illusion. It does not follow, however, that politicians are required to neglect the most rudimentary principles of financial prudence. Yet in many countries, the pursuit of rapid social and economic progress led to the abandonment of all caution. To comprehend such reckless over-optimism we need to look at the international encouragement which Third World leaders received.

Foreign aid and the development debate

We do not know much about the epidemiology of politics: why some political ideas spread and others remain confined to their countries of origin. We do know, however, that the necessary optimism of Third World politicians was powerfully reinforced by the wider intellectual milieu of western, particularly United States, liberalism. Within the Commonwealth, a modest start with development planning had been made during the 1930s in an attempt to contain the damage inflicted by the Great Depression. After the Second World War, seemingly impervious to the speed at which the colonial rout would be completed, the British strengthened the sterling area and introduced a number of economic schemes designed to save dollars during the post-war shortage. Such *ad hoc* responses to immediate problems groomed colonial administrations in the habits and techniques of economic intervention which, once learned, were unlikely to be abandoned by successor governments. Even so, they hardly amounted to a guarantee of future prosperity.

It was primarily to the United States rather than Britain that Third World governments, including those of ex-British colonies, looked to support their belief that intractable problems of social and economic development could be solved in short order. From the American government's point of view the question was how to use its power and wealth to advance political development as both it and the influential academic community had defined it.[13] Two contrasting policies emerged. The first was to use financial aid in support of national security. 'Aid was seen as a cold war tool that could be used to promote political stability, win alliances to the United States, and impede the emergence of radical or communist regimes.'[14] The second linked Third World political development directly to economic growth. Packenham describes the reasoning:

Economic and technical assistance contributed to economic development; and economic development in turn was seen as contributing to political development. Economic growth was defined in terms of growth of per capita product and other conventional measures; political development was defined in terms of stability, democracy, anti-communism, 'world community', peace, pro-Americanism.[15]

The origins of American liberal economism can be traced to the Marshall Plan and the Truman Doctrine, but it was its extension to the non-aligned countries during the Kennedy Administration (1960–3) that contributed most to Third World optimism. What mattered to Asian and African governments, of course, was not the laborious processes whereby Americans justified their policies to themselves, but the availability of financial aid. In his autobiography, Ayub Khan makes it clear that he considered an anticommunist alliance irrelevant to Pakistan's security but a price worth paying to buttress the country's economic and military strength against India.[16] Similarly, the Indian government was more concerned to advance its own development priorities, than with theoretical arguments about political stability.

Nonetheless, Kennedy's aid policy was influential in shaping the climate of opinion in the Third World for two reasons. First, the freeing of American aid policy from the requirement that recipients should demonstrate loyalty in the cold war allowed those countries to accept aid from both sides and so maximise the flow of resources. The American government itself had difficulty in selling its new aid policy to Congress; but while admitting that there was 'no guarantee that improved political institutions will follow in any automatic way', it insisted that 'without economic progress the chances for strengthening democratic processes in the less developed countries would be greatly diminished'.[17] Perhaps! For the recipients, the real advantage was that in domestic political terms, the policy rendered western aid cost free. The Indians, for example, took full advantage of the economic possibilities of their non-aligned foreign policy. American aid was channelled to the private sector and provided general balance of payments support, while Soviet assistance was concentrated in the development of heavy industry, particularly steel. Since India already had a mixed economy, and the government had decided in 1956 to reserve all future investment in heavy industry to the public sector, the acceptance of aid required neither a major reassessment of its economic strategy nor the scaling down of its development plans to offset shortages of foreign exchange.

The second way in which the Americans influenced Third World opinion was by promoting the doctrine that economic development was primarily a matter of bridging the shortfall between domestic savings and a country's 'legitimate' investment requirements. Economic development was presented as a technical problem to which a solution, namely foreign aid, was available. Walt Rostow, the author of a celebrated tract on this theme,[18] argued that there were five historical stages in the development of a modern economy culminating in the stage of self-sustaining growth. Thus, in the Foreign Assistance Act of 1961, the Kennedy Administration concluded that history could be cheated, claiming that, through the agency of foreign aid, 'more than half the people of the less developed nations' could be moved 'into self-sustained economic growth' and that the rest could be moved significantly nearer that goal.

Rostow's concept of economic 'take-off' was an apt emblem of the times. The implicit metaphor suggested that the problems of society as much as the mysteries of space could be resolved by rational analysis and the application of technology. The concept also had obvious attractions for Third World leaders who aspired to close 'the gap' between their own societies and those of the industrial west. Finally, 'take-off' was admirably suited to the Administration's purposes in dealing with a sceptical Congress, since it implied that foreign aid to the Third World, like the Marshall Plan, was a strictly limited liability. Given a strategic infusion of capital, economic growth would become self-generating within a relatively short period. Third World governments would then be in a position to play their part in the open world economy without fear or favour. It was not a question of throwing good money after bad, or so the argument ran. This was what everybody wanted to hear; it was a comfortable and seductive fiction.

Within the Commonwealth, India and, to a lesser extent, Ghana were the chief beneficiaries of President Kennedy's determination to pursue America's ideological competition with the Soviet Union in the Third World by economic rather than by direct military means. By the time the majority of African, Caribbean and Pacific countries achieved independence, the climate had changed and foreign aid was both more difficult to come by and more problematic in its political entailments. In order to ensure the passage of the 1963 Aid Bill through Congress, Kennedy had appointed a commission of inquiry to advise on the relationship between aid and national security. The tactic was successful, but the commission advised that, in the interests of burden-sharing, primary responsibility for development assistance to African countries should henceforth be borne by the former colonial powers.[19] After the Cuban missile crisis, the superpower competition for influence amongst non-aligned countries temporarily eased off. It was in this context that the focus of the development debate shifted from bilateral relations to multilateral diplomacy.

The Third World in the liberal economic order

The European powers dismantled their empires within an international context which was structured, not only informally through the bipolar balance of power, but legally through a network of international institutions. If, as its critics have sometimes argued, the Commonwealth was an organisation designed to conceal from the British the realities of lost power and influence, the United Nations Organisation (UNO) was well designed to flatter the self-importance and exaggerate the influence of its new members. With its emphasis on co-operation rather than power, multilateralism was an inherently optimistic approach to world affairs.

The new states of Asia, Africa, the Caribbean and the Pacific entered at birth into the UNO which immediately conferred on their representatives both dignity and status. Outside the Security Council, the UN system operated on the basis of the sovereign equality of its members. Consequently, with the constant swelling of the ranks of new members, the UN was soon dominated by Third World problems and interests. It was on the floor of the General Assembly, in its committees and the UN Specialised Agencies that the Afro-Asian bloc continued the anti-colonial struggle into the era of independence. At the centre of this collective enterprise was an assault on the liberal economic order. It came to a head in 1964 with the establishment of the United Nations Conference on Trade and Development (UNCTAD). Commonwealth countries did not act as a separate unit within the Group of 77, which was formed to advance the Third World case in UNCTAD.

But they were prominent, at least initially, in urging a global solution to the development problem, against the francophone African states in particular, who were determined to maintain their privileged access to the EEC.

After 1945, the liberal economy had itself been subjected to institutionalised management to an unprecedented degree. The Bretton Woods institutions (IMF and IBRD) and GATT were set up to police an open market order on the basis of a compromise between neo-classical and Keynesian economic principles. An open trading system would only work, it was believed, under three conditions. First, the right of governments to pursue full employment policies would have to be explicitly recognised. This involved the tacit admission that a revival of protectionism could only be avoided if economic growth rates were maintained at a high level. Secondly, both growth and liberal trade policies required a degree of predictability in exchange rates. Without a fixed exchange rate, the temptation to engage in beggar-your-neighbour policies by allowing rates to float downwards might prove irresistible whenever countries faced balance-of-payment problems and rising unemployment. Thirdly, if governments were to commit themselves to liberal trade policies, full employment and stable exchange rates, they would need credit to tide them over periods of structural adjustment.

These modifications to the liberal idea of a self-regulating capitalist economy were at the time consistent with the interests and perceptions of Third World governments. Nevertheless, the institutional framework set up as a result of the Bretton Woods and Havana Conferences did not, in their view, go far enough in the direction of international (and multilateral) management. As they saw it, the underlying theory of the modified liberal order did not address the problem of development directly. The exceptions to the GATT, which allowed governments to reimpose protectionist measures during balance-of-payments crises, or to defend domestic industry against a sudden surge of imports, were designed to give the authorities in the already developed states time to adjust without having to abandon their macro-economic policies or the objective of full employment. The drawing rights provided by the IMF were designed with the same Keynesian objective in mind.[20]

So far so good. But, as Benjamin Higgins has noted, from a Third World perspective, Keynesianism had certain drawbacks. First, it was primarily a domestic theory. The *General Theory*

> does not advance much beyond comparative statics. It contains no real theory of development. It is much more concerned with the mechanisms with which economies react to events and shocks than with what makes an economy grow. It retains the basic neo-classical assumption that growth is 'natural' in a capitalist society, and concentrates on how to make that growth 'steady' within acceptable rates of unemployment and inflation.[21]

Keynes's influence on the economics profession was so pervasive that it hardly mattered that he was not personally concerned with development. The growth of development economics owed much to the shift to macro-economic theory that he had pioneered, and many of his followers became actively involved in Third World planning both directly and within the UN system. But the early United Nations forays into the issues of development shared the original Keynesian preoccupation with national rather than international priorities. In the first UN report on the issue published in 1950, 'development was essentially, indeed almost exclusively a matter for domestic action'.[22]

A second drawback to the Bretton Woods system and GATT concerned the way the system operated in practice. In theory the three institutions were universal, open to all members of the international community. In practice, Stalin for one concluded that they were intended to form the economic infrastructure of the western alliance, and many Third World governments believed them to be an exclusive rich countries' club. At the end of the 1950s, when the IMF finally began to operate more or less along the lines originally agreed, the spectre of a liquidity crisis arose to threaten the future growth of the world economy. During the 1960s there was a prolonged debate about ways and means of avoiding this disaster. Third World governments took part in this debate, but they were effectively excluded from influencing the outcome The major industrial countries developed informal practices of consultation and co-operation outside the IMF, which was increasingly used as an instrument of ratification for decisions taken elsewhere. Moreover, when they finally agreed on the creation of a new international asset, the Special Drawing Right (SDR), western governments vetoed the favoured Third World proposal of linking monetary reform to development.

The GATT was also more open to Third World influence in theory than in practice. At first sight, western governments seemed more willing to accommodate Third World trading interests than to heed their advice on monetary reform. Under the GATT, world trade was to be liberalised by a reciprocal exchange of concessions. Since most Third World countries were either forced to protect their economies because of persistent shortages of foreign exchange, or wished to protect their 'infant industries', as the GATT permitted, or relied heavily on exports of raw materials which already entered into western markets duty free, they had very little with which to bargain. In theory, under the most favoured nation principle (MFN), they stood to gain from a general abolition of quota trade and reduction of tariffs; in practice, the GATT largely ignored their interests.

By the end of the 1950s the special trading problems of developing countries had been recognised. In 1962 a new Chapter was added to GATT in the hope of meeting their legitimate grievances. The contracting parties conceded that, in future trade negotiations, the developing countries would be entitled to bargain on the basis of non-reciprocity, and to seek improved access to western markets for commodities of special interest to them.

This reform was strongly supported by Commonwealth countries. Its theoretical significance, however, was more impressive than its actual consequences. The new Chapter added a principle of positive discrimination to the MFN principle on which the system of multilateral commercial diplomacy was ostensibly based. Improving market access for Third World exports was then made one of the objectives in the US Trade Expansion Act of 1962, the enabling legislation for the Kennedy Round of Tariff Negotiations. This was the first multilateral negotiation to be conducted following the addition of the new Chapter. In practice, it proved so difficult to achieve agreement between the United States, the EEC and Japan that the Third World was bypassed. When Britain finally joined the EEC in 1973, the African, Caribbean and Pacific members of the Commonwealth, led by Nigeria, were instrumental in ensuring that the Lomé Convention (which replaced the previous Association agreement) incorporated the reformed GATT principle of non-reciprocity. Thus, while in reality the new Convention signalled the acceptance of a special post-colonial relationship by a large part of the Commonwealth Third World – by mutual consent, the South Asian countries were excluded – in theory, the idea of a non-discriminatory multilateral solution to North–South trading problems was upheld.

By the mid-1980s, however, little progress had been made in

overcoming the two major commercial problems which developing countries faced within GATT, and under the Lomé Convention. Western countries continued to impose 'escalating tariffs' under which they increased the level of protection for their domestic industries with each stage of industrial processing, thus inhibiting Third World efforts to develop their own processing and manufacturing capacity to exploit their raw materials at source. Secondly, international trade in textiles, a sector in which latecomers have traditionally been able to achieve a comparative advantage, has been regulated by the western consumer countries since the 1950s in defiance of GATT rules. The Multi-fibre Agreement (MFA), the most recent of the regulatory instruments, has assumed the character of permanent and institutionalised protection, even though it was originally conceived as a temporary measure and was negotiated under the purview of the GATT itself.

The campaign for structural reform

Long before the Kennedy Round tariff cuts were implemented in 1970, it was clear that the Bretton Woods system was too closely wedded to western interests to satisfy Third World demands for rapid social and economic change. It was also too firmly attached doctrinally to the primacy of domestic measures to satisfy those who argued that the major constraints on development were the result of economic structures established during the colonial period, and the emergence of new forms of economic dependence. No doubt, for many leaders, western economic domination was a convenient scapegoat for their own failures in economic policy; but with their continued dependence on distant and volatile world commodity markets over which they had little or no control, it was an understandable perception.

At any rate, the view that Third World development was shackled by the nature of the western economic system became widespread. It was coloured by dependency theory which gradually established an ascendancy over development studies. At the core of the theory, in all its varieties, was a pessimistic assumption about the possibilities of, and prospects for, economic development within the world capitalist system. Dependency theorists maintained that underdevelopment was not merely a description of traditional societies prior to industrialisation. Nor was it a matter of arrested development, a technical problem to be overcome, à la Rostow, by an infusion of foreign capital. Underdevelopment was directly caused by the development of the advanced industrial countries. It followed that economic progress was not possible within the existing system.

'The new approach', writes Kenneth Dadzie,

> asserted the existence of a process of inequalising exchange between the North and South, as the latter's terms of trade of primary commodities exports for manufactured imports consistently deteriorated, as economic surplus was transferred from the South to the North through transnational enterprises, as mercantilist policies restricted access to technology, and as international capital limited structural change and the potential for growth.[23]

Taken to its logical conclusion, dependency theory suggested that the only way forward was to break the links which bound the ex-colonial states to the international economy.

Since powerful external interests were involved, and many Third World élites had been co-opted into the system, few governments were either able or willing to follow this advice. We can only speculate as to why the politicians refused to accept the conclusions to which the fashionable new doctrines pointed. The most probable explanation is that in the Third World, as elsewhere, practical men adopt a utilitarian attitude towards all theory: they take what is useful for their immediate purposes and discard the rest. In this case utility was buttressed by two further considerations.

The first concerns the 'rationalism' which is inherent in multilateral diplomacy. Decolonisation enabled the new states to form a loose revisionist alliance to challenge western domination of the international system, at least within the United Nations where each state had an equal vote. The cold war temporarily gave the non-aligned movement a political salience which it might not otherwise have enjoyed. Their political weight in the United Nations in turn enabled Third World governments to join with the Soviet Union in forcing the west to agree to a new international organisation to deal with trade and development. From the start in 1964, the UNCTAD was dominated by Third World demands and its secretariat was responsible for developing the intellectual framework within which these demands were advanced.

Raul Prebisch, the Argentinian economist who was the first

Secretary General of the UNCTAD, shared with more radical dependency theorists the assumption that there was no possibility that spontaneous self-correcting forces might overcome the structural constraints facing the developing countries.[24] But, unlike them, he believed that rational analysis could persuade the major industrial states to modify the system. Since multilateral agreement between sovereign states has to reflect a consensus, the crucial prerequisites are an acceptable definition of the problem and a possible solution which offers something to all sides. If it was true, as Prebisch argued, that Third World terms of trade would continue to deteriorate, it followed that the western goal of an open world economy could only be achieved if deliberate corrective measures were adopted. Prebisch's rationalism was thus firmly grounded in an appeal to western self-interest.

Multilateralists have always wanted to believe that international society could be reformed peacefully in much the same way as those western social democracies which evolved without the catharsis of violent revolution. On this view, the creation of new states would exercise a similar pressure on the bastions of privilege as had the extension of the franchise in western Europe and north America. The hope was that, as in the latter case, an extension of political rights would be followed by a redistribution of income in the interests of equity. In practice, western governments never accepted the domestic analogy on which multilateralism was based. They also disputed the central assumption of the Prebisch thesis, namely that there was an irreversible decline in the terms of trade between raw materials and manufactures. But they accepted enough of the argument to keep alive the hope of a multilateral solution to the development problem. In particular, they recognised that Third World governments had to be given some incentive to stay within the liberal order.

Between 1964 and 1970 the focus of the development debate shifted from the need for foreign aid to improving the access of Third World manufactures and semi-manufactured exports to western markets. The protracted negotiations which led to the establishment of the General Specialised Preference Schemes(GSP) consumed international and diplomatic resources out of all proportion to the outcome. The GSP negotiations maintained the impression that progress was being made, and the scheme itself entrenched the concept of positive discrimination in international society more firmly than the GATT. But the immediate benefit was felt only by the few countries which already had an industrial sector with a latent export potential. Within the Commonwealth, the GSP had little to offer the majority of African, Caribbean and Pacific states. Like most other developing countries, they would continue to rely on the production and export of raw materials and tropical foodstuffs.

In sum, the immediate outlook for most Third World countries at the beginning of the 1970s was bleak. However, a second UN Development Decade (to be followed by a third) was declared, in an apparent effort to urge the international community to learn from its mistakes. Hope was able to triumph over the dead hand of dependency theory by shifting the emphasis from the rationalism of multilateral diplomacy to the scope that it provided for pressure group politics. The analogy with western social democracy was maintained, but attention was now fixed less on its constitutional arrangements than on the circumstances which had persuaded the European ruling classes to widen the franchise and eventually share power with the population at large. On this view the European bourgeoisie had been primarily motivated by fear. Their nervousness was occasioned by the organisation and solidarity of the working class, which could threaten to withhold its labour, or worse still imperil the institution of private property. The Third World stood in the same relation to the countries of the OECD as the European working classes to the bosses on the eve of the First World War. Such, broadly, was the argument that greeted the sudden quadrupling of the oil price in 1973/4.

With hindsight, the weaknesses in this version of the domestic analogy seem obvious. There is no international equivalent to the obligations that working class citizens had to accept in return for a share in power, such as the duty to pay taxes or to be conscripted in time of war. And where workers in a single industry might share an interest in standing together in an effort to force improvements in their pay and conditions, Third World commodity producers were more often in competition with one another for the same markets. Nonetheless, circumstances conspired to lend a superficial plausibility to the comparison.

Looking back with scarcely concealed nostalgia in 1987, the Secretary General of UNCTAD recalled the cathartic impact of OPEC's success on North/South relations:

> It lent credence to the possibility of fundamental change and to the aspiration that a world of economic equity and justice, as envisaged by the developing countries, might actually be created. The 1974 Declaration on the Establishment of a new International Economic Order (NIEO) and its accompanying Programme of Action convey a new message of strength and purpose ... essentially, they underscored the developing countries' conviction that change was needed in the operation of the international economic system, and that the change could be effected through a process of global negotiation in a context of strength and bargaining power on the part of the developing countries and of the concrete demonstration by OPEC of world interdependence. It is worth noting, for example, that the NIEO was ostensibly proclaimed to reassert and strengthen the 'spirit, purposes and principles of the Charter of the United Nations'.[25]

It is certainly true that, for a season, western governments were amazed at the redistribution of economic power that the oil producers had brought about. They were also fearful of the demonstration effects that OPEC's success might have on other commodity producers. The Americans attempted to kill the virus before it spread by organising a consumers' cartel. But they failed to win the support of the allies: West European countries and Japan were more dependent on imported raw materials and less well protected than the United States by long-established strategic stockpiles.[26] Nature also conspired to strengthen the impression of a seismic shift in the structure of the world economy. The frost which wrecked the Brazilian coffee harvest in 1974 not only quadrupled the coffee price but led other 'soft' commodity prices to harden in sympathy.

In the end, after several false starts, the western powers agreed to negotiate with the Group of 77 in UNCTAD on an Integrated Programme of Commodities (IPC). The centrepiece of this negotiation was to be a new institution (the Common Fund), with the power to intervene directly in the market and with resources to promote new international commodity agreements. It was clear that western co-operation was motivated more by a desire to limit the damage to their own interests than by a conversion to the principle of managed commodity markets. Western governments reacted to proposals by the Group of 77, rather than initiating or lobbying for proposals of their own. This was partly because there were major differences of approach between them. France ostensibly favoured a concept of administered commodity prices, while the Federal Republic of Germany was deeply suspicious of political interference in the market. Britain was prepared to support individual commodity agreements where these could be agreed between producers and consumers but was opposed to any attempt to raise prices artificially above their market clearing level. But if, collectively, the western response to the IPC was negative, it was also because fundamental reforms would require legislative and policy changes for which there was little domestic support.

As soon as market conditions allowed, western governments retreated to the *status quo ante* with an almost audible sigh of relief. Arrangements to set up an emasculated Common Fund were eventually agreed, very largely as a result of efforts within the Commonwealth to find the basis of a compromise.[27] This demonstration of the Commonwealth's ability to bridge the North/South divide, and assume a catalytic role within the wider international community, would have been more impressive if its timing had been better. The Secretary-General admitted that the Commonwealth could not negotiate for the world, but insisted grandly that it could help the world to negotiate. It all came to nothing: in the event, the Fund never materialised, and in the straitened circumstances of the 1980s came to seem increasingly irrelevant to the immediate problems facing developing countries.

The impact of the oil price rise on the Third World was not universally disastrous. Amongst Commonwealth countries, India survived surprisingly well. The new price not only stimulated domestic exploration and production but led, indirectly, and against the trend in many parts of the world, to an improvement in the country's balance of payments. Proximity allowed India to meet the growing demand in the oil-rich Gulf for both skilled and unskilled labour. India remains one of the poorest countries in the world, but many individual Indians and their families prospered from the new remittance economy.

In Nigeria, the major African producer, the sudden oil wealth – rising from a low base before 1967 to over 90 per cent of export earnings by 1974 – led to a fatal neglect of agriculture and dangerously raised the stakes in an already turbulent polity. But wealth also had positive consequences. It probably helped to heal some of the wounds inflicted by the civil war. It certainly enabled the Nigerian government to play a leading part in both regional affairs and North/South relations. Hope feeds on the illusion as much as the reality of progress. Where substantive advance is blocked, well-meaning activity may still be useful in maintaining a sense of purposeful movement. The establishment of the Economic Community of West African States (ECOWAS) as the result of a Nigerian initiative is a case in point. Its record of achievement has so far been unimpressive, but it has at least charted a rational framework of future development on the basis of regional co-operation. More significantly, as we have seen, Nigeria took the lead in the negotiation of the first Lomé Convention in 1975. Its ability to forego claims on the European Development Fund (EDF) in favour of its less fortunate partners also overcame one of the main obstacles to a successful negotiation – the EEC's refusal to enlarge the size of the EDF.

For the majority of the developing countries, however, the oil crisis had dire consequences. No amount of multilateral dialogue could shield their fragile economies from the impact of soaring fuel bills. As the following, fairly typical, figures show, most countries were unable to balance their current account before 1973; afterwards they had no practical alternative but to incur massive new debts.

Current account balance
(millions of US dollars)

	1970	1976
Sri Lanka	−13	−59
Kenya	−38	−61
Ghana	−58	−72
Jamaica	−145	−248

Source: World Development Report 1978

The Third World's response to OPEC's triumph cannot easily be explained if it is conventionally assumed that states act (and react) in defence of their immediate national interests. The vast majority of developing countries do not produce their own oil: the quadrupling of the price therefore inevitably led to a massive deterioration in their balance of payments. Yet, for the most part, they welcomed the advent of 'oil power', viewing the OPEC victory as their own.

Many Third World leaders probably saw the oil prices as an

important victory in the Afro-Asian revolt against the West, on a par with the Japanese defeat of Russia in 1905, or the collapse of France in 1954 at the battle of Dien Bien Phu. Viewed in this light, the long-run benefits could be expected to outweigh the inconvenience and costs of higher oil bills. More specifically, many hoped what the West feared, that OPEC could provide a model for other commodities. Admittedly none was of such strategic importance to the economies of the industrial states. The prospect of 'banana power' never seemed likely to keep the lights burning in the State Department or the Chancelleries of Europe. But some other commodities, such as copper or bauxite, were widely used in the industrial world, were not quickly substitutable and were produced by relatively few countries. Producer organisations, loosely modelled on OPEC, seemed to offer a way forward. Jamaica, under Michael Manley, played a leading part in the formation of the International Bauxite Association (IBA) and Zambia joined the major Latin American producers to form a similar organisation for copper. For the rest, the best hope seemed to be to exploit the changed international climate to negotiate a more broadly based set of reforms to the world economy.

The campaign to establish a 'New International Economic Order' (NIEO) was a gigantic gamble. The odds were always against its success, partly because it required the boom conditions, which had precipitated the oil crisis, to continue, and partly because success required the oil producers to act cohesively, not merely on their own behalf but on behalf of all developing countries. In the event, not only did western demand for Third World exports fall, but western governments took steps to reduce their dependence on what they regarded as politically unreliable sources of supply, a rising proportion of western investment in the exploration and extraction of strategic minerals shifting from the Third World, particularly Africa, to North America and Australia. The oil producers, it is true, emerged as major aid donors, and even Nigeria briefly entered the lists.[28] But they were no more prepared to underwrite Third World (or in the Nigerian case, Commonwealth African) solidarity where it ran counter to their own interests than the western powers. It is not surprising, therefore, that when the gamble failed, the hope for a multilateral solution to Third World development problems also faded.

The new realism

The election of Margaret Thatcher as Prime Minister of Britain in 1979 and Ronald Reagan as President of the United States in 1980 marked the opening of an era in which the major western powers distanced themselves from the institutions and mores of multilateral diplomacy. In large measure this change in the political landscape provides the answer to the final question raised at the beginning of this chapter. How are we to account for the loss of confidence in development as an attainable political goal, and as an instrument of political mobilisation on which Third World leaders can base their claims to legitimate authority?

The attempt to solve the development problem by international economic reform required the co-operation of the major capitalist powers. The emphasis in the NIEO on the need for greater South/South co-operation was window dressing. The crucial policy changes concerned commodity prices, the terms of access for Third World exports into western markets, the transfer of technology from North to South and the implementation of a code of conduct for transnational corporations. All required action by western rather than Third World governments. The UNCTAD Secretariat continues to analyse the world economy in terms which suggest the urgent need for global negotiations; but without an audience their appeals make little impact.

In 1981, an independent Commission under the chairmanship of Willy Brandt published the *North/South Report: A Programme for Survival* in an attempt to rekindle international concern for the plight of the Third World. Its central policy prescription consisted of a grandiose form of global Keynesianism: the way out of the recession for both North and South required western scientific know-how to be harnessed to Arab petro-dollars and Third World manpower. But, despite a distinguished list of retired prime ministers and world statesmen on the Commission (none of whom had been conspicuously active in promoting international economic reform while in office), the Brandt report also fell on deaf ears. The leading western governments had broken with the post-war Keynesian consensus at home and were not about to resurrect it abroad. The multilateralist party was over. The emergence of the radical right in Britain and America followed the failure of centrist governments to maintain growth and curb inflation simultaneously. The new orthodoxy involved a symbolic attempt to 'roll back' the state, a selective return to neo-classical economics and a resurgence of realist dogma in foreign policy.

The multilateralist enthusiasm of the 1970s had been accompanied by a reasonably buoyant economic performance over much of the developing world. Despite appalling disasters such as famine in the Sahel, and the even more ominous failure of predominantly agricultural countries, particularly in Africa, to feed themselves on a regular basis, economic growth remained largely unaffected by the slowdown in the industrial countries, averaging 5·4 per cent for the decade. Indeed, arguably, it was because many Third World countries were beginning to challenge western industrial hegemony that the major powers felt compelled to take the NIEO demands seriously. It was one thing to have accommodated the Japanese economic miracle within the liberal order, but quite another to contemplate its total transformation to facilitate the takeover of the world economy by successive waves of industrial latecomers. Revolutions, it has often been said, are made by the frustrated, not by the destitute: it is the pace of change, not its absence, which ignites the flame.

The NIEO campaign, however, took place in circumstances which were much more precarious than those which had accompanied the rise of Japan. In the latter case, during the 1950s and 1960s, the United States was still the undisputed hegemon, dominating world capital markets, underwriting the gold exchange standard and providing a market for distress goods. Japan's industrial recovery tested the system and imposed strains in strategic sectors (e.g. the automobile and electronic industries), but it did not threaten its basic structure. By contrast, inflation, the collapse of the Bretton Woods monetary system in 1971 and the oil price shock in 1973 undermined its foundations. The relatively strong performance of the Third World during the 1970s could only be achieved by a rapid accumulation of external debt and – in many countries – by the accumulation of domestic imbalances, such as fiscal deficits, inflation, and over-valued currencies.

In the harsher economic and political environment of the 1980s, the high cost of offering these hostages to fortune could no longer be concealed. The World Bank sketches 'the present climate of economic uncertainty' in a few sombre brush strokes:

Growth has slowed substantially in the developing countries. Some African and highly indebted middle income countries have suffered significant declines in per capita income. Their investments have fallen to levels at which even minimal replacement may no longer occur in important sectors of their economies. Their debts are growing, but they still face negative net resource transfers because debt service obligations exceed the limited amounts of new financing. In some developing countries the severity of the prolonged economic slump already surpasses that of the Great Depression in the industrial countries, and in many countries poverty is on the rise.[29]

It is not surprising in these circumstances that exaggerated beliefs about the links between political independence and rapid economic development have been quietly abandoned. The temper of the times in the Third as much as the First World is realist; these days governments are more concerned with survival than with progress. The new realism, however, lacks the autarkic impulses of the old: the international economy is recognised to be a system from which there is virtually no escape. As the solidarist assumptions on which the NIEO was based fade from view, they have been replaced by a new international orthodoxy emanating from the IMF and the World Bank. The idea of 'debtor power', a concerted Third World strategy to force international reform by threatening the world's banking system with massive default, has occasionally been floated, but has never taken off. Some indebted governments, such as Nigeria, have played for time and insisted on devising their own programme of structural adjustment rather than immediately accepting the IMF package in return for international relief. But the range of policies – devaluation, the relaxation of import controls and a reduction of urban food subsidies – does not vary greatly. The wheel has come full circle: in the 1980s, as in the 1950s, development is seen very much in terms of self-help.

The scaling down of Third World expectations about the possibilities of multilateral diplomacy may in the end have beneficial consequences for international co-operation. Within the Commonwealth, the Secretariat has moved with the times, shifting the emphasis of its work from advocacy of broad international reform to providing more modest assistance to its member states (particularly the smaller ones) in defending their interests in order to get the best possible deal for themselves in trade and financial negotiations.[30]

An international solution to the problem of African debt is just conceivable on the basis of the new orthodoxy. The United Nations Emergency Session on the African crisis in 1986 did not yield immediate results; but it did produce an unprecedented admission by African governments that their plight was in large measure their own fault. By 1988 there was a growing consensus, endorsed by the Toronto summit of western leaders, that the international community should recognise the efforts that African governments had made to implement the reforms recommended by their western creditors and by international financial institutions. A UN report concluded that, in its turn, the West should 'acknowledge that the severe damage which developments in the 1980s have inflicted on African economies have made these changes very difficult to implement'.[31] Whether the consensus will prove strong enough to generate the additional financial support which the UN experts called for remains to be seen. But on the precedent of 1987 when large increases were organised through the IMF, the World Bank and the African Development Bank, there is at least room for hope.

The price that will be exacted for future North/South co-operation of this kind – adherence to a domestic economic strategy dictated by the western powers and by international financial institutions – is unlikely to do much for the legitimacy of Third World governments. The original ideal of rapid economic development was good for the self-esteem of the rulers and promised to bind the people to their government. The assumption was that independence would release the energies of the people and allow the country's own resources to be exploited for their benefit. This ideal survived the first shock of independence: the realisation that the rhetoric of sovereign equality and mutual economic interdependence concealed the reality of a rigid international hierarchy. Politically, however, the intractable nature of the development problem was perceived as a challenge rather than as evidence that the goal of 'closing the gap' between the developing and industrial countries was misconceived. The numerical majority of Third World countries in international organisations allowed them to press the case for fundamental economic reform. There were also age-old dividends to be drawn from the argument that misfortune was someone else's fault, that Third World poverty was a direct consequence of the affluence, exploitation, and greed of the major industrial powers. And for a short time the spectacular success of the oil-producing countries in demonstrating the vulnerability of industrial society to external pressure rekindled the hope that the problem of economic justice had an attainable international solution.

It is difficult to sustain this belief. In the 1930s the Great Depression witnessed a widespread retreat from economic liberalism. Governments everywhere became avowedly nationalist, sometimes for aggressive and sometimes for defensive reasons. The prolonged slump of the 1980s has seen a combination of nationalist behaviour and liberal dogma. It is probably incorrect to assume that, throughout the Third World, the rediscovery of the virtues inherent in market forces is always and necessarily the result of a forced conversion by the IMF. In India, with its genuinely mixed economy, the business class has grown in size and, in recent years, in political influence also. It is not so much the government's failure to alleviate rural poverty that worries them, as its own inability to compete effectively with the fast industrialising countries of East Asia. Deregulation is both fashionable and, up to a point, in their own interests. In Nigerian society the capitalist (or at any rate the proto-capitalist) ethic has always had deep roots, so that national (or state) liberalism seems a natural response to the country's predicament, except of course to the office-holding class which finds its additional sources of income curtailed under the new austerity. And in many of the smaller African and Caribbean countries the manifest failure of collectivist policies to solve the twin problems of insolvency and agricultural decline has left the ruling élites genuinely puzzled about what to do next.

Liberal economic doctrine prescribes a series of policies required to generate wealth. Broadly, governments should maintain a firm hold on law and order, suppress corruption and other forms of malpractice and keep out of the market place as much as possible. If the prescription works, over the long run political stability may return to many parts of the Third World from which, recently, it has been conspicuously absent. In that event, governments may recommend themselves to their populations by creating an environment in which enterprise can prosper, rather than by promising to redistribute an income which they do not possess and cannot create.

It is possible, but it seems unlikely. Notoriously, politics take place in the short run. In the capitalist democracies, governments were converted to economic liberalism after, not before, industrialisation, and after, not before, the development of strong central government and national politics. In the contemporary Third World the order is being reversed. Where liberal policies help generate growth and industrial diversification, the evidence suggests that success is more likely to sharpen ethnic and class antagonisms than to resolve them. Where the level of economic dependence is such that market discipline by itself can do little to restore the economy to minimal health, even the state may be at risk.

The future of the Commonwealth Third World may not be any worse than at other times since the transfer of power. Nor perhaps are the prospects of rapid economic development any worse. But whether they will prove any better seems doubtful. The development debate gave rise to two illusions – that a 'quick fix' could be achieved either with the help of overseas aid or, alternatively, by structural reform. Both have been shattered. If societies, like men, need illusions to live by, it is not clear where a third is to be found.

Notes

1 A. H. Hansen, 'Power shifts and regional balances' in Paul Streeton and Michael Lipton (eds.), *The Crisis of Indian Planning*, Oxford University Press for IIA, Oxford, 1968, p. 43.

2 Cf. Ernest Gellner, 'So, looking back on our *belle epoque*, I would say that in basic outline, our situation has not changed so very much; but the new balance of power and demoralization have made it much more frightening.' 'Recollection in anxiety, thought and change revisited', in *Culture, Identity and Politics*, Cambridge University Press, Cambridge, 1987, pp. 111–22.

3 World Bank, *World Development Report, 1978*, Oxford University Press for the World Bank, Oxford, 1978.

4 Richard S. Reid, 'Protecting Africa's children,' paper presented to the Conference to celebrate the Silver Jubilee of the Organisation of African Unity, Cairo, 25–7 January 1988.

5 J. P. Dreze and A. K. Sen, *Hunger and Public Action* (forthcoming).

6 'Decolonization, development, dependence: a survey of changing attitudes', in Prosser Gifford and William Roger Louis (eds.), *The Transfer of Power in Africa: Decolonisation 1940–1960*, Yale University Press, New Haven, CT, and London,' 1982, pp. 483–514.

7 Stephen Krasner, *Structural Conflict: The World Against Global Liberalism*, University of California Press, Berkeley, 1985, pp. 98–9.

8 Ibid., p. 104.

9 See Chapter 1, pp. 1–16 and Chapter 5, pp. 72–105.

10 Jawaharlal Nehru's speeches, Vol. 1, 2nd edition, Government of India, New Dehli, 1958, quoted in A. Appadorai, *Essays in Politics and International Relations*, Asia Publishing House, London, 1969, pp. 38–9.

11 Julius Nyerere, *Freedom and Unity: A Selection from Writings and Speeches, 1952–65*, Oxford University Press, Dar-es-Salaam, 1966, pp. 103–4.

12 Eric Williams, *Economic Problems of Trinidad and Tobago*, Public Affairs Pamphlet No. 1, 19 July 1955, quoted in Carl Parris, 'From populist nationalism to national corporatism' in Basil A. Ince (ed.), *Contemporary International Relations of the Caribbean*, Institute of International Relations, University of West Indies, St Augustine, Trinidad and Tobago, 1979, pp. 243–59.

13 Robert Packenham, *Liberal America and the Third World*, Princeton University Press, Princeton, NJ, 1973, p. 7. See also D. E. Apter, 'The passing of development studies', *Government and Opposition*, Vol. 15, Nos. 3–4, Summer/Autumn 1980, pp. 263–75.

14 Ibid., p. 5.

15 Ibid., p. 4.

16 Ayub Khan, *Friends, not Masters: A Political Autobiography*, Oxford University Press, London, 1967, p. 138.

17 David E. Bell, *Testimony on Foreign Assistance Act 1963*, Committee on Foreign Affairs, United States House of Representatives Hearings, 88th Congress, First Session, Part II, 23–6 April 1963.

18 W. Rostow, *The Stages of Economic Growth: A Non-Communist Manifesto*, Cambridge University Press, Cambridge and New York, 1960.

19 *Report to the President of the United States from the Committee to Strengthen the Security of the Free World: the Scope and Distribution of the United States Military and Economic Assistance Programmes*, Department of State, Washington, D.C., 20 March 1963.

20 Richard N. Gardner, *Sterling–Dollar Diplomacy*, Columbia University Press, New York, 1980.

21 Benjamin Higgins and Donald J. Sairoice (eds.), *Regional Economic Development*, Unwin Hyman, Boston, 1988, pp. 37–8.

22 Kenneth Dadzie, 'The United Nations and the problem of economic development' in Adam Roberts and Benedict Kingsbury (eds.), *United Nations, Divided World*, Clarendon Press, Oxford, 1988, p. 140.

23 Ibid., p. 142.

24 *Towards a New Trade Policy for Development: Report by the Secretary-General of the United Nations Conference on Trade and Development*, UN, E/CONF, 46/3, New York, 1964.

25 Cited in Dadzie, in Roberts and Kingsbury, *United Nations, Divided World*, p. 144.

26 Philip Connelly and Robert Perlman, *The Politics of Scarcity: Resource Conflicts in International Relations*, Oxford University Press for RIIA, London, 1975.

27 Geoffrey Goodwin and James Mayall (eds.), *A New International Commodity Regime*, Croom Helm, London, 1979, pp. 111–39.

28 James Mayall, 'Oil and Nigerian foreign policy', *African Affairs*, Vol. 75, No. 300, July 1976, pp. 317–30.

29 *World Development Report, 1988*, Oxford University Press for World Bank, Oxford, 1988, pp. 2–3.

30 *Report of the Commonwealth Secretary-General, 1979*, Commonwealth Secretariat, London, 1979, pp. 31–2.

31 *Financing Africa's Recovery: Report and Recommendations of the Advisory Group on Financial Flows for Africa*, United Nations, New York, 1988, p. 43.

10 *Anthony Payne*

Full bellies in Freedom House: universal human rights, cultural relativism and the Commonwealth Third World

The very existence of so many new states forged out of the ruins of the British Empire is of itself a tribute to the force of belief in the modern world in a certain sort of human rights. Hoist by its own doctrine of the 'civilising' mission, hooked latterly on the notion of 'preparing' colonies for self-government, Britain could in effect find no moral basis for its continued rule of the Empire when eventually faced with the joint demand for political freedom and economic development from non-enfranchised societies and aspirant nations. These new states thus took up their place in international society as victors in a struggle but also as graduates of a school of liberal human rights – sometimes, it should be said, disgruntled and dismissive of the colonial legacy, but in the vast majority of cases committed to the fuller implementation of the very social, economic and political values by which imperial rule was first legitimised and ultimately destroyed.

Given that these were the circumstances of their birth, it is important in any review of the post-colonial experience of ex-British Third World states to ask hard questions, and give honest answers, about their human rights record after independence was achieved and the restraining hand of colonial control was removed. This chapter devotes itself to this task. The problem is that it is far from easy to establish what evidence is appropriate to the discussion or how it should be evaluated when gathered. These matters need to be considered most carefully before any empirical data are introduced into the discussion. We can sensibly begin by looking at the longstanding debate within the western political tradition about the universality of human rights.

The universality of human rights

The alleged universality of human rights can be approached at the level of both theory and practice. At the theoretical, or philosophical, level, the natural rights perspective is that human rights must be universal: they are inherent in one's humanity and do not depend on either the fulfilment of obligations or the granting of rights by states or other bodies. They simply express what is essential about the nature of human beings. The tradition of natural rights thought is well enough established. It is conventionally traced back to the Stoics and their belief that the individual belonged to a universal community which existed by nature and was governed according to reason; it proceeds via the Christian gospel, Renaissance humanism and the Reformation's assertion of the right of resistance to its glorious period, that of Locke, the American and French Revolutions and the Declaration of the Rights of Man and of the Citizen. There was added in the nineteenth century the contribution of German romantic thought which took exception to what it saw as the exaggerated individualism of the French revolutionary doctrine and elevated group rights, such as national self-determination, to equal status.

There also exists in western political theory an equally articulate tradition of attack on the idea of natural rights, embracing *inter alia* Burke's emphasis on the importance of organic and sentimental communities, Hegel's not dissimilar assertion of the real unity of the group, and Marx's claim that the theory of natural rights reflects only the special language of particular interests. What is striking, though, about the development of human rights thinking over time is its capacity to absorb criticism in a way that enriches the theory. To a considerable degree, modern twentieth-century theorising on human rights has embraced many of the classic criticisms. Hegel's strictures, for example, have flowered in the attention now paid to group rights, and Marx's condemnation of the narrowness of the eighteenth-century view of civil and political rights has spawned the new category of social and economic rights.[1] In this way the theory of human rights has endured and grown over many generations and in our era has arguably produced something close to a working philosophical consensus, whereby the argument is reduced mainly to one about the relative vitality of differing constituent strands.

At the practical, or political, level, the international system has enshrined human rights on a universal basis within the Universal Declaration of Human Rights, passed by the General Assembly of the United Nations in 1948. Supplemented by the two International Covenants on Civil and Political Rights and Economic, Social and Cultural Rights, which were set out in 1966, this document has become the internationally recognised standard of human rights behaviour.[2] Yet, as a matter of fact, the original Declaration was first and foremost a political construct – a statement of principles and objectives agreed as a compromise between the conflicting interpretations of human rights advocated by the three major groupings of states within the United Nations at the time: the Soviet bloc, the liberal democracies of North America and Western Europe, and the independent Third World countries of Latin America, Asia and the Near East. What is more, most of the conflict derived from the different politics of the first two groups. In a similar way, the two Covenants derived from the Declaration were products of the cold war era and directly reflected the insistence of the United States government that civil and political rights be split off from social and economic rights.[3] In other words, the nature of the world's first global regime of universal human rights was shaped, in origin at least, by the balance of international political forces at the time of enactment, rather than by a coherent philosophical view as to the proper content of such an instrument.

As a consequence, there was infiltrated into the whole regime a definite bias in favour of political, as against economic, rights. The former were set out at some length in Articles 3–21 of the Universal Declaration and included the right to a fair trial; the right to protection from slavery, servitude and torture; the basic freedoms of thought, religion, movement, assembly and participation in government; and the rights to marry, have a family and enjoy nationality. By comparison, social and economic rights were squeezed into Articles 22–7 and comprised essentially the rights to social security, work, education and free participation in the cultural life of the community. Moreover, the Covenants further distinguished between the two categories by expecting the immediate attainment of civil and political rights but only gradual implementation of economic, social and cultural rights. Finally, it was clearly the case that individual rights were stressed more firmly than group rights.

These and other criticisms of the United Nations regime were widely voiced in the 1970s as more ex-colonial states joined the international community and gained the confidence to speak out forcibly in its councils. The dominant argument, which came to be referred to as the 'full-belly thesis' and was closely tied to the call for a New International Economic Order, asserted that the achievement of political rights and civil liberties had to wait until economic rights had been realised.[4] Indeed, such was the numerical predominance of new states conceiving of themselves as owing common allegiance to a Third World position that a United Nations resolution passed in 1977 demanded that, in future, priority in human rights policy be given to group rights, such as the assertion of national sovereignty, and to the whole economic and social agenda associated with the call for international economic reform. Interpreted literally, this took redress of the former imbalance too far and provided a mask for the abuse of individual human rights in the name of social and economic radicalism. Interpreted in practice, however, within the United Nations human rights system, it established an appropriate blend of political and civil considerations, on the one hand, and economic and social ones, on the other. A working consensus was forged which has generally enabled the argument on the global stage about human rights to move on from basic matters of definition.

In short, the answer to the question posed at the beginning of this section as to the universality of human rights is that, at both the level of theory and practice, sufficiently convincing affirmative cases have been made – at least within the framework of western political analysis, which can be said in philosophical terms to embrace Marxism. The next step is to extend the discussion beyond the realms of Europe and North America and to consider whether the consensus we have sought to establish about what human rights universally are survives the transition.

Cultural relativism[5]

The doctrine of cultural relativism undoubtedly mounts a fierce challenge to the claimed universality of human rights. In Vincent's apt formulation it can be set out in three logical steps:

In the first place, it asserts that rules about morality vary from place to place. Secondly, it asserts that the way to understand this variety is to place it in its cultural context. And, in the third place, it asserts that moral claims derive from, and are enmeshed in, a cultural context which is itself the source of their validity.[6]

As such, the doctrine considers even the attempt to argue the existence of a universal morality to be a form of imperialism (or more fashionably ethnocentrism) and counterposes against this cultural arrogance an acceptance of the 'equally valid patterns of life which mankind has created for itself from the raw materials of existence'.[7] As Vincent again nicely puts it, 'cultural egalitarianism seems to follow from cultural relativism'.[8] The intellectual challenge hereby mounted against the existence of universal human rights has understandably proved to be popular amongst modern Third World nationalists seeking to throw off not only the politics and economics of imperialism but also its cultural associations. The claim of cultural specificity has thus been made in many forms, but perhaps one formulation, the most prominent in the literature, can be taken as a test of the validity of the general argument. It makes a bid for continental exceptionalism and asserts that there is a specifically African concept of human rights which differs in a meaningful way from the western ideal.

Those who advance this argument tend to take as the key to that difference the alleged existence of a communitarian ideal in Africa.[9] For example, President Kenneth Kaunda of Zambia, who styles himself an 'African humanist', has written in a fashion typical of this approach:

> The tribal community was a mutual society. It was organised to satisfy the basic human needs of all its members and, therefore, individualism was discouraged ... Human need was the supreme criterion of behaviour... social harmony was a vital necessity ... Chiefs and tribal elders ... adjudicated between conflicting parties, admonished the quarrelsome and anti-social and took whatever action was necessary to strengthen the fabric of social life.[10]

In this extract are to be found all of the characteristic claims of the cultural relativist argument as applied to Africa – that the group is more important than the individual, that decisions are made by consensus rather than by competition, and that economic surpluses are conventionally generated and disposed of on a redistributive rather than capitalistic basis.

However, in an important commentary on this thesis Rhoda Howard has carefully unpicked virtually all of its major tenets.[11]

She argues persuasively that the traditional African concept of 'personhood', by which 'persons become persons only after a process of incorporation'[12] into the obligations of communal life, is more properly a theory of human dignity than of human rights, and is in any case breaking down as, to take one example, more African women develop individualistic orientations towards the many customary practices which pertain to marriage. Equally, in her view the consensual model of decision-making in traditional society is not only exaggerated but quite wrong as a description of the kinds of feudal bureaucracies that existed in Ashanti, Buganda and Northern Nigeria. It also cannot be sustained in its modern guise, that of the 'palaver' state talking out its problems and policies within the framework of the single party. Lastly, Howard is just as unromantic in insisting that, whatever may have been the case in the past with respect to the communal ownership of property and the distribution of welfare according to need, the African political economy today is not noted for its commitment to the redistributive ideal, even in states with genuine socialist aspirations such as Tanzania. In sum, as she puts it, the cultural distinctiveness in respect of human rights still claimed for Africa by virtue of its commitment to a communitarian ideal 'is based on inadequate understanding of pre-colonial African societies and an ignoring of the profound structural changes which have taken place in African societies as a result of British colonialism and Africa's incorporation into the capitalist world economy'.[13]

The argument here is essentially sociological. What Rhoda Howard is saying is that the 'African human rights' thesis rests on bad sociology. There is a sense, however, in which this is not really the issue at stake at all. For it is, of course, possible to stand her criticisms on their head and offer as the answer to the question of whether or not there are universal human rights the view that there has come to exist in the contemporary world a single culture which has spread itself across all indigenous cultures, overwhelming them in the name of modernisation or world capitalism or whatever else it might be thought to be. As individuals all over the world have been detached from their traditional ties with their local communities, the international culture of human rights has emerged as 'the natural response to changing conditions, a logical and necessary evolution of the means for realizing human dignity'.[14] Or so, at least, it can be argued. The difficulty here is again precisely sociological: it is not easy to argue with any conviction that there *is* just such a common culture which has shaped, or is in the process of shaping, the whole world. It would be something of an understatement to say that, for all the force of globalism, differences still look to be quite marked and, if so, the argument about cultural relativism and the universality of human rights is once more reduced to the actions (differently observed, inevitably) of human beings in what remain different cultural contexts.

This suggests, therefore, that ultimately the argument is a moral one, on which a stance has sooner or later to be taken. From this perspective there is merit in the distinction drawn by Jack Donnelly between 'weak' and 'strong' cultural relativism. The former is located at the universalist end of the continuum and merely observes that 'culture may be an *important* source of the validity of a moral right or rule'.[15] The latter, by contrast, presumes that 'rights (and other social practices, values, and moral rules) are culturally determined' and would 'allow such a wide range of variation for most rights that two entirely justifiable sets might overlap only slightly'.[16] The conclusion to which this leads is that universal human rights are indeed compatible with a weak view of cultural relativism but that, from the strong version, two things follow which must be rejected. The first is that all cultures create equally valid patterns of life: for this is to argue that anything done by any culturally distinct group of people is worthy of respect by another. The second is that moral claims deriving from outside a culture have no validity within it: for this is to argue that the rest of the world should have no say about a society which brutalises its children. For all of the radical chic with which cultural relativism has been surrounded in Third World hands, pushed to this extent, the doctrine is a resurrection of what John Stuart Mill called the 'despotism of custom'.[17] As Mill observed, the person who 'devolves upon his own world the responsibility of being in the right against the dissentient world of other people' is never troubled by the fact that 'mere accident has decided which of the numerous worlds is the object of his reliance, and that the same causes which make him a Churchman in London, would have made him a Buddhist or a Confucian in Pekin'.[18]

In the final analysis, then, we have elected to place ourselves within the moral boundaries of universal human rights theory, albeit qualified by the weak version of cultural relativism. We have also come to the end of this preliminary discussion of definition and meaning and can now turn to consider the actual human rights record of Commonwealth Third World states.

The indices game

Yet this too is far from straightforward. The investigation of human rights performance inevitably requires the establishment of a systematic basis for assessment and comparison. For many, this need is met by the development of indices, defined as 'relatively objective efforts to assess a particular condition'.[19] Sceptics of the merits of quantitative social science may take some convincing, but supporters of the enterprise argue that indices are implicitly part of our thinking whenever we say that something is improving or deteriorating and claim accordingly that the endeavour to make them explicit is simply a more rigorous way of proceeding. The human rights field is certainly replete with such efforts and it makes sense to look at some of them to see what illumination they can shed on the Commonwealth Third World record.

Perhaps the best-known, albeit controversial, attempt to report qualitative information about human rights in numerical form has been Freedom House's regular Comparative Survey of Freedom, prepared under the direction of Raymond D. Gastil.[20] The two dimensions of the survey are political rights, by which is meant 'the right of all adults to vote and compete for public office, and for elected representatives to have a decisive vote on public policies', and civil liberties, which are 'rights to free expression, to organize or demonstrate, as well as rights to a degree of autonomy such as is provided by freedom of religion, education, travel, and other personal rights'.[21] Each country is rated on these criteria on seven-point scales, constructed comparatively between countries rather than against absolute standards, and is then judged to be 'free', 'partly free' or 'not free' on a composite of the two.

What emerges? Taking the data for 1986, of forty-five Commonwealth Third World states, no fewer than twenty-one are deemed to be free (although only four receive the highest scores on both scales – Barbados, Belize, St Kitts-Nevis and Tuvalu); nineteen are considered partly free; and only five are ranked not free – Ghana, Malawi, Nigeria, the Seychelles and Tanzania – although it should be said that none got the 'double-seven' then awarded across the board to the states of the Soviet bloc![22] At face value, it is not a bad performance. Nearly half the countries in question 'pass out' of Freedom House's school, only just over 10 per cent fail the exam, and the rest are still working at it. It is noteworthy too that Africa is as strongly represented amongst the failures as the Caribbean is amongst the bright boys at the top of the class. The metaphor is appropriate because the survey is fundamentally authoritarian and patronising: this is what has made it controversial.[23] In the end, it takes a view of human rights that is too narrowly political and too passionately ideological to stand service as a general framework for assessment.

Another survey, which is not dissimilar to the Freedom House study in its results, is the so-called World Human Rights Guide produced by Charles Humana, a former volunteer-worker for Amnesty International.[24] Humana initially selected some forty rights, all drawn from and supported by the various United Nations declarations and covenants, to prepare the questionnaire with which he aimed to compare the human rights performances of countries. In order to be able to give a rating in percentage terms to each country, he subsequently 'weighted' the rights according to his judgement about priorities. Seven major rights – all characterised by 'freedom from', variously, slavery, extra-judicial disappearances or killings, torture, work conscription, capital punishment, court sentences of corporal punishment, and indefinite detention without trial – were given three times the weighing of the rest, which included the other more positive 'freedom to' rights. Humana defended his choice in the terms of Amnesty International and the popular mood. His belief, simply stated, was that 'an individual screaming while subjected to torture or locked for years in an unlit cell because of his or her opinions is enduring a degree of physical or mental suffering greater than the denial of a vote or of having his or her newspapers censored'.[25]

The ratings, which reflect the period up to the end of 1986, certainly produce interesting findings regarding the Commonwealth Third World, from which sixteen countries are considered fully. The 'top four' – some way ahead of the rest – were Papua New Guinea (91 per cent), Trinidad and Tobago (79 per cent), Botswana (78 per cent) and Jamaica (77 per cent); the worst cases were Bangladesh (44 per cent), Zimbabwe (45 per cent), Ghana (46 per cent), Tanzania (47 per cent), and Kenya (48 per cent);

and the rest bunched somewhere in the middle – Sierra Leone (64 per cent), India (60 per cent), Singapore (59 per cent), Malaysia and Nigeria (both 53 per cent), Sri Lanka (52 per cent) and Zambia (51 per cent). The Commonwealth Third World average was 59 per cent, compared to a world average of 55 per cent, pushed up by the inclusion of all the developed liberal democracies and the exclusion of many other Third World states with 'bad' records for which insufficient data was available to Humana. All in all, the Commonwealth Third World may again be said, in comparative terms, to have done quite well.

The findings of Freedom House and Humana, in fact, correlate fairly closely. This is because they both concentrate on political rights at the expense of social and economic rights. Freedom House is explicit about this; Humana is more defensive, conceding that only three of his forty rights derive from the International Covenant on Economic, Social and Cultural Rights but claiming that this was unavoidable, given the extent to which the latter are often couched in terms of promises and aspirations rather than specific pledges. Nevertheless, he ultimately admits that his questionnaire reflected 'the Western liberal bias'[26] of the Universal Declaration and the International Covenant on Civil and Political Rights. Yet the quantitative analysis of human rights does not have to be bound in this way. The indices game is also played on social and economic terrain and other surveys can be drawn upon to redress the balance of the discussion.

One body of social indexing work which has lately received a good deal of attention is that produced by Morris D. Morris and his colleagues at the Overseas Development Council in Washington. His team constructed a Physical Quality of Life Index (PQLI), calculated from an average of life expectancy at the age of one, infant mortality and adult literacy. For the thirty-seven Commonwealth Third World countries for which the calculation was done in 1982, the PQLI average was 65·8, almost as high as the world average of 68 and substantially in excess of the average for all developing countries of 59.[27] Indeed, some states were close to the average for developed countries of 94 – namely, Barbados and Grenada (both 92), Malta, Jamaica and Trinidad and Tobago (all 89), the Bahamas, Guyana and St Vincent (all 87), Cyprus, Singapore and Western Samoa (all 86) and Fiji and Tonga (both 85). The Caribbean, the Mediterranean and the Pacific generally did well, whilst the poor performers were almost all to be found in Africa and Asia – the Gambia (20), Sierra Leone (24), Malawi (31), Bangladesh (35), Nigeria (38), Ghana (41) and India (42) being the worst. The averages for Commonwealth Africa and Asia (48 and 66 respectively) were at least higher than those for the two regions as a whole (43 and 58), although the 'lead' can hardly be said to be statistically significant in either case.

The PQLI data are once more quite intriguing and undoubtedly point up those countries with the most pressing social needs. Yet the very simplicity and attractiveness of the model is also its major weakness. Of the three indicators used to construct the index, two (rates of infant mortality and years of average life expectancy) are essentially measures of the quality of national health care services, whilst the third (rates of adult literacy) assesses the adequacy of basic educational provision. The PQLI makes no reference to other equally important social and cultural rights, such as the status of women and children, the quality of housing and the living environment, or matters of personal and family security. It is not, in other words, a comprehensive index for the measurement of social rights.

This is perhaps more nearly achieved in the last effort at global indexing we shall look at – the analysis of the Social Progress of Nations undertaken by Richard Estes.[28] Ambitiously, he rates, and in essence ranks, countries in relation to forty-four welfare-relevant social indicators distributed over eleven wide-ranging sub-indices – education, health, status of women, defence effort, economics, demography, geography, political stability, political participation, cultural diversity and welfare effort. From these emerged, via the computer, the Index of Social Progress (ISP) for the year 1979/80, represented as a composite score ranging from the world's best (Denmark at 201) to the world's worst (Ethiopia at –12). The average for the Commonwealth Third World (based on the fifteen states in this category surveyed by Estes) comes out at 65, lower than the average for developing countries as a whole (89) but higher than that for his grouping of least developing countries (41). This is the first time in the indices that we have examined that Commonwealth developing states have been at a disadvantage when compared with the category as a whole. Otherwise, the regional pattern previously noted reappears – the Caribbean at the top of the league, with Jamaica scored at 132 and Trinidad and Tobago at 126, and Africa at the bottom, with Uganda at 21,

Tanzania at 29, Nigeria and Zimbabwe both at 33, Zambia at 37 and Ghana at 39.

At this point in the argument, with numbers spinning between the different indices, it is as well to retire from the fray. Two points must have emerged clearly from the discussion. Firstly, there is no single index available which properly reflects the broad view of human rights argued for earlier; they are all predisposed to either the civil and political or the social and economic dimension. Secondly, the indicator game tells us many things which are interesting and relevant to the analysis of human rights performance, but it does not spare us from the task of judgement. The figures still have to be interpreted; opinions have to be offered on the relative weighting of different criteria; and, above all, some sense of context, both geographical and historical, has to be entered into the debate.

The case-study approach

Put another way, what we have to do is to retreat into the case-study approach. It is actually an advance. The proper assessment of human rights conditions requires that analysts should map out the entire spectrum of the performance of human rights in any country where these conditions are being examined. Such a comprehensive mapping does not mean either that all rights have to be deemed equal or that some will have to be neglected at the expense of others. It demands instead a simple sensitivity to trends, both admirable and damnable – in other words, qualitative rather than quantitative analysis. Ideally, such an approach should be undertaken country-by-country and on the basis of detailed research.[29] However, for the purposes of this analysis, a sketchier region-by-region tour of the Commonwealth Third World will suffice.

Africa

The African record has been the worst; indeed, it has been nothing less than appalling. Quite apart from the instances of atrocity which have acquired international notoriety, it is the case that the *norms* of political life in Commonwealth African states since independence have come to include the following: single-party or military rule without opportunity to organise in opposition, surveillance, detention and beatings of political opponents, deployment of the machinery of state security for political purposes, state ownership of the media, exchange of political refugees between states and widespread use of the death penalty in political cases. Add to this list a regional economic performance which has been almost universally poor and a pattern of child labour and discrimination against women (including in some countries the continued practice of female circumcision and infibulation), and it is clear that, by any standards, human rights have been very poorly protected in many parts of Africa over the past twenty or thirty years.

Moreover, as indicated, this is not to mention the most grotesque abuses, of which it has to be said there have been many. The case of Uganda is obviously the most renowned, witnessing the systematic mass murder of innocent people, not only under General Amin (whose brutality captured the headlines) but, if anything, even more widely under the regime of Milton Obote which followed that first reign of terror. Ghana has seen three former heads of state (and many other political figures) publicly executed by firing squad; Nigeria has lived through a civil war which provoked allegations of genocide against the Biafrans and, of late, has become used to military tribunals dispensing 'justice' in a brusque and highly physical way; Zimbabwe has experienced the massacre by sections of the army of many Ndebele-speaking residents of Matabeleland, an area of political opposition to the government. And so one could go on.

On the positive side, Botswana and the Gambia have maintained forms of multi-party politics which have preserved some of the traditional freedoms of opposition, and Tanzania has worked harder than most single-party states to make a reality of internal party democracy. For that matter, no observer of the Nigerian political scene could deny that long years of military rule have manifestly failed to subdue a lively 'culture' of criticism and dissent in the hearts and minds of many of the country's citizens. For many years too, Kenya could claim that it had a tolerable human rights record. Violence sporadically marked its politics (as in the murders of Mboya and Kariuki) and a one-party state emerged, as elsewhere, whilst clearly the distribution of economic growth was characterised by uneveness between classes and ethnic groups. But there was economic improvement over the post-independence period and the most unattractive features of single-party rule were largely avoided. In this light the most depressing recent feature of Commonwealth Africa's human rights record has been Kenya's descent into repression. Torture, political detention, unfair trials, police raids on the University of Nairobi – all these tactics have been deployed by the government in the last two or three years in its efforts to intimidate and eradicate the opposition Mwakenya organisation. The lesson is how easily and quickly in contemporary Africa even the better human rights cases can slide towards the regional norm.

Asia

Asia's record is not significantly better, especially in respect of the three Commonwealth states of the Indian subcontinent. India itself has preserved a kind of democracy against what can only be described as considerable odds, which is a not unheroic achievement. Yet, as a state, it was born amidst intercommunal violence and has always had to live with tensions between its various component communities. In recent years, many deaths have been brought about as a result of the Sikh conflict which in 1984 prompted the Indian army to attack and enter the Golden Temple in Amritsar. The existence of a continuing politics of violence in the country has also led to the passage of special 'antiterrorist' legislation and preventive detention laws which have lacked the legal safeguards required by international human rights standards and have consequently allowed people to be detained even for non-violently expressing dissenting opinions. What is more, despite elaborate constitutional protection offered to human rights, the hold of traditional customs and prejudices within Indian society is such that these commitments are habitually vitiated. The caste system, religious constraints on intermarriage and general discrimination on the grounds of sex cannot but work against the achievement of the free and equal society to which the western-educated Indian élite formally aspires. Widespread poverty, notwithstanding real agricultural and industrial growth, also limits economic rights and makes the proportion of child labour used in India the highest in the world.

Yet, in the final analysis, India is rescued by the undoubted and longstanding vitality of the country's electoral process and, on the whole, its overall human rights performance probably exceeds that of either Bangladesh or Sri Lanka. In the former the level of human rights is shaped above all by the grim realities of mass poverty. Military governments have also predominated since independence and martial law operated between 1982 and 1986. Evidence of unlawful killings and torture of the peoples of the Chittagong Hill Tracts by military and paramilitary personnel further confirms a dismal record. In the latter the recent escalation of communal tension to embrace terrorism and virtual warfare has shattered a functioning democratic system. The activities of armed Tamil groups seeking a separate state in the north of the island have been met with arbitrary killings and arrests of Tamil civilians by government forces, often in direct reprisal against terrorist attacks on the majority Sinhalese population. Hundreds of deaths have taken place in circumstances which make a mockery of the language of human rights.

By comparison, the record of Commonwealth states in South-East Asia is an improvement, but it is still far from good and may perhaps be said to be deteriorating. Malaysia retains a commitment to competitive party democracy, except that it bans the existence of a communist party. Many political detainees with alleged communist connections have been held without trial, some of them for over ten years, under the terms of a rigorous internal security act introduced in the midst of intercommunal conflict in 1969. Singapore has had much greater economic success, contributing to the expansion of human rights in that sphere, but it has increasingly been accompanied by authoritarian behaviour on the part of the government which has systematically harassed the two opposition members of parliament elected in 1984. Recent new restrictions on freedom of the press contribute to a growing disquiet about the protection of political rights in the country. Social rights have long been limited by virtue of the government's insistence on the compulsory dissemination of traditional Confucian ideas which intrinsically discriminate against women.

The Caribbean

By comparison with other parts of the Commonwealth Third World, the Caribbean is a haven of decency. The states of the region are characterised, on balance, more by social and political cohesion than conflict. They have a sound record of administration and they are generally highly democratic in their political cultures and practices. Competitive elections take place freely and fairly, and are most vigorously contested; political leaders voluntarily relinquish office in the face of electoral defeat. Freedoms of thought, expression and assembly are generally well established. Parliaments exist widely and they function, even if they remain weak by comparison with executives. The military mostly keeps out of politics. The bureaucracy and the judiciary are not generally subject to excessive or unreasonable public interference. Indeed, many honourable and dedicated public servants work long and hard in the service of the state and region. Inequalities of race, culture, sex and class are present, but they are not systematically entrenched and the position of women in Caribbean society could hardly be described as downtrodden. Grinding poverty is not absent, especially within the shanty-towns of Kingston and Port of Spain, but these are not, by a long way, the poorest societies in the Third World. Nobody has starved to death in the Commonwealth Caribbean in the last thirty years. In short, the general human rights record of the region is good.

Nevertheless, there is the danger of becoming a little too lyrical when looking at the Caribbean in direct comparison with parts of Africa and Asia. Specific exemptions to all of the claims previously made can be entered. Jamaican society, in particular, is unquestionably violent, both culturally and politically: some 750 people died in political conflicts leading up to the 1980 election. Attempted coups took place in Trinidad in 1970 and in Jamaica in 1980. The government of the Bahamas is corruptly involved in the drugs business and many have been the improper deals struck between the leaders of the smaller islands and nefarious business operators. In elections, the gerrymandering of constituency boundaries, the disruption of opposition meetings and the buying of votes are all common practices across the region, with the result that it is certainly easy to demonstrate that the quality of democracy enjoyed in the Caribbean leaves much to be desired. Yet none of these points can do more than shade the general argument which reports favourably on the Caribbean's post-independence performance in respect of human rights. What more seriously damages the region's record are the two exceptional cases – Guyana and Grenada.

Both have blotted the otherwise relatively civilised landscape of the Caribbean, but in different ways. In Guyana, the post-independence record of the government of Forbes Burnham was one of corruption, malpractice, ballot-rigging, political thuggery and ultimately alleged assassination. It is relevant that the population of the country has long been bitterly divided between African and East Indian elements, for the essence of the authoritarianism of the Burnham regime was an attempt to maintain a racial ascendancy. In Grenada, the nasty, petty brutality of Eric Gairy created the circumstances whereby a revolutionary regime could take power by non-constitutional means. By definition, as it were, the revolution's own goals aroused counter-revolutionary opposition which, in turn, led it to imprison opponents without trial, the spiral eventually generating the grotesque sequence of events by which Maurice Bishop and other leading figures of the government were put up against a wall and shot by members of the revolutionary army. Even then, the trajectory of degeneration initiated by Gairy was not at an end: the sovereign rights of all the Grenadian people were violated by the invading forces of the United States and the revolutionary leaders were captured, subsequently tried and sentenced to death, in circumstances which themselves involved the breach of many of the expected rights of defendants. The only feature of the whole affair which was encouraging was the genuine revulsion caused all round the Caribbean by the trauma of Bishop's murder, for it showed the extent of the culture of tolerance which generally pervades the region.

The Mediterranean

The Mediterranean Commonwealth states, Cyprus and Malta, although not conventionally classified as belonging to the Third World, nevertheless share many of the social, economic and political problems of developing states. By and large, Malta has prospered since independence and operated a real, if somewhat tough-minded, democracy, the two major parties exchanging office in open, electoral competition. Cyprus, however, has been subject to considerable levels of ethnic conflict, political violence and external interference in its modern history. The development of passive ethnicity into active nationalist consciousness on the part of both the Greek and Turkish communities stood in the way of a peaceful transition to independence, giving rise to the bitter EOKA struggle of the late 1950s. After independence, violent clashes between the two communities continued as ethnic politics became ever more established, until in July 1974 the National Guard, guided by the

Greek military junta, intervened to overthrow the elected president, thereby provoking in response Turkish invasion and annexation of about 40 per cent of the island. The action created some 200,000 Greek Cypriot refugees (as well as a smaller number of displaced Turkish-Cypriots) who had to be housed inadequately in camps supported by international funds. The political pursuit of a rhetoric of 'return' also served to lock this refugee group into a culture of impermanency and confirmed their position at the bottom of the socio-economic structure. In human rights terms, therefore, Cyprus falls into a distressingly familiar tradition of analysis.

The Pacific

The Pacific has not, until recently, attracted much attention from human rights analysts. Although many societies remained attached to tribal and chiefly forms of organisation which limited equalities of opportunity between citizens, they appeared to have adapted these structures fairly successfully to the forms of open, competitive democracy. Traditional customs discriminating against the rights of women and children still prevailed in the more remote, mountainous parts of Papua New Guinea or the outer islands of Melanesia, but they tended to be seen as anachronistic features of another age, rather than as specific abuses of rights. However, this complacency was shattered in 1987 by the two coups effected in Fiji in that year by Lt. Colonel Sitiveni Rabuka. Responding to the victory of the multiracial Fiji Labour Party in elections in 1985, the army's intervention restored, by force, the traditional Melanesian dominance of the political system which had been interrupted by the success of a political party in which the majority Indian section of the population enjoyed a significant, although not exclusive, role. The consequence has been the crushing of democracy, the abrogation of the constitution, the harassment and imprisonment of judges, the virtual abolition of political dissent via the passage of a draconian internal security decree and the exodus of large numbers of ethnic Indians for whom Fiji has become a place of fear. Reports also testify to a sudden increase in the number of rapes of women in the period since the coups. The ending of the era of Pacific innocence thus came quickly and comprehensively, destroying what remained of the region's relative detachment from some of the more illiberal and least desirable aspects of modern times.

Conclusion

What can be said, by way of conclusion, about human rights in the Commonwealth Third World? What picture emerges from this brief survey of its different regions? Something of an answer can be given at three levels. At the descriptive level, the answer is obviously a mixture of the good and the bad: the range of countries considered includes Uganda as well as Barbados, as well as all points in between on the human-rights scale. Clearly, there is nothing about the particular legacy of British colonialism which *ensures* the maintenance of human rights. At the predictive level, there is the question of the trend. Examples do exist of improving records – Uganda under President Museveni is a case in point – but there are, it seems, even more examples where the trend is in the other direction. Too many functioning Third World democracies, like Fiji and Sri Lanka, which have until lately worked hard to protect human rights, have been broken in recent times for the argument to be put in any other way. At the comparative level, the evidence is not stark and incontrovertible, but it is just about firm enough to be able to say that the Commonwealth Third World has done a little better in the human rights sphere than the Third World more broadly defined.

Put these points together, and the following conclusion can be tentatively suggested. It is to claim that there can be detected a residual effect of the ideological commitment of British colonialism to at least a version of human rights theory. These ideas, and the consequential institutional apparatus set up in most ex-British colonies at or around the time of independence, did act as a constraint – albeit only loosely – on the behaviour of successor regimes in the post-colonial era. The degree of constraint was always limited; it could be, and was, easily overcome; but it was, nevertheless, an obstacle which *had* to be overcome. And the lesson is too that the longer the colonial experience lasted, and the longer the ethic had to be internalised in the minds of élites, then the more likely it was that the post-colonial era would continue to be marked by a measure of human rights protection. In a nutshell, this is what separates the poor record of Africa (with barely sixty or seventy years of colonialism under its belt) from the relatively good record of the Caribbean (with its experience of over 300 years of British rule). At best, something of the ideology of British colonialism stuck and held in the Commonwealth Third World, protecting human rights to the degree that they have been preserved; at worst, though, it still provided a measure by which abuses could be highlighted and ventilated. The peoples of the Commonwealth Third World know what are the rights they want to see protected, even if they do not currently enjoy them, and that is itself an achievement not to be dismissed. In this connection, the hopes are not so much fallacious as eternal.

Notes

1 See Kenneth Minogue, 'The history of the idea of human rights' in Walter Laqueur and Barry Rubin (eds.), *The Human Rights Reader*, Temple University Press, Philadelphia, 1979.
2 See Richard B. Lillich, *International Human Rights Instruments*, William S. Hein, Buffalo, New York, 1983.
3 Henry Shue, *Basic Rights: Subsistence, Affluence, and US Foreign Policy*, Princeton University Press, Princeton, 1980, p. 6.
4 For a fuller discussion, see Rhoda Howard, 'The full-belly thesis: should economic rights take priority over civil and political rights? Evidence from sub-Saharan Africa', *Human Rights Quarterly*, Vol. 5, No. 4, November 1983, pp. 467–90.
5 The argument in this section draws closely on the insightful analysis of this problem provided in R. J. Vincent, *Human Rights and International Relations*, Cambridge University Press, Cambridge, 1986, pp. 37–57.
6 Ibid., p. 37.
7 Ruth Benedict, *Patterns of Culture*, Routledge, London, 1935, pp. 200–1, quoted in ibid., p. 38.
8 Ibid., p. 38.
9 See, amongst others: Asmarom Legesse, 'Human rights in African political culture' in Kenneth W. Thompson (ed.), *The Moral Imperatives of Human Rights: A World Survey*, University Press of America, Washington, D.C., 1980; Lakshman Marasinghe, 'Traditional conceptions of human rights in Africa: the Nigerian experience' in Claude E. Welch Jr. and Robert I. Meltzer (eds.), *Human Rights and Development in Africa*, SUNY Press, Albany, New York, 1984 and Chris C. Mojekwu, 'International human rights: the African perspective' in Jack L. Nelson and Vera M. Green (eds.), *International Human Rights: Contemporary Issues*, Human Rights Publishing Group, Standfordville, New York, 1980.
10 Kenneth D. Kaunda, *A Humanist in Africa*, Longman, London, 1966, pp. 24–5.

11 Rhoda Howard, 'Is there an African concept of human rights?' in R. J. Vincent (ed.), *Foreign Policy and Human Rights: Issues and Responses*, Cambridge University Press, Cambridge, 1986, pp. 11–32.
12 Ifeanyi A. Menkiti, 'Person and community in African traditional thought' in Richard A. Wright (ed.), *African Philosophy: An Introduction*, University Press of America, Washington, D.C., 1979, p. 162.
13 Howard in Vincent (ed.), *Foreign Policy and Human Rights*, p. 20.
14 Jack Donnelly, 'Human rights and human dignity: an analytical critique of non-western conceptions of human rights', *American Political Science Review*, Vol. 76, No. 2, 1982, pp. 312–13.
15 Jack Donnelly, 'Cultural relativism and universal human rights', *Human Rights Quarterly*, Vol. 6, No. 4, 1984, p. 401.
16 Ibid.
17 John Stuart Mill, *On Liberty*, in Mary Warnock (ed.), *Utilitarianism*, Collins/Fontana, London and Glasgow, 1962, p. 201.
18 Ibid., p. 144.
19 Jorgé I. Dominguez, 'Assessing human rights conditions' in Jorgé I. Dominguez, Nigel S. Rodley, Bryce Wood and Richard Falk (eds.), *Enhancing Human Rights*, McGraw-Hill, New York, 1979, p. 21.
20 Raymond D. Gastil, *Freedom in the World: Political Rights and Civil Liberties 1986–7*, Greenwood Press, New York, 1987.
21 Ibid., p. 6.
22 Ibid., pp. 29–33.
23 See Harry Scoble and Laurie Wiseberg, 'Problems of comparative research on human rights' in V. P. Nanda, J. R. Scarritt and G. W. Shepherd (eds.), *Global Human Rights: Public Policies, Comparative Measures and NGO Strategies*, Westview Press, Boulder, 1981, pp. 147–72 and Lars Schoultz, review of *Freedom in the World: Political Rights and Civil Liberties*, *Universal Human Rights*, Vol. 1, No. 2, January–March 1980, pp. 94–6.
24 Charles Humana, *World Human Rights Guide*, Pan, London, 1987.
25 Ibid., pp. 3–4.
26 Ibid., p. 5.
27 Statistical Annexes in John P. Lewis and Valeriana Kallab (eds.), *US Foreign Policy and the Third World*, Praeger with the Overseas Development Council, New York, 1983, pp. 210–21.
28 Richard J. Estes, *The Social Progress of Nations*, Praeger, New York, 1984.
29 Examples of how this might be done, in the cases of Cuba and Mexico, are provided in Dominguez et al., *Enhancing Human Rights*, pp. 49–85.

Index